The Economics of
Communication

Pergamon Titles of Related Interest

PERGAMON POLICY STUDIES ON INTERNATIONAL DEVELOPMENT

The Economics of Communication
A Selected Bibliography With Abstracts

Karen P. Middleton
Meheroo Jussawalla

Published in cooperation with the
East-West Center, Hawaii

Pergamon Press
NEW YORK • OXFORD • TORONTO • SYDNEY • PARIS • FRANKFURT

Pergamon Press Offices:

U.S.A.	Pergamon Press Inc., Maxwell House, Fairview Park, Elmsford, New York 10523, U.S.A.
U.K.	Pergamon Press Ltd., Headington Hill Hall, Oxford OX3 OBW, England
CANADA	Pergamon of Canada, Ltd., Suite 104, 150 Consumers Road, Willowdale, Ontario M2J 1P9, Canada
AUSTRALIA	Pergamon Press (Aust.) Pty. Ltd., P.O. Box 544, Potts Point, NSW 2011, Australia
FRANCE	Pergamon Press SARL, 24 rue des Ecoles, 75240 Paris, Cedex 05, France
FEDERAL REPUBLIC OF GERMANY	Pergamon Press GmbH, Hammerweg 6, Postfach 1305, 6242 Kronberg/Taunus, Federal Republic of Germany

Library of Congress Cataloging in Publication Data

Middleton, Karen P   1945-
  The economics of communication.

  (Pergamon policy studies on international development)
  Bibliography: p.
  Includes indexes.
  1. Communication—Economic aspects—Bibliography.
  I. Jussawalla, Meheroo, 1923-   joint author.
II. Title. III. Series.
Z5630.M5 1981 [P96.E25]   016.3803   80-20505
ISBN 0-08-026325-9

Printed in the United States of America

Contents

Acknowledgments

This bibliography was inspired by the ongoing work of the Communication Policy and Planning Project of the East-West Communication Institute. We would especially like to thank S. A. Rahim, Project Leader, John Middleton, and D. M. Lamberton for their contribution to the conceptualization of the bibliography. George Beal, Georgette Wang, Marcellus Snow, and Godwin Chu made many helpful comments and suggestions. Jack Lyle, Communication Institute Director, lent his support to the work. Sumiye Konoshima brought many readings to our attention, and conducted a computer search of the Institute's document collection to find materials for the bibliography. Special thanks are due to Phyllis Watanabe, Wendy Nohara, and Mildred Ching, who typed the manuscript.

Foreword

We live in "The Age of Communication," in which people speak of "communication explosion," "communication gaps," "communication imperialism," and the "New Communication or Information Order."

The Communication Institute of the East-West Center is dedicated to the study of how communication systems facilitate (and impede) development in different cultures through the exchange of information. Communication Research is a relatively young tradition. It traces its genesis primarily to the traditional disciplines of psychology, sociology, and political science. Using the research tools of these disciplines, it has been shown that communication can be used effectively as a component of development programs. As the Institute's program has developed, we have seen a necessity to add economics to the portfolios or disciplines represented within our staff resources.

The promise of communication systems for development has attracted funding - frequently in large amounts - from governments, foundations, and technical assistance agencies. But as large-scale projects have developed, inevitably questions have been raised concerning efficiency and cost-effectiveness.

After all, program planners and funders usually face decisions not only regarding optional choices of media systems, but also of whether to substitute media for traditional and nonmedia distribution systems. A rational basis for making choices in such option situations must include information on costs, inputs, and outputs. And so the "economics of communication" is emerging.

As the compilers of this bibliography indicate, the economics of communication is a new field. Pertinent literature is relatively scarce and scattered. But there is ample reason to believe that the economics of communication will receive rapidly

expanding interest and that its importance will mushroom.   If
this is truly the Age of Communication, it cannot be otherwise.
     The   East-West   Communication   Institute   supported   the
compilation of this bibliography in the hope that it will provide
a basic building block for this new field.

                         Jack Lyle
                         Director
                         East-West Communication ·Institute
                         East-West Center
                         Honolulu, Hawaii

                         April 1980

Introduction

BACKGROUND AND PURPOSE

The economics of communication is a new interdisciplinary topic stemming from two quite distinct areas of inquiry. The first is the economics of information. In a seminal volume of readings published in 1971, editor D. M. Lamberton pointed out that "an economics of information and knowledge starts by recognizing that an economic system is activated by decisions which link information flows to objectives; traditional [economic] analysis bypassed the problem [of information]."(1) Economic analysts had tended to assume the availability of perfect information when constructing models of economic systems. In the 1960s economists began to explore the implications of the existence of incomplete and imperfect information. For example, George Stigler wrote on the variance in prices of similar and even homogeneous goods, "Price dispersion is a manifestation of ignorance in the market."(2) In 1966 R. A. Jenner developed a model of perfect competition based in information theory.(3)

In this growing body of work, information is treated as a variable in economic models; another thrust to the economics of information places information at the focus of the analysis. According to Michael Cooper, the economics of information is the examination in economic terms of the entire chain of events that begins with the creation of new information, continues through its dissemination, and ends with the processing (or use) of information by individuals.(4) The economics of communication is emerging from this latter view of information economics. For the purposes of this bibliography, communication is considered to be the transmission of information; thus, the economics of communication is concerned with the economic analysis of communications media and channels. The focus is on channels rather than on other aspects of the communication process (such as effects) for several reasons: first, in developing nations there is currently a burgeoning interest in purchasing and implementing advanced communications systems; second, since the media are more amenable to economic analysis than are other aspects of the communication process, there is more economic literature extant on this subject. Examples of the type of work included in this bibliography that are considered to be part of the economic analysis of communications include studies of the demand for teleconferencing, the financing of communication satellites, the pricing of telephone service, and economies of scale in the postal service.

The economics of information and communication can be further distinguished by the fact that the former, for economists, is concerned primarily with the economics discipline itself, while the latter seeks to apply economic tools to another area of interest. Lamberton predicts that since economics of information is embedded within economic analysis, "its life as a separate subject should be short-lived . . . the discussion will be integrated with general economics which will hopefully be transformed for the better."(5) The economics of communication, as currently perceived, will be an interdisciplinary topic with a pragmatic focus, that of economic development.

The second area of inquiry that has stimulated the economics of communication is communication and development. Since World War II, problems of economic growth and development have received increasing attention in rich and poor nations alike. Numerous theories and models have been set forth and billions of dollars have been spent, but many difficulties still remain. Even the terms "growth" and "development" are not clear; Robert Flammang points out in a recent journal article that, according to some definitions, "growing is apparently something that a rich country does, and developing is something that a poor country does."(6) After surveying a number of alternative interpretations, Flammang suggests that "to most of us, economic growth is a process of simple increase, implying more of the same, while economic development is a process of structural change, implying something different if not something more."(7) Viewing development as a process of structural change, communication scholars in the 1960s began looking for connections between development and communication; the availability, use, and efficiency of communication goods and services were seen to have a necessary role in national development. Frederick Frey(8) cites a number of statistics from Unesco and other data showing relationships between such communication indicators as newspaper circulation, mail flow, and number of telephones and such development indicators as gross national product (GNP).

Colin Cherry(9) has also shown correlations between communi-
cations media and wealth indicators.   Communication scholar
Wilbur Schramm wrote Mass Media and National Development(10)
in 1964, and in 1967 he and Daniel Lerner co-edited a book on
Communication and Change in the Developing Countries.(11)
In 1976 they updated their previous work in Communication
and Change: The Last Ten Years -And the Next.(12)   Everett
Rogers has written on Modernization Among Peasants: The
Impact of Communication.(13)   In several industrialized countries attempts have been made to measure the contribution of
the information/communication sector to GNP.   In the United
States some 53 percent of all labor income is earned by infor-
mation/communication workers; 46 percent of a two trillion
dollar GNP is generated by the information/communication
sector.(14)   Recent rapid advances in communication technology
promise significant effects on the socioeconomic systems of
both developed and less developed nations.
     Economists have been almost exclusively involved in the
first area of inquiry, the economics of information, while
communication and political science specialists have undertaken
the second.   According to Kenneth Boulding, "the recognition
that development, even economic development, is essentially a
knowledge process has been slowly penetrating the minds of
economists, but we are still too much obsessed by mechanical
models, capital-income ratios, and even input-output tables, to
the neglect of the study of the learning process which is the
real key to development."(15)   Because of this neglect,
because of the major role the economics discipline plays in
development theory, and because the communication of information is increasingly viewed as fundamental to all sorts of
economic systems, the possibility of establishing a fruitful new
interdisciplinary area of study led the authors to undertake a
search for literature bearing on the interaction of economics
and communication.   This bibliography is the product of that
search; it is intended to pave the way for economists and
communication specialists to engage in collaborative research on
problems of mutual interest.

Economics of Communication as an Interdisciplinary Study

Interdisciplinary studies are becoming more widespread as
problems such as economic development prove intractable to
methods and solutions offered by one discipline alone.   In the
most common type of interdisciplinary research members of
several disciplines contribute their expertise to the study of a
mutual practical problem.   "More intimate relations arise when
the variables of one field begin to play a part in the explanations of the other, and most intimate when one field
is integrated within another in explanatory processes."(16)

Communication scholars have often demonstrated correlations between communications variables and indicators of economic growth, but so far no definitive statement on a cause/effect relationship has been made.

As Ronald Coase has pointed out, economists have begun moving into other social sciences because of the precision and usefulness of their analytic techniques. The view of economics as the study of human choice in a world of limited resources gives economists an advantage in the study of social problems.(17) An interdisciplinary subject with similarities to the economics of communication is the economics of education. It involves both the economic analysis of schools and the impact of schooling on the occupational structure of the labor force and the size and distribution of personal income, which are major aspects of economic development. According to Mark Blaug, the basis of the economics of education is that "the acquisition of education in a modern economy provides opportunities for individuals to invest in themselves."(18) Communication also provides opportunities for people to "invest in" themselves; however, it is at the same time a much more diffuse and pervasive phenomenon, and therefore harder to isolate for study.

Economic development provides the particular focus for this bibliography. Therefore, in choosing items from both the economics and communications disciplines for inclusion in the bibliography, a major criterion was whether the item had something to say in the economic development context. Because the economics of communication is a new topic, the authors tried to be inclusive and extensive in selection, rather than exclusive; the boundaries of a new topic are necessarily uncertain. Most of the items included were not written from a specifically interdisciplinary viewpoint, and many of the items are implicitly rather than explicitly related to economic development. In the selection process, the question was asked whether a given item contained information about the economics of communication that would be useful to a national development planner.

SUBJECT CLASSIFICATION

In a bibliography, materials are grouped according to the purposes of those who will use the bibliography. This classification scheme therefore stresses features of importance to economists, communication researchers, and planners who are working on economic development problems. Development of the classification was guided by the purpose behind the bibliography, that of gathering materials useful in the context of economic development. The classification scheme essentially built itself from the materials available on the economics of communication; that is, as materials were gathered, they coalesced around certain topics.

An outline of the classification is presented below, together with the number of items to be found in each section. The number of items can be a useful indicator of gaps in knowledge, and can point to directions for further research.

(11)   1.   Definitions: Economics of Communication;
                 Information/Communication Sector
(28)   2.   Economic Descriptions of Communications Indus-
                 tries
(259)   3.   Economic Analysis of Communications
   (4)   A. General
   (38)   B. Competition/Monopoly Issues
   (22)   C. Other Regulatory Aspects*
   (32)   D. Demand Studies
   (41)   E. Pricing Studies
   (17)   F. Financing
   (69)   G. Approaches to Resource Allocation
   (16)   H. Production Functions/Productivity/Economies
                     of Scale
   (20)   I. Future of Communications**
(60)   4.   Impact of Communications on Economic Systems
(18)   5.   International Exchange of Communication
                 Goods/Services
(10)   6.   Social/Political Implications of Communication
                 Economics

*Concerns regulatory issues aside from competition/monopoly problems.
**Includes materials in which the future is predicted, forecasted, or hypothesized about.

The first section of the bibliography contains materials that seek to _define_ the topic or the concept of an information/ communication sector of the economy. Grouped in the next section are materials that _describe_ various communications industries, stressing economic factors. The third section contains materials, primarily written by economists, in which an economic _analysis_ of some aspect of communications is provided; this very large section is subdivided by the analytical tool or particular economic problem that is emphasized.

The fourth part contains items in which the _impact_ of communications on _economic systems_ and _development_ is described and sometimes measured. This section is called "Impact of Communications on Economic Systems," rather than "communication and development," to emphasize its inclusive nature; that is, development is frequently taken in conjunction only with Third World countries, but this section contains materials relating to both the so-called "developed" and "developing" countries. The next section includes materials on the international exchange of communications goods and services. In the final part are found items that describe some political implications of the economics of communication.

COMPILING THE BIBLIOGRAPHY

To be selected for inclusion in the bibliography, an item had to be concerned with some economic aspect of communications; it had to define, describe, analyze, or show the economic impact of communications. Given these criteria, all types of communications media in the print, broadcasting, and telecommunications industries are included. Materials concerning such communications equipment as satellites, cables, and computers are included. There are analyses of such communications distribution channels as libraries, information systems, and post offices; school systems could belong here, but are not included, except in connection with the use of radio and TV, because the economics of education has become an area of analysis in its own right. Educational, informational, and cultural/entertainment purposes of communications are included.

Because the economics of communication is a new interdisciplinary topic, the literature search was quite complex. The subject itself cannot be looked up in a card catalog or an indexing tool. A great deal of basic work on the definition of the subject remains to be done; materials included in this bibliography will contribute to the definitional work. The materials were found by looking up specific pertinent aspects of economics or communication, since the two fields are not generally thought of or indexed together. Most items were found by searching under quite specific headings: television, satellites, telephones, public utilities, monopoly, and competition.

The following indexing tools proved to be the most useful: Social Sciences Index, Public Affairs Information Service, Journal of Economic Literature, Library Literature, Current Contents, and Selected Rand Abstracts. Some items were found in Communication Abstracts, Sociological Abstracts, and a bibliographical portion of Journalism Quarterly called "Articles on Mass Communication." Recent issues of journals that are not well indexed in common tools were hand searched, including Telecommunications Policy, Telecommunication Journal, and Satellite Communications. A number of Asian journals published in English, and Australian journals, were also hand searched, including Indian Economic Journal, Indian Journal of Economics, Asian Economic Review, Philippine Economic Journal, <u>Economic Record</u> (Australian), <u>Japanese Economic Studies</u>, <u>Malayan Economic Review</u>, <u>Asian Economies</u>, and <u>Australian Economic Papers</u>.

However, the most productive search method was to utilize footnotes, references, and bibliographies of relevant items already found. Since this is a new topic there is naturally no organized body of literature with appropriate subject headings. Citations are an excellent way to trace the development of a new topic back to its origins.

As was discussed above, development of the classification scheme and gathering of materials proceeded together; each reinforced and directed the other. When the classification scheme was completed, each bibliography item was classified into one subject area. In cases where more than one subject is treated in a particular item, that item was classified according to the subject which received the major emphasis. In some items only certain portions were relevant to the economics of communication; these items were classified according to those relevant portions.

The preponderance of materials from the economics literature is found in Sections 2 and 3, while the communication literature is concentrated in Sections 4, 5, and 6. However, it is interesting to note that a significant number of readings from both disciplines can be found in all sections of the classification; scholars in both fields have begun developing this new interdisciplinary topic.

FEATURES

Three hundred eighty-six items were selected; they are numbered consecutively through the bibliography. All were available to the compilers in Honolulu. Most have been published since 1970, although a few relevant items from the 1960s seemed too important to omit. All are written in English.

An abstract is provided for each entry. The individual abstracts are nonevaluative summaries of the original material; they are an objective presentation of the author's main thesis, methods, and findings. When another relevant title is mentioned within an abstract, it is included in the bibliography and can be located through the author index.

Besides the organization provided by the classification scheme, there are author and subject indexes to the bibliography. In the subject index the relevant items are indicated by their number.

Certain abbreviations are used for the sake of brevity throughout the bibliography (see List of Abbreviations).

Details as to the physical location of items in the bibliography, especially unpublished papers, can be obtained by writing to Dr. Meheroo Jussawalla at the East-West Communication Institute, East-West Center, Honolulu, Hawaii 96848.

NOTES

(1) D. M. Lamberton, "Introduction," in Economics of Infor-
     mation and Knowledge, ed. D. M. Lamberton (Middlesex,
     Eng.: Penguin Books, 1971), p. 8.
(2) George J. Stigler, "The Economics of Information," The
     Journal of Political Economy 69 (June 1961) 214.
(3) R. A. Jenner, "An Information Version of Pure Com-
     petition," in Lamberton, Economics of Information and
     Knowledge, p. 83.
(4) Michael D. Cooper, "The Economics of Information," in
     Annual Review of Information Science and Technology,
     1973 (Washington, DC: American Society for Information
     Science, 1973), p. 5.
(5) D. M. Lamberton, "The Economics of Communication," in
     Planning Methods, Models, and Organization: A Review
     Study for Communication Policy Making and Planning
     (Honolulu: East-West Center, 1978), p. 55.
(6) Robert A. Flammang, "Economic Growth and Economic
     Development: Counterparts or Competitors?" Economic
     Development and Cultural Change 28 (October 1979) 48.
(7) Ibid., p. 55.
(8) Frederick W. Frey, "Communication and Development," in
     Handbook of Communication, ed. Ithiel de Sola Pool and
     Wilbur Schramm (Chicago: Rand McNally, 1973).
(9) Colin Cherry, World Communication: Threat or Promise?
     A Socio-Technical Approach (Chichester, Eng.: John
     Wiley, 1978).
(10) Wilbur Schramm, Mass Media and National Development
     (Stanford, CA: Stanford University Press, 1964).
(11) Daniel Lerner and Wilbur Schramm, eds., Communication
     and Change in the Developing Countries (Honolulu: East-
     West Center Press, 1967).
(12) Wilbur Schramm and Daniel Lerner, eds., Communication
     and Change: The Last Ten Years - And The Next (Hono-
     lulu: University Press of Hawaii, 1976).
(13) Everett M. Rogers, Modernization Among Peasants: The
     Impact of Communication (New York: Holt, Rinehart and
     Winston, 1969).
(14) Marc U. Porat, "Global Implications of the Information
     Society," Journal of Communication 28 (Winter 1978) 70.
(15) K. E. Boulding, "The Economics of Knowledge and the
     Knowledge of Economics," in Economics of Information and
     Knowledge, p. 27.
(16) Abraham Edel, "Introduction: Trends in the New Social
     Sciences," in Trends in the New Social Sciences, ed. B.
     N. Varma (Westport, CT: Greenwood Press, 1976), p. 9.
(17) Ronald H. Coase, "Economics and Contiguous Disci-
     plines," in The Organization and Retrieval of Economic

Knowledge, ed. Mark Perlman (Boulder, CO: Westview Press, 1977).

(18) Mark Blaug, An Introduction to the Economics of Education (London: Penguin Press, 1970), pp. xv-xvi.

List of Abbreviations

AID	Agency for International Development
ASEAN	Association of South East Asian Nations
AT&T	American Telephone & Telegraph Co.
BBC	British Broadcasting Corporation
CATV	Community Antenna Television (Cable Television)
Comsat	Communications Satellite Corporation
EBU	European Broadcasting Union
EEC	European Economic Community
ESCAP	Economic and Social Commission for Asia and the Pacific
ETV	Educational Television
FCC	Federal Communications Commission
GDP	Gross Domestic Product
GNP	Gross National Product
IBM	International Business Machines Corporation
Intelsat	International Telecommunications Satellite Organization
I-O	Input-Output
ITU	International Telecommunication Union
LDC	Less developed country
MHz	Megahertz (one million cycles per second)
NASA	National Aeronautics and Space Administration
OECD	Organisation for Economic Co-operation and Development
OPEC	Organization of the Petroleum Exporting Countries
PBS	Public Broadcasting Service
PTT	Post, Telegraph, and Telecommunications Authority
R&D	Research and Development
STV	Subscription Television
TV	Television
UHF	Ultra high frequency
U.K.	United Kingdom

UN   United Nations
UNDP   United Nations Development Programme
Unesco   United Nations Educational, Scientific and Cultural
                Organization
U.S.   United States
USP   Usage-sensitive pricing
USPS   United States Postal Service
U.S.S.R.   Union of Soviet Socialist Republics
VHF   Very high frequency
VTR   Videotape recorder
WARC   World Administrative Radio Conference (of the
                ITU)

Section 1

Definitions: Economics of Communication; Information/ Communication Sector

1. International Commission for the Study of Communication Problems. <u>Interim Report on Communication Problems in Modern Society</u>. Paris: Unesco, 1978.

Information, concepts, and questions valuable to the study of communication economics can be found throughout this report. In a portion descriptive of established communication structures and actors, ownership patterns in print and broadcast media are discussed, and the worldwide trend to concentration of press ownership is pointed out. Commercial forms of communication - advertising and entertainment - are looked at as businesses, and data on world production and exports are provided. In "The Actors Involved," the roles of private and financial interests, governments as regulators and owners, and transnational companies are described.

A section on "Economic Aspects and Implications" raises the following points: (1) communication systems are linked to, and even subordinate to, economic systems; (2) communication is governed by economic factors and structures; (3) communication is linked to national development, especially in regard to its pace and philosophy; (4) communication is an industry, which raises questions of how much capital to invest in it, who should control it, and how to finance it; (5) communication is growing into a fourth sector of the economy; it is continually employing more people and contributing more to GNP.

In "Communication Problems Today," a section on "Material Imbalances and Inequalities" points out irregularities in international tariff structures that have made rates lower from developed to developing countries than vice versa. Paper production and consumption is another major issue here. In "Communication Tomorrow," the necessity for communication policies and planning is pointed out. Financial resources for communication growth must be increased.

1

2. Karunaratne, Neil D., and Cameron, Alan. "Input-Output Analysis of the Australian Information Economy." Paper presented at the Seventh Conference of Economists, Sydney, Australia, Macquarie University, 28 August-1 September 1978.

Because of the public goods aspects of information, government policy is required to deal with the optimal allocation of resources to information activities. The structural analysis undertaken in this study is intended to begin the generation of empirical data needed for the formulation of public policy. Australia is shifting toward an information economy, due to such factors as: (1) the lower unit cost of information processing; (2) greater demand for information commodities as physical demands are satiated; (3) recognition of the value of information in production and markets.

The authors define a "primary information sector" within the Australian economy and list the varied industries that belong to it. The structure of this sector is simulated by an input-output matrix to show interindustry intermediate information transactions. The matrix is further analyzed using a modified triangularization technique. Output and income multipliers are calculated, and the position of the information sector within a national input-output model is also analyzed. The study suggests that continued growth of information activities is required to sustain growth in productive activities; the high degree of interdependence among information industries suggests the need for balanced growth to avoid structural bottlenecks.

3. Lamberton, Donald McL. "The Economic Dimensions of the Right to Communicate." In Evolving Perspectives on the Right to Communicate, pp. 209-215. Edited by Jim Richstad and L.S. Harms. Honolulu: East-West Center, 1977.

Using the approach of traditional economics, a taxonomy of communication can be developed. Communication activities can be classified according to the type of information transmitted, the type of participant, the nature of the response to be elicited, or the communication medium/technology. Input-output tables can be used to analyze information flows, which in the past have been relegated to "residual" categories. In the explanation of the potential of input-output tables for the analysis of communication, three points are clear: (1) we lack understanding of the process of information flow; (2) economies of scale arise in information processes; (3) new communication technologies will bring cost reductions.

Communication contributes to economic growth in many ways: (1) it reduces the use of other resources; (2) it enables more efficient use of work and leisure time; (3) it helps people plan education, adjust to change, and make or contribute to public decisions; and (4) it helps people get the most value from their income. People must have the capacity to use information. If the purpose of establishing the right to communicate is to reduce inequalities, it must be emphasized that equality of access will not mean equality of benefit when there are disparate capacities to use information/communication.

4. Lamberton, Donald McL. "The Economics of Communication." In Planning Methods, Models, and Organization: A Review Study for Communication Policy Making and Planning, pp. 21-97. Honolulu: East-West Center, 1978.

Literature relevant to the role of communication in economic growth is reviewed; most of the authors considered are economists. Contributions to the development of the information sector approach are reviewed, stressing the work of Marc Porat, who attempted to measure the primary and secondary information sectors of the U.S. economy. The limitations of conventional economic theory in relation to information processes are pointed out. A review of the current state of economic development theory shows that informational aspects are now being considered. However, there are still very few discussions by economists of the role of communication in development; communication planning has not been integrated into development planning.
The economics of information is an important innovation in analyzing the dynamic processes of the real world; this new subject is so pervasive that it should eventually be integrated with general economics.
Discontents with development planning are discussed, and then some specific readings on communication in development are considered. Information sector analysis provides an important new approach to communication and development planning. The major unsettled question is the identity of the information sector.

5. Lavey, Warren G. Toward a Quantification of the Information/Communication Industries. Cambridge, MA: Harvard University Program on Information Technologies and Public Policy, 1974.

For the benefit of public and private decision makers, Lavey has gathered and organized statistics to present a picture of the information/communication industries in the

United States. There is no rigid scheme or framework, but rather an attempt to present a self-portrait for each industry and also to initiate further thought on that industry. The 11 industries studied are television, radio, telephone, telegraph, postal service, newspaper, periodical, book publishing and printing, motion pictures, computer software, and cable television. Data were collected in four categories: (1) revenues and net income; (2) employment and compensation; (3) messages handled; and (4) other industry descriptors. The third category comes the closest to actually describing what each industry does, but it is difficult to use it for interindustry comparisons because of the problem of converting various message units to a common denominator.

6. Machlup, Fritz. "Stocks and Flows of Knowledge." Kyklos 32:1/2 (1979) 400-411.

In economics, a distinction is made between stocks and flows of goods; the same distinction can be applied to knowledge. Machlup discusses ways to measure the stocks and flows of knowledge. For estimating the stock of knowledge he distinguishes between knowledge on record and knowledge in the mind. Attempts have been made to measure the stock of knowledge by counting numbers of journals and books, but such measures seem inadequate.

There are three kinds of knowledge flows: transmissions from person to person, person to record, and record to person. With economic goods, flows are measured by estimating changes in stocks; that method cannot be applied to knowledge, because when one person transmits knowledge to another the first person's stock is not reduced. With knowledge, every flow increases the total stock. In some areas of knowledge transmission, physical units can be counted, such as books, movies, and telephone calls. However, these units are not comparable; total dollars spent or collected for knowledge transmission could be one way to measure knowledge flows.

7. Marschak, Jacob. "Economics of Inquiring, Communicating, Deciding." American Economic Review 58:2 (May 1968) 1-18.

According to Fritz Machlup, in 1958 the U.S. knowledge industry contributed between 23 and 29 percent of GNP; its growth rate was 10 percent, twice that of the GNP. The United States is experiencing an "informational revolution." Marschak discusses the economics of the kinds of services and instruments used in meta-decision making, which he breaks down into three components: inquiry, communication, and decision. The components are defined and examples given for each. Communication is the link between inquiry, or data gathering, and decision. Communication consists of two services: the first, encoding and decoding, uses person power; the second, transmission, uses equipment. From an economics point of view, optimally efficient decisions are based on the theory of joint demand for all three components. The problem facing the meta-decision maker is to transform the inputs of data production, communication, and decision into outputs.

The user of information wants to maximize the net value of data-producing and decision-making services. The economist is concerned with the distinction between the production and transmission of data, which is analogous to the distinction between the production and transportation of goods. As a result, economists emphasize the joint demand aspect of communication series, while engineers isolate the communication problem from the production of data. Statisticians omit the communication component of decision making. The economies of mass production apply to communication, because economically significant results can be derived from measuring information in bits.

Essentially Marschak urges a multidisciplinary approach to the economics of communication for the use of decision makers, the disciplines involved being engineering, statistics, and economics.

8. Oettinger, Anthony G., and Shapiro, Peter D. Information Industries in the United States. Cambridge, MA: Harvard University Program on Information Resources Policy, 1975.

Information industries are defined as those having as a sole or primary product a service that involves one or more of the functions of creating, processing, collecting, or communicating information. In the early 1970s, for every $5 spent in the United States, over $1 was spent on an information service; such services also play a significant role in stimulating economic growth and distributing its benefits. Oettinger discusses several important issues confronting the information industries today; the issue most pertinent to the communications industry is the dislocation of traditional market patterns due to both the emergence of cable TV and the threat to AT&T's monopoly from the advent of competition. Another major issue is the determination of society's priorities in allocating information service dollars; for example, just where should research and development money be spent?

9. Porat, Marc Uri. The Information Economy. 9 vols. Washington, DC: Department of Commerce. Office of Telecommunications, 1977.

A summary and discussion of Porat's findings are found in volume 1 of this report series; the other eight volumes contain the detailed tables and matrices which support this work. The first volume, which is subtitled "definition and measurement," is abstracted here.

The United States is now an information economy because of the large share of national wealth originating from information activities. Information activity "includes all the resources consumed in producing, processing and distributing information goods and services." There are two major types of information activity: in the primary information sector, information goods and services are sold on the market; in the secondary sector, information is embedded in some other good or service. Porat builds a set of income and product accounts for both sectors.

Looking at the value-added side of national accounts, in 1967 25.1 percent of GNP originated in the primary and 21.1 percent of GNP in the secondary information sectors.

Categories of information workers are presented, and the changing composition of the U.S. work force over time is illustrated. In 1967, 45 percent of the work force were information workers, earning over 53 percent of all labor income.

A large number of information policy issues stemming from the applications of information technology are listed. Porat concludes with two major recommendations: (1) a federal organization should be established to coordinate interdepartmental policy formulation; (2) the Bureau of Economic Analysis should consider constructing permanent information sector accounts.

10. Smith, Alfred G. "The Primary Resource." Journal of Communication 25:2 (Spring 1975) 15-20

The communication economy is the way we trade messages and allocate information. Information is now our primary resource; it is a new kind of resource, requiring new concepts of production, distribution, and consumption. We are ignorant of our total investment in communication hardware and software; we seek a return on this investment in the form of social benefits, but these are very hard to measure. We can at least compare different investments and returns, which will require a form of cost-benefit accounting. The study of the communication economy will become a very complex part of the field of public finance.

There is a very uneven distribution of information and communication throughout the world; the poor do not have access to the most important form of meta-communication, information about information, because they have no knowledge of the use of libraries, computers, and organizations.

Smith concludes with five predictions: (1) a communication oligopoly will arise; (2) the communication economy will be a regulated software utility; (3) we will measure a communication national product as part of the GNP; (4) the study of the communication economy will becme a policy science; and (5) a communication elite will emerge.

11. Tomita, Tetsuo. "The Information and Communications Policy in Japan." Studies of Broadcasting no. 14 (1978) 37-61; reprinted in pamphlet form by the Nippon Hoso Kyokai.

Modern society is established on the basis of information networks, but we must not overemphasize the possible impact of information technology; information is not a fundamental of human life, and furthermore it is difficult to quantify and assess. Nor is information orientation particularly a manifestation of modern life; Japan has always been an information society. Tomita presents a three-way classification of information industries: (1) manner of operation - whether an industry transmits, processes, or sells information; (2) means by which information is transmitted - telecommunications or nontelecommunications services; 3) ways information is handled - whether the information is more for the benefit of individuals or more on a mass basis.

Tomita states that the primary objective of an information/communication policy is to guarantee people's freedom to utilize information. He then presents and discusses policy options to fulfill this objective, including ways of arranging the information supply system, monopolistic versus competitive market structures, and rates and costs.

Section 2

Economic Descriptions of Communications Industries

12. "Back With the Mailcoach, Forward With Electronics." The Economist, 30 December 1978, p. 45.

National post, telegraph, and telecommunications indus-tries (PTTs) are currently facing a number of changes. Industrialized western European nations and the United States are discussed in this survey. All the postal services are government-run, and this highly labor-intensive industry is finding it difficult to stay in the black without huge price increases; postal charges do not reflect the cost variations of distance. Comparative prices for first-class letters and also business and residential telephones are given.

Most national PTTs (except in the United States) run a government monopoly telephone service. They differ widely in the extent to which customers are allowed to buy their own equipment. PTTs may become more like electricity boards, supplying the basic service on which a huge private goods industry is based. PTTs in the future will become more like regulatory agencies and less like monopoly suppliers. Economies of scale can be gained through such devices as combining rural bus services and posts.

13. Baer, Walter S., and Pilnick, Carl. Pay Television at the Crossroads. Santa Monica, CA: Rand Corp., 1974.

Commercial interest in pay TV is increasing due to the installation of cable distribution systems and such factors as: (1) an easing of regulatory constraints; (2) a belief that programming available on "free TV" has grown stale; (3) the decreased cost of "unscrambling" equipment; (4) the existence of a strong market for pay TV movies among hotel/motel

guests.   Current   (1974)   FCC   regulations,   however,   still
severely limit the type of programming that can be offered via
pay TV; pay TV has virtually no competitive edge in programming.

Baer and Pilnick outline FCC regulations and pose policy
issues affecting pay TV; a major issue is whether pay TV
should be allowed to compete openly against advertiser-
supported free TV.   Broadcasters and theater interests want
to keep pay TV restricted to specialized, minority-taste programming.

The bulk of the report is a description of pay cable home
subscriber systems, pay cable hotel/motel systems, broadcast
pay TV, and pay TV networking.   In 1973 more hotel/motel
rooms were equipped for pay TV than were homes.   Compati-
bility between systems is a future concern; for now there will
be much duplication of effort and waste of resources until
competitive forces work themselves out.

14. Bernstein,   Peter   W.   "Television's   Expanding   World."
    Fortune 99:13 (2 July 1979) 64-69.

The $10-billion-a-year   U.S.   television   industry   will
expand dramatically in the near future, both in traditional
broadcasting and in such innovative areas as cable TV, pay
TV, videotapes, and videodiscs.   Pay TV is spurring the
growth of cable TV; however, it is currently forecast that no
more than 40 percent of households will sign up for cable.
Therefore subscription TV (STV), the broadcast version of
pay TV, also has an excellent future.   At present, about 20
percent of TV households have cable TV.   The heaviest
restrictions on cable have been removed by the FCC and the
courts.

Cable   operators   are   very   selective   in   choosing   new
markets; factors include population density, costs of construction, demographics, and the number of broadcast signals
available.   A good choice means a 16 to 20 percent return on
investment; however, the return on investment for a broadcast
station is usually 20 to 30 percent.   Methods for financing a
cable company are described; local interests are usually invited
to participate.   Very soon, all the desirable franchises will be
taken, and future expansion will depend on programming.   A
study is cited that indicates that CATV has had little impact
on the network's leadership in programming.

15. "Briefing/Telecommunications." Asiaweek 4:46 (24 Novem-
    ber 1978) 28, 31-32, 34-36, 38.

Several brief articles provide an overview of the telecommunications industry in Southeast Asia, focusing on the five
ASEAN (Association of Southeast Asian Nations) countries (Indonesia, Malaysia, Philippines, Singapore, Thailand).   All five
ASEAN countries belong to Intelsat. Progress in the implementation of telecommunications plans for each ASEAN country is
described in detail; there is an in-depth report on the Philippines, which is unique in that private corporations are in
charge of its system due to its American colonial background.
In the Philippines, the telegram has been found to be a most
economical means of communication for an island country; there
has been heavy investment in computerized international
message-switching centers in the hopes of making Manila the
center of international communications in the Far East.
    A symbol of ASEAN cooperation is the establishment of a
submarine co-axial cable network; the first segment, between
the Philippines and Singapore, was inaugurated on October 3,
1978.   Telecommunications cooperation will yield great transnational economic and social benefits.   The cable system is
complementary to satellites which are sometimes vulnerable to
atmospheric disturbances.
    The overview is concluded with a look at telecommunica-
tions growth prospects and competition among the Southeast
Asian nations.

16. Chapuis, R.   "Common Carrier Telecommunications in the
    World Economy."   Telecommunication Journal 39:10 (1972)
    601-620.

Telecommunications is typically viewed as an ancillary
activity; Chapuis has gathered and presented extensive
statistics for a number of representative ITU members to point
up the importance of telecommunications as a major economic
activity.   Common carrier telecommunications is defined as all
message transmissions for public needs, normally between fixed
points; this excludes broadcasting to undetermined stations
and also private networks.   Data were gathered from annual
reports of government administrations and private operating
agencies; gaps were filled in with estimates.
    The tables cover the years 1969 and 1970; for each
country shown, basic financial data for telephone, telegraph,
and telex services are given.   From Table 4, a summary of the
total turnover of common carrier telecommunications throughout
the world, it can be deduced that in 1972 world turnover
would be $42 billion U.S.   This may be the first global-level
estimate ever made.

Capital assets, or total gross investment, are compared to annual revenues; the ratio is found to be roughly 3, which is much higher than in ordinary commercial undertakings. The proportion of revenue accounted for by international service is shown to be growing very rapidly. International telecommunications should grow at an annual rate of 20 percent or more during 1970-1985.

17. Colburn, John H. "Economics of the Press." In Proceedings: Education for Newspaper Journalists in the Seventies and Beyond, pp. 101-139. Sponsored by American Newspaper Publishers Association Foundation. Washington, DC: ANPA Foundation, 1974.

The U.S. newspaper publishing industry has achieved a prosperity unforeseen 20 years ago, due to such factors as fewer competing dailies in one city, better economic planning, new technology, and more professional management. A sound economic base is the key to the survival of the American free press; Colburn outlines costs, which are primarily for personnel, newsprint, and ink, and shows how newspapers plan their profits.

Broadcasting has successfully competed for newspaper readers and advertisers, but newspapers still retain the largest percentage of advertising among the mass media. The possibility of two-way cable TV is a threat to the future of newspapers. Information, in the form of news or advertising, is the lifeblood of the newspaper. Newspapers allocate a portion of their budgets for the acquisition of information; a large city daily will spend 8 to 10 percent of total revenue on its newsroom. To be successful, a journalist must understand the "economics of the press."

18. "The Common Market Rewires its Phones." Business Week, 13 April 1974, pp. 42, 44.

The Common Market countries are far behind the United States in terms of telephone penetration, and much of their telephone plant is obsolete. Due to public demand and massive technological changes, Europe is now investing heavily in the most modern telephone equipment. Manufacturers expect a 25 percent annual growth rate in the private market segment during the rest of the decade. This sudden boom may be beyond the capacity of European suppliers, and such U.S.-based multinationals as IBM are trying to edge into the market. IBM has been concentrating on new equipment for the business telephone market. This article describes the traditional marketing patterns for phone equipment and speculates on the impact on the market of the rather sudden high rate of demand.

19. "Computers: High Growth That Goes On and On."   Business Week, 8 January 1979, pp. 39, 42, 46.

Although the U.S. economy faces a possible slowdown in 1979, the manufacturers of information-processing equipment have had two years of record-shattering growth and feel that their performance this year should be as good.   Many companies have large backlogs of orders.   The main trend in the business is declining prices coupled with enhanced performance; one company has been reducing its prices 20 percent every year.   The largest equipment market, general-purpose main-frame computers, grew the slowest in 1978, while minicomputers and small business systems grew the fastest; the market for small business systems is expected to grow by 40 percent in 1979.   The elasticity of demand for more cost-effective computers seems endless.

IBM dominates the market and has kept up competitive pressure with new products and price cutting.   An important new trend is distributed processing; when IBM entered this market it legitimized the trend.   This approach shifts a customer's data processing out of centralized operations into smaller computers and terminals that do the processing at local sites.   Another important trend is the introduction of systems that do both data and word processing, which are traditionally separate markets.   IBM also dominates this business, but its existing product line is facing fierce competition.

Japan is seen as a threat to the future of the American industry.

20. Curwen, Peter J.   "The Economics of Academic Publishing in the U.K."   The Journal of Industrial Economics 25:3 (March 1977) 161-175.

It is difficult to measure "academic" publishing since statistics are not collected under this heading.   In this study, "adult non-fiction" books are used as roughly equivalent to academic books.   Price indices for the period 1964-1975 show that the general trend is rising prices; from 1964 to 1970, however, prices actually increased only for the most expensive books, thus raising the average - for most books, prices remained static.   In the early 1970s, average prices declined due to the upsurge in paperback publishing; since then, there have been sharply rising prices.

It is inappropriate to speak of the demand for books, as each book is a unique product.   The crucial issue is whether

people buy books primarily because of their price; Curwen
feels that in academia demand for books is price-inelastic
except above an upper threshold.

Production costs have been rising sharply, especially for
paper and printing. Publishers must tie up large sums in the
production process, giving them a cash flow problem. Publishers have been pursuing a variety of options to offset
this problem: (1) concentrating on profitable books; (2) concentrating on textbooks rather than monographs; (3) raising
prices and selling exclusively to libraries; (4) cutting
production runs; (5) concentrating on booklists, as it is
cheaper to produce a new edition than a new book. Publishers
feel that in the early 1970s there was overproduction of books
and that this period of retrenchment is healthy.

21. "Dishy Offer for Satellite Television." The Economist, 7
    July 1979, pp. 103-104.

RCA Americom has offered a free satellite receiver to
every U.S. commercial TV station. Over 200 of the 725 stations have accepted the $50,000 receiver so far. Through
this aggressive marketing strategy, Americom will make a
profit if more than half of the stations accept. Currently,
networks and other program suppliers must use air freight,
air mail, or AT&T's land lines to deliver their product;
Americom is particularly interested in challenging AT&T's
virtual monopoly on reliable, instant national service. Americom offers large savings over the price of AT&T's services;
for a one-hour transmission from New York to 20 cities,
Americom would charge $1,100 - AT&T charges $8,000.

The new system is going to be tested for six weeks,
beginning in October 1979. Other potential competitors will be
watching, including Western Union with its Westar satellites.

22. "Electronic Post." The Economist, 4 August 1979, pp.
    76-77.

In the near future all offices will have an electronic mail
system. Intelpost, a current experiment in international
electronic mail, is showing itself to be relatively cheap.
Electronic mail can be transmitted along conventional telephone
lines or digital networks; various types of terminal equipment
are described, including teleprinters, facsimile machines,
communicating copiers, and communicating word processors.
American companies are forging ahead in both the provision of
network services and in terminal equipment; current marketing
activities of such companies as IBM, Xerox, Exxon, and AT&T
are described.

The transformation of business communications depends on "technology push" and the rapidly declining costs of machine intelligence. By 1987 the price of a communicating word processor will be half of what it is today.

Electronic mail has not yet been justified on purely economic grounds; experiments on its costs and benefits have been inconclusive. Nor has it been conclusively proven to raise office productivity; new management techniques must be developed for maximizing the efficiency of the automated office.

23. Greaser, Constance U. Alternatives to Traditional Forms of Scientific Communication. Santa Monica, CA: Rand Corp., 1976.

Journals are the major medium for disseminating scientific information; rapid increases in the number of journals and their processing costs are making it necessary to find ways to lower costs and increase efficiency of information dissemination.

Experiments in faster, cheaper ways to publish the traditional paper journal include: (1) a cooperative called an "editorial processing center" formed by publishers of small journals to share the costs of automating certain functions and gain economies of scale; (2) "no-frills journals," unedited and nondescript in appearance, concentrating solely on high-quality scholarship; (3) a "synoptic," a brief article containing the key ideas, results, and data from a longer article – the reader can use it and can also order the longer article; (4) "miniprints," standard-length articles in very small type that can be read by the naked eye; and (5) selective dissemination, a method for cutting down on distribution costs.

Two major alternatives to paper journals are micrographics and the electronic journal. Micrographics are very cheap, but there is a negative bias toward their use. The electronic journal is a futuristic concept; a central data bank would contain articles that could be accessed through remote terminals. Cost has been a prohibitive factor for this development, but it is predicted that by the 1990s the electronic journal should cost less than a paper journal.

24. International Data Corporation. "Business Communications: The New Frontier." Fortune 98:7 (9 October 1978); 18 pages of text in advertising supplement pp. 25-80.

The communications industry is on the threshhold of a period of vigorous expansion that will benefit both suppliers and users; the hottest sector of the market will be in business communications. This "White Paper to Management" is particularly intended to alert communications managers to available and potential opportunities for streamlining and cutting costs in communications systems. In some businesses, such as airlines, hotels, and banking, communications can give the organization a competitive edge. Electronic business communications will become as crucial to business growth and development as electronic data processing has been.

User spending on business communications grows by 15 percent per year. Growth rates in supplier revenues are given for all sectors of the telecommunications industry: voice revenues grow about 8 to 10 percent per year; total data revenues are much smaller but are growing three times as fast; business rates are growing faster than residential, as new services and equipment reach the high-volume users first. Many new services and new markets are described: digital technology, word processing, facsimile, electronic mail, and teleconferencing are among the new technologies that will have a major impact on business communications. Business communications, computers, and office products will eventually intertwine to become one market; the "information age" will have arrived.

25. Irwin, Manley R. "The Communications Industry." In The Structure of American Industry, 4th ed., pp. 380-418. Edited by Walter Adams. New York: Macmillan, 1971.

The U.S. communications common carrier industry is regulated, which distinguishes it from other industries, shapes its structure, and affects its performance. Irwin presents a concise description of the industry under the following headings: market structure, market entry, market conduct and performance, and public policy. Statistical data are included in each section.

Structure is considered from both the supply and demand side. The Bell system, the independents, and Western Union are described; holding companies are a characteristic structure. On the demand side, services offered are classified by customer groups, as between toll and local service, business and residential service. Irwin speculates that demand is price-inelastic, although local service may be sensitive to personal income.

Major factors in market entry are the capital-intensiveness of the industry, scale economies, availability of frequency spectrum, and the regulatory process. Under the market conduct heading, Irwin considers the price competition that exists in some submarkets, such as the private lease market, and policies that protect the carriers from price competition in other markets.

Performance considerations include pricing for services and equipment, profits, rate of return, research and development, productivity, and incentives/disincentives to innovation. Public policies that have led to the formation of holding companies are reviewed; Irwin suggests that the holding company is an impediment to the industry's ability to adjust to technological innovation.

26. "Japan's New Electronics Goodies." The Economist, 22 April 1978, pp. 84-85.

Japanese consumer electronics goods are exported throughout the world; North America is the biggest market, having imported 45 percent of the total in 1976. By product, tape recorders constituted 28 percent of consumer electronics exports, color TV 19 percent, audio systems 17 percent, and radios 11 percent. During the ten-year period 1967-1977 the output of this industry quintupled, from $2 billion to $10 billion. There are two significant reasons for this phenomenal growth: (1) the Japanese maintain a high ratio of R&D spending to total sales - Sony's ratio is 5 percent, which in 1978 meant $125 million for R&D; (2) the Japanese seem able to create mass markets where none existed. A major example is VTR systems; while sales of European and U.S. systems lagged, the relatively cheap Japanese Betamax has been very successful, especially in Japan. The Japanese are working on many new products and technologies for the 1980s; promising prospects include flat television technology, laser-based audio systems using pulse code modulation, and home facsimile systems.

27. Kuczun, Sam. "Ownership of Newspapers Increasingly Becoming Public." Journalism Quarterly 55:2 (Summer 1978) 342-344.

U.S. newspapers have traditionally served two publics, readers and advertisers. In 1967, when Gannett Company offered 500,000 shares over the counter, a third party became involved, the investing public. In 1960 only 11 newspaper companies had stocks or bonds that could be purchased publicly; by 1977 five companies were listed on the New York Stock Exchange and five on the American. Of the top ten newspaper groups in terms of daily circulation, half are publicly owned. Kuczun presents statistics detailing this trend to public ownership.

In the past it has been difficult for researchers to obtain economic data about newspapers because the papers were privately owned. Publicly owned newspapers are within the jurisdiction of the Securities and Exchange Commission and are required to disclose information concerning their financial affairs. Researchers will now be better able to study the economic behavior of newspaper firms.

28. LeDuc, Don R. "The Common Market Film Industry: Beyond Law or Economics." Journal of Communication 29:1 (Winter 1979) 44-55.

    In the nine Common Market countries, film has remained a nationally oriented and marketed commodity, while Common Market laws and policies have encouraged and even compelled the production and distribution of other goods at Common Market-wide levels. Film companies behave as if national trade barriers still existed. The Common Market Cinema Industry Committee maintains that film cannot transcend cultural barriers and will not benefit from a combined market; it also claims that film is acting in compliance with Common Market industry exemptions. The Commission (the executive body of the Common Market) has tried to overturn national policies that act as tariffs to restrict the movement of many goods, but it has made no such moves against film. The Commission has requested the cessation of national subsidies for film, with no results.
    The Common Market film industries are in a great deal of financial trouble due to the divergence of earnings through multinational corporations to interests outside the Community and due to drastically declining attendance. There is a growing dependence on national governments for financial support, which could curtail artistic integrity as effectively as any possible legal actions by the Common Market Commission.

29. Lemasters, John N. "Earth Station Market - The Picture Today; Prospects for the Future." Satellite Communications 2:11 (November 1978) 30-32.

    Five major segments of the international market in satellite communications are described. In the INTELSAT network there are presently 205 earth stations, with 30 to 40 being added per year; this market is worth some $200 to $300 million a year. The network has provided smaller nations with a direct means of international communication; previously, external communication had to be routed through neighboring countries. In the U.S. television market, satellites have been used for CATV and special news and sports events; approximately 50 percent of the capacity of American satellites is used for TV. Commercial TV stations are now getting into the earth station market.

Growth in the dedicated network market in the U.S. has been held back by the fact that services are already available through the telephone system; this is a replacement market. Also, the FCC has not licensed the smaller earth stations required for this application. The U.S. data communications market looks very promising for the 1980s. The largest market is for domestic satellite networks that provide in-country long-distance service; the market consists primarily of the developing nations that do not have a highly developed terrestrial system. A satellite system can be operational in two years, as compared to at least ten for a terrestrial system, and at lower cost; also, upkeep and maintenance costs are lower.

30. Maddox, Brenda. Beyond Babel: New Directions in Communications. London: André Deutsch, 1972.

New developments in communication technology are described from an economic and sociopolitical point of view. The potential of satellites, cable television, and telephones is emphasized because they will offer cheap, two-way communication, the main thrust of the communication revolution. Many technological innovations have not been implemented for general use because of the enormous costs of new equipment, and also because of profound social inertia. There is such a pent-up demand for all types of communication services that it is difficult to predict the future of any one technology.

Satellites have revolutionized the economics of communication because distance between senders and receivers on the ground becomes irrelevant. Maddox describes the creation and organization of Comsat and Intelsat, regulatory issues, satellite capabilities and rate structures, the economics of cable and satellites as rival technologies, and the contribution of satellites to educational technology.

Current industry structure and regulatory problems of cable TV and telephones in the United States and Britain are described. The potential of cable TV lies in its enormous capacity, but will people be willing to pay for television? Telephones are the basic instruments of the new technology, with possibilities for many new services.

Maddox recommends the centralization of responsibility for national communication; governments must perceive communication as a social need, parallel to housing and education. Also recommended is a complete renovation of telephone pricing; cheap flat rates for calls anywhere in the world must be set.

31. Marvin, Carolyn. "Computer Systems: Prospects for a
    Public Information Network." Journal of Communication
    28:4 (August 1978) 172-183.

    The major obstacle to a U.S. national public access in-
formation network is the high cost of software. Only users
with large capital resources, characterized as Big Government,
Big Business, and Big Science, have been able to reap the
benefits of information retrieval on a large scale. Commercial
data base suppliers show little concern for intersystem com-
patibility; they prefer to keep their systems mutually exclusive
to cut down competition from other companies. They duplicate
among each other the fixed costs of software and maintenance
and the marginal costs of marketing and administration and
pass these costs on in the form of high prices.
    Traditionally free public libraries are becoming the clients
of commercial vendors and charging fees for new services to
recover costs. Only larger libraries have the volume of use
providing the economies of scale that make such services
feasible; it is possible that smaller libraries will be squeezed
out of business by such developments.
    The Library of Congress has been trying to develop a
public access network using its own MARC (Machine Readable
Cataloging) format; this format, however, was constructed to
handle books and serials, not such other types of information
units as journal articles. The Library has provided a free,
local information system linked to computer files containing
cataloging data, information on pending legislation, and data
on organizations that provide information services. Marvin
concludes, however, that there is little prospect for a unified
public network on the horizon.

32. Miller, Frederick W. "Electronic Mail Comes of Age."
    Infosystems 24:11 (November 1977) 56, 60, 62, 64.

    Electronic mail is a system in which messages are trans-
mitted in electronic form; various implementations are described
in this article. Systems differ in the types of messages sent,
scope of the delivery system, and system justification. Speed
and cost are overriding concerns in all systems. An early
system was Western Union's Mailgram service which began in
1971-72 to deliver business messages overnight; it has grown
25 percent a year. Datapost is a prime competitor to Mailgram
and is an unregulated mail/communication service; it is provided by TDX Telecommunications of Houston. Services,
costs, and marketing of several other firms are described.
The future of electronic mail. depends on the development
of cost-effective terminals, low-cost satellite transmission
networks, and adaptability to the new equipment by office

workers. Efficient use of electronic mail could improve office productivity, but workers must become accustomed to less face-to-face oral communication.

33. "The New New Telephone Industry." Business Week, 13
    February 1978, pp. 68-71, 74, 78.

Recent decisions by the FCC have opened many sectors of the U.S. telephone industry to intense competition. New products and services offered by new competitors make it the fastest-growing new market in the United States. Telecommunications technology is racing ahead, threatening the premature obsolescence of much existing telephone plant. Two major markets are: (1) consumer telephones - subscribers can now purchase their own equipment and save 70¢ a month on their service rates if they do; (2) business communications - the mix of communications and information systems will yield the electronic office of the future. There will also be major expansion of telecommunications systems abroad; it is predicted that the number of telephones in the world will triple to 1.4 billion by the year 2000.

The two biggest U.S. competitors are AT&T and IBM; their marketing moves, and those of other competitors are described. Regulatory problems caused by the increasingly blurry distinction between the regulated communications industry and the unregulated computer industry are outlined. The FCC and Congress are determined to maintain competition in this potentially $400 billion industry, and will try to keep AT&T and IBM from splitting the market between themselves.

34. Oettinger, Anthony G. Elements of Information and Re-
    sources Policy: Library and Other Information Services.
    Revised ed. Cambridge, MA: Harvard University Pro-
    gram on Information Technologies and Public Policy, 1976.

This report was prepared for the National Commission on Libraries and Information Science, which has a mandate to develop and recommend plans for library and information services adequate to meet the needs of the American people. The report is a study of information providers and their clients, to find out what economic, institutional, and technological factors determine how people get the information they need. Extensive information on both the private-sector information industry and the library world is provided. Some important findings include: (1) the primary users of libraries and of direct fee services are the economically better off; (2) virtually all information services are supported to some extent by the government; (3) some information resources are unique; natural monopolies must be identified, and economies of scale should be preserved through avoidance of duplication; (4) the size and cost of information services have risen faster than such basic indexes as population size and consumer prices; and (5) accounting practices are poor, and it is very difficult to assess costs and particularly benefits of information services.

35. Smith, Datus C., Jr.   The Economics of Book Publishing in Developing Countries.   Reports and Papers on Mass Communication, no. 79.   Paris: Unesco, 1977.

The concentration of book production and consumption in a few advanced countries is an obstacle to social progress. Self-sustaining national publishing enterprises must be developed.   In this survey of 55 publishers in developing countries, economic problems peculiar to the book industry are identified and discussed.   The survey data include manufacturing costs and their distribution among composition, presswork, binding, and paper; editorial costs, overhead costs, retail prices and how they are set; profits; and the determination of a break-even point.
To develop a large-scale book industry, low prices and large quantity production are required; also, the public interest case for books is stronger if books reach large audiences, not just elites.   Thanks largely to Unesco there are now few import-duty restrictions on the flow of books to developing countries; however, there are often large duties on printing machinery and paper.   National governments must change this policy if they wish to develop a book industry. Few developing nations have treated book industries well in terms of supplying finance capital.   Governments also influence the book industry through special postage rates, purchase of books by government institutions, and literacy programs. Co-publishing arrangements are suggested among smaller countries to achieve the economies of larger markets.

36. Soma, John T.   The Computer Industry: An Economic-Legal Analysis of its Technology and Growth.   Lexington, MA: Lexington Books, 1976.

The impact of the interaction of economic, technological, and legal factors on the growth of the computer industry is analyzed.   The first chapter concerns the economic development of the U.S. computer industry.   Soma outlines the "computer development cycle," which began in the 1940s on the basis of a large underlying demand for information processing; extensive federal funding was provided to early computer projects.

The next chapter reviews several issues in the legal environment: (1) the regulatory interface between communications and computers, networks, the dependence of computers on communications, and the difference between data processing and message switching; (2) antitrust and barriers to entry; (3) patents, copyrights, and trade secrets; (4) leasing of computer equipment; (5) regulations and policies affecting exports and imports of computer equipment and various international markets; (6) U.S. federal procurement policies (the U.S. government buys over 10 percent of industry output).

Finally, a technological forecast for the next 15 years is made. A long-term trend towards structural atomization of the industry is predicted.

37. "Striking It Rich in Radio." Business Week, 5 February 1979, pp. 58-62.

The U.S. radio business is currently enjoying great prosperity, and countless investors are seeking to buy into radio stations. Radio now earns more advertising dollars than the magazine industry. Radio advertising rates appeal to advertisers in these inflationary times; because radio is relatively neither capital- nor labor-intensive, as compared with television and print, rates are not climbing as quickly. The FCC is moving toward almost total deregulation of radio and is encouraging a more competitive atmosphere and expansion in the number of stations. FM stations are doing very well and have shown that with revamped formats they can have parity with AM stations. There has been an increase in specialized programs aiming at certain segments of the radio audience, comparable to the growth of specialized magazines.

38. "Telecommunications Gets a Ring of Confidence." The Economist, 28 October 1978, pp. 82-83.

A very profitable future for the telecommunications equipment industry is projected; in 1977 world sales were $30 billion, and by 1987 they should reach $65 billion. The change to computerized, fully electronic switching equipment has been accomplished and will lead to demand for sophisticated services. Developing countries will have the fastest growth in demand for equipment, about 10 percent a year.

A major problem for European producers is how to pay for the huge investment required by new systems. Money for growth has to be spent before the new revenues start coming in. The European PTTs must get their funds from finance ministries, which leads to political complications. If prices are pushed up now to pay for future services, subscribers will object; private capital could be obtained, but investors are wary of state-controlled monpolies. A possible solution might be an international network linking the nine EEC countries, using the .lucrative revenues from international calls, but the national PTTs are not enthusiastic.

Types of equipment and their percentage of the market are given; concentration among both buyers and sellers is described.

39. Udell, Jon G. The Economics of the American Newspaper. New York: Hastings House, 1978.

Setting the newspaper industry in the context of the American free enterprise system, the author discusses the problems of private enterprises that perform a public service. Newspapers try to produce an informative, quality product, free of bias, and at the same time earn enough money to survive. Profits and how they function to maintain newspaper quality, costs, and revenues are described in detail. The marketing of newspapers to readers and advertisers is ana-lyzed. The new technology of newspaper production is pre-sented together with its capital requirements. The concluding chapter is a look ahead to new technology, the ever-evolving role of the newspaper, and American economic problems that affect newspapers.

Section 3

Economic Analysis of Communications

A. GENERAL

40. Dobell, A. Rodney; Taylor, Lester D.; Waverman, Leonard; Liu, Tsuang-Hua; and Copeland, Michael D.G. "Telephone Communications in Canada: Demand, Production, and Investment Decisions." Bell Journal of Economics and Management Science 3:1 (Spring 1972) 175-219.

In this econometric model of the telecommunications industry in Canada, attention is focused on demand, production, and investment decisions in the telephone sector. As background information, Canada's telephone network is described, including ownership patterns, regulatory bodies, and the process of rate regulation. The overall model is briefly explained before a detailed analysis of each of the three components. Demand is assumed to be dependent on general macroeconomic conditions; output is assumed equal to demand, so in the production section of the paper the problem is to determine the necessary inputs to produce the output; output and demand forecasts establish expected future capital requirements, which determine the necessary level of investment.

A dynamic model is used to estimate demand for local and long distance, residence, and business calls. Revenue is used as the dependent variable. Important conclusions are that in the short run there is little response to changes in income or price; in the long run, the income elasticity of demand is greater than one. Demand is homogeneous across regions of Canada.

Three types of relationships were estimated to characterize production: a production function of the Cobb-Douglas form, an input requirements function, and productivity functions giving inputs as functions of relative factor prices.

A modified accelerator model was found to best explain the level of investment expenditures, which is consistent with the behavior of a regulated industry. In conclusion, it is noted that a consistent pattern was found linking demand to production decisions to capital formation. (See also Fishelson, entry 268).

41. Dordick, Herbert S., ed. Proceedings of the Sixth Annual Telecommunications Policy Research Conference. Lexington, MA: D.C. Heath, 1979.

Four themes reflecting current policy issues and trends in policy research were selected as topics for the conference: (1) TV - its social effects and the policy issues they create; (2) computer-communication networks and the emerging information economy; (3) spectrum allocation; and (4) economics of regulation and the economics of pricing of telecommunications services. The latter three contain papers relevant to the economics of communication.

Marc Porat's research on the information economy is reviewed by Albert Walderhaug; he also suggests applications and tests for Porat's theories. R. Michael Tyler discusses the costs of and potential demand for teletext systems. The costs of computer mail and computer conferencing are reviewed by Robert Johansen.

The need to structure a theory or model for rational allocation of the electromagnetic spectrum is stressed; the resource is becoming increasingly scarce. John Robinson proposes that an auction be used instead of a hearing to chose among competing applicants for multipoint distribution service channels. Charles Jackson presents "a market alternative for the orbit-spectrum resource."

Yale Braunstein finds that when states regulate cable TV, subscription rates are greater than in states without state regulation. John Panzar compares flat-rate tariffs and usage-sensitive pricing, and Bridger Mitchell surveys pricing policies in five European telephone systems.

42. Lewin, Leonard, ed. Telecommunications: An Interdisciplinary Survey. Dedham, MA: Artech House, 1979.

The purpose of this book is to present the basic course material in the University of Colorado at Boulder's interdisciplinary program in telecommunications. Such a program is necessary because the size and shape of the telecommunications industry are determined by such a variety of forces: the technical aspects of design and operation, economics, government regulation, management, and legal and social impacts. In the introduction, interdisciplinary programs at several universities, including Boulder, are described. Twelve chapters by various contributors cover such areas as the ITU, the FCC, broadcast control and regulation, constitutional law, the information society, international aspects of telecommunications operations, telecommunications systems, signal transmission, and the computer in telecommunications.

Of particular relevance to the economics of communication are the chapters on engineering economy and the telephone rate structure. The first treats the economics of technical alternatives; economy is viewed as a design parameter. In the second, marginal cost pricing, usage-sensitive pricing, and value of service pricing are discussed; such pricing problems as the presence of externalities and decreasing costs are treated.

43. Owen, Bruce M.; Grey, David L.; and Rosse, James N. A Selected Bibliography in the Economics of the Mass Media. Research Memoranda Series, no. 99. Stanford, CA: Research Center in Economic Growth, Stanford University, 1970.

The authors have provided an extensive list of books and journal articles published primarily in the 1960s which, in their view, have made a significant contribution to the literature. The list is divided into two sections; the first is arranged alphabetically by author, and the second is a subject arrangement. The seven subject areas are: (1) theory and concepts; (2) analysis, description, empirics; (3) law, regulation, public policy; (4) data sources; (5) trade publications, professional journals; (6) technology and development; (7) general and miscellaneous. Within each subject area, materials are grouped by medium, as follows: (1) electronic (radio, TV, cable, satellites); (2) newspapers; (3) magazines; (4) advertising; (5) general, other.

B. COMPETITION/MONOPOLY ISSUES

44. Abel, J.D.; Hill, R.A.; and Spicer, M.W. "The Political Economy of Broadcasting." Lloyds Bank Review, no. 119 (January 1976) 23-37.

In this description of the structure of the British broadcasting system, it is noted that its outstanding characteristic has been stability. Certain factors threaten this stability: (1) cable systems that will make more channels available; (2) low revenues and rapidly increasing costs that are threatening finances; (3) a lack of consensus on social values, and criticism of both the BBC and commercial broadcasters for their stance on public issues.

The authors suggest that it is time for changes in the system. From broadcasting we want a diverse mixture of information, education, culture, and entertainment. Diversity is crucial; besides a variety of programming, we also need a wide range of values, opinions and ideas and the opportunity to communicate ideas. Many factors influence diversity; the authors show the effects on diversity of monopolistic and competitive industry structures. Three proposals to increase diversity are discussed: (1) reducing competition; (2) pay television; (3) increasing the number of channels.

45. Baer, Walter S.; Geller, Henry; Grundfest, Joseph A.; and Possner, Karen B. Concentration of Mass Media Ownership: Assessing the State of Current Knowledge. Santa Monica, CA: Rand Corp., 1974.

Two principal questions are addressed in this literature review of some 500 items: (1) what is the extent of concentration of U.S. mass media ownership? (2) how does media ownership influence performance? There are three general forms of concentration: (1) consolidation of local media outlets of the same type; (2) cross-ownership of different media in the same market; (3) group or chain ownership of media outlets in different communities. Government interventions to limit concentration are based on the objective of maintaining competition in the marketplace of ideas; government policies dealing with concentration are outlined.

Using one index of concentration, cable TV is the most concentrated medium, followed by newspapers, then TV stations. Group-owned TV stations account for three-fourths of the average daily audience. There are many documented cases of abuse by media owners, such as presenting one-sided versions of the news or violating the antitrust laws, but no patterns of behavior among classes of media owners emerge.

In assessing evidence of the effects of ownership on media performance as economic units and information sources, the authors conclude that most research is inconclusvie due to methodological problems. The size of a market, demographic characteristics, and the number of local competitors are more important factors than ownership.

An extensive bibliography listing items published since 1945 concerning media ownership is included.

46. Baer, Walter S., and Mitchell, Bridger M. "Impact of Competition on an Independent Telephone Company." Public Utilities Fortnightly 96:9 (23 October 1975) 23-29.

Continental Telephone System is the third largest telephone company in the United States; it serves two million telephones in 41 states, with exchanges located principally in small towns. Continental serves as the subject of this case study. FCC decisions in the late 1960s opened up competition in two areas: (1) terminal equipment; and (2) private-line interconnecting services. Because of the separations principles used to divide toll revenues between AT&T and the independents, the independents may be even more affected by the new competition than Bell.

Revenue/cost relationships are analyzed to determine the real effects of competition. The authors used a fully distributed cost method, based on separations principles, which allocates investment and operating and overhead expenses according to relative usage. A crucial question was whether business subscribers support residential services, or vice versa; the data clearly showed that in the Continental system business exchange and toll service supported residential service. The biggest impact will be that direct competition will reduce the subscriber line usage factor used in determining settlement revenues, leading to large losses in toll settlements revenues for the independents. Losses will require increased revenues from basic exchange service, or other charges such as usage-sensitive pricing. Competition will reduce the costs of some business users, but most methods of repricing services in response to competition will make some subscribers worse off.

47. Baer, Walter S.; Geller, Henry; and Grundfest, Joseph A. Newspaper-Television Station Cross-Ownership: Options for Federal Action. Santa Monica, CA: Rand Corp., 1974.

In the early 1970s the FCC was considering a rule that would prohibit newspaper-television station cross-ownership in the same geographic market. As of July 1974 there were 79 pairs of daily newspapers and TV stations under common ownership. The U.S. government is concerned with maintaining a diversity of information sources available to the public. The authors first review antitrust and congressional actions leading up to the proposed rule. In discussing the extent of cross-ownership, they point out how difficult it is to measure or index concentration of ownership; market and media definitions have a strong effect on any index.

Arguments for and against cross-ownership restrictions are summarized; the authors claim arguments on both sides are weak and repetitive. Issues include whether combinations give superior service, whether they lead to monopoly abuses, and whether divestiture would disrput the industry.

Six major options for FCC action are briefly examined. The most difficult decision will be whether to require divestiture of all combinations, or only future combinations, or only in cases showing undue concentration and abuses.

48. Beebe, Jack H. "Institutional Structure and Program Choices in Television Markets." Quarterly Journal of Economics 91:1 (February 1977) 15-37.

This article deals with the absence of competition in TV programming, the attempts made by economists to construct models of program choice, and the welfare implications of such choice. The institutional framework used by Beebe is one of limited channel capacity and advertiser-supported broadcasting. He considers the implications of viewer preference intensities and makes a formal comparison of monopoly and competition in terms of consumer surplus and total surplus for producers and consumers. The assumptions for this analysis include: (1) the TV market is in partial equilibrium; (2) advertising is the only source of revenue; (3) program costs are the only costs; (4) the program is a free good to the viewer.

The calculations of program patterns make use of the facts that monopolists never duplicate programs and that they try to attract viewers from non-TV activities, not from other channels. Also, the monopolist will choose a program that promises maximum net addition to total audience. The competitor has to solve an "n"-person non-zero sum game in which "n" is so small that decisions of one firm affect the profits of other firms.

In calculating consumer surplus using ordinal preferences, the programming structure providing more first choices is superior. Under limited channel capacity either monopoly or competition may give greater consumer surplus. The total surplus is the sum of consumer and producer surplus. The latter is the total advertising revenues minus total program costs.

The welfare implications for advertiser-supported broadcasting support the expansion of channels as a necessary condition for viewer attainment of preferred choices. If this is possible then a competitive channel structure is favored.

49. Boyd, Marjorie. "Getting a Handle on AT&T." The Washington Monthly, January 1979, pp. 37-47.

American Telephone and Telegraph, the world's largest company, is partly regulated and partly private; 80 percent of its operation consists of running the phone network, the other 20 percent consists of the unregulated subsidiaries Bell Laboratories and Western Electric. The Justice Department has filed an antitrust suit against AT&T, which will come to trial in 1980, seeking divestiture of Western Electric and the division of the system into its component parts.

Utility rates are based on the amount of investment by the company; a rate-making commission sets prices for the telephone company that will ensure a reasonable return on the investments that make up the rate base. In 1976 the FCC released a four-year study showing that AT&T had hundreds of millions of dollars of wasted investment in excess capacity and overbuilt facilities. The only barrier to this "expansion-by-investment" is the regulatory commission, and AT&T is so huge that the commissions can't police it effectively. An example of excess investment is the videophone, for which demand simply has not materialized.

50. Crandall, Robert W. "The Economic Case for a Fourth Commercial Television Network." Public Policy 22:4 (Fall 1974) 513-536.

A network triopoly is limiting diversity in U.S. television programming. This triopoly is caused by the FCC's local-station allocation plan which limits the number of VHF stations to three in most markets, thus blocking the entry of a new network. The first section of this study shows the effect of network concentration on audience size; results show that as more signals are added, audiences increase but at a declining rate. The number of network signals has a significant but small impact upon total viewing. In the second section, the value of increased viewing options is estimated. Cable TV data can be used to estimate consumer demand; the author's econometric study shows a projected benefit to consumers of nearly $1 billion for a fully competitive fourth network.

Operating costs and revenues in a four-network structure are outlined; profits would become leaner for all networks. However, to be economically viable, the new network would have to reach as many homes as the existing networks. This is impossible under existing allocations; Crandall recommends that the FCC increase the number of commercial VHF stations in the largest markets by transferring public broadcasting to the UHF band. Diversity will come from expanding the number of commercial networks, not by expanding noncommercial stations offering programs that relatively few people watch.

51. Crandall, Robert W.   "The Postwar Performance of the Motion-Picture Industry."   The Antitrust Bulletin 20:1 (Spring 1975) 49-88.

In 1972 the U.S. Justice Department filed suit against ABC and CBS for restraint of competition in the production/ distribution of movies. Using extensive data, Crandall analyzes the film industry to learn just how competitive it had become by the 1960s, and for what reasons the TV companies had entered the market. He first describes the structure of the industry, which can be divided into three separate markets: production, distribution, and exhibition. Since the Paramount antitrust decision of 1948, distributors have been forbidden to own theaters. During the period 1948-1967, however, new entrants didn't enter the market, and in 1966 the seven Paramount defendants held 74 percent of the U.S. market.
    Crandall's analysis shows that the distributors have maintained market power by controlling the number of films released, which has decreased dramatically. Admission prices have shot up, but the distributors have been in a strong position to negotiate for a large share of admission revenues. In the 1960s a rise in foreign rentals of U.S. films and the emergence of TV networks as film customers made the industry attractive to new entrants. The wave of new entries caused increased film output and declines in returns per film; many companies suffered losses, and in 1972 CBS and ABC exited. The Justice Department suit possibly hastened the exit. The chief danger of monopolistic power in this industry is an insufficient number of films.

52. Day, John W.   "The Paper Price Outlook: Opaque." Finance Magazine 93:4 (April 1975) 43-46.

Developments in the United States-Canada newsprint industry in the early 1970s are reviewed. The industry is a highly competitive one, but at the time the article was published Abitibi Paper had just bought a majority interest in Price Co., making the combined Canadian company the largest producer of newsprint in the world. Consumers had been hoping for a paper price war, but the new company should give the paper industry the clout to maintain prices at a reasonably profitable level. If demand does soften, industry leaders say they will cut production rather than price. Effects on newsprint consumers are shown: newspaper publishers are planning to revise formats, going to smaller pages and fewer columns, and to use lighter-weight paper.

53. Eversole, Pam. "Concentration of Ownership in the Communications Industry." Journalism Quarterly 48:2 (Summer 1971) 251-260, 268.

A merger movement between conglomerates and communications companies is leading to increased concentration of the U.S. mass media. A conglomerate is made up of a group of companies in diverse fields; it is hard to prove anticompetitive effects against conglomerates since they don't decrease competition within a given industry or directly eliminate a competitor. During the 1960s, fewer than 1 percent of mergers were formally protested by antitrust agencies; new legislation may be required to combat conglomerates. Many examples of mergers between broadcasting and nonbroadcasting companies are cited; the newest industries, such as CATV and microwave communications, are included. Companies are seeking a wider investment, profit, and technological base.

A major problem caused by mergers is the potential alliance between corporations with large government contracts and the mass media; critics are concerned over effects on news and cultural values transmitted through the media. The statement that only larger units can compete successfully shows indifference to all but economic factors in the communications industry. The FCC has proposed a "one-to-a-customer" rule barring common ownership of any two stations in the same market, but it is very far from becoming a reality.

54. Grotta, Gerald L. "Consolidation of Newspapers: What Happens to the Consumer?" Journalism Quarterly 48:2 (Summer 1971) 245-250.

The concentration of newspaper ownership in the United States has resulted from mergers and the acquisition of newspapers by chains. There has been controversy over whether the public benefits from concentration; this study centers on the economics of the issue, rather than the ethics. It is felt that economies of scale make concentration inevitable in this industry; a study by James N. Rosse ("Daily Newspapers, Monopolistic Competition, and Economies of Scale," entry 276) shows evidence for a decreasing average cost curve. Grotta asks what happens to certain price and output variables when ownership is concentrated, and whether consumers receive any benefits in terms of price or improved quality; his hypothesis is that they do not.

The study was conducted in two phases: (1) changes from two-newspaper competition to one-newspaper monopoly, and (2) changes from independent ownership to chain ownership. One hundred fifty-four newspapers were included, and multiple regression was used to analyze the data; variables included advertising space price, subscription price, and several "quality" variables such as change in number of editorial employees. Results showed that consumers receive no benefits from consolidation; they actually pay higher prices, including much higher prices for advertising space, with no compensating increases in quality. In the case of newspapers, monopoly effects seem to overide economies of scale effects.

55. Hall, W. Clayton, Jr., and Batlivala, Robert B.D. "Market Structure and Duplication in TV Broadcasting." Land Economics 47:4 (November 1971) 405-410.

Television is often criticized for duplication of programs; this problem is related to U.S. industry organization. Broadcasters have discovered that they attract more viewers by sharing the audience for the most popular program types rather than broadcasting to smaller minority groups. The authors have developed an index to measure the extent of duplication: D (Duplication) = $(X-P)/(X-1)$, where X = number of channels and P = number of program types. The index was applied to geographic areas with various numbers of channels, and results show that the number of program choices increases much less rapidly than increases in the number of channels.

Since competition is apparently not reducing duplication, it is suggested that it may be necessary to experiment with other market structures. In Britain, BBC is now running two channels; BBC-1 competes with Independent Television, while a second complementary service is provided by BBC-2. The Index of Duplication shows that the British system provides more choice than an area in the United States with three channels. It is recommended that the FCC permit or even require more than one station under the same ownership to operate in each viewing area; the second station must be required to show program types that do not duplicate those shown on the first.

56. Irwin, Manley R. <u>The Telecommunications Industry:</u> <u>Integration vs. Competition</u>. New York: Praeger, 1971.

Vertical integration is complete for the entire U.S. domestic communications industry; suppliers of telecommunications equipment are owned or controlled by telephone carriers, and the carriers buy most of their hardware from their affiliates. This industry structure has been defended in terms of systemic integrity and economies of scale; however, rapid technological change has brought competitive substitutes for many types of equipment, challenging the natural monopoly premise. An important issue is the blurring of boundaries between communication technology and digital technology; it is possible that the computer industry will be kept out of the communication market by the current market structure.

Irwin shows how direct and indirect government policies have promoted integration and restricted competition. He also provides a review of the literature on the economic implications of vertical integration in the cases of both nonregulated and regulated firms.

Irwin concludes that current market structure extends the defects of utility regulation into the equipment market with no compensating advantages; monopoly power is created in an unregulated market, which disrupts the incentives of the captive supplier. Among policy options for the future, Irwin would prefer to restore competition through divestment of suppliers from carriers; the innovative process would thus be encouraged, ultimately providing benefits to the consumer. Antitrust laws do provide the means for restoring competition; the FCC has simply not yet tried out its antitrust enforcement power.

57. Johnson, Leland L. "Boundaries to Monopoly and Regulation in Modern Telecommunications." In <u>Communications</u> <u>for Tomorrow: Policy Perspectives for the 1980s,</u>   pp. 127-155. Edited by Glen O. Robinson. New York: Praeger, 1978.

The development of the U.S. telecommunications industry has been guided by three propositions: (1) only one entity can economically serve a single geographic area; (2) cost averaging would contribute to rapid development; and (3) a single entity should have responsibility for providing end-to-end service. New technologies and service demands call all three propositions into question; digital computers, terrestrial microwave transmission, and communication satellites may require different types of networks, which may not need to be supplied by a single, regulated monopolist.

The FCC has permitted competition in the private-line and terminal markets. Emerging policy issues include: (1) cross-subsidization, the most fundamental problem in telecommunication policy - Johnson provides an extensive discussion of costing methodology; (2) potential harm to technical integrity of systems; (3) defining the scope of competitive entry; (4) the possibility that users of basic services will have to pay higher rates if competition in other areas reduces revenues.

Johnson recommends deregulation of the terminal market (where there are no strong economies of scale), the creation of "arm's length" subsidiaries of Bell for competitive services, and improved cost methodologies using incremental cost principles for competitive services. Telecommunications is a vigorous industry unlikely to be harmed by competition, which has already brought forth exciting innovations.

58. Johnson, Leland L. "Technological Advance and Market Structure in Domestic Telecommunications." American Economic Review 60:2 (May 1970) 204-208.

The U.S. domestic telecommunications industry is a mixture of monopoly and competition. The Bell System dominates, serving 84 percent of telephone subscribers. The industry is characterized by rapid technological advance; new demands for telecommunications services have been created, especially by the growing computer industry. The FCC has responded by allowing more competition in the industry; economists feel that competition is more likely to yield experimentation with pricing and new products.

Some inherent complications arising from competition include: (1) disparities between rates and costs: potential entrants worry that existing carriers will be able to cut prices below incremental costs for competitive services because they have protected revenues from monopoly services and thus will be able to drive out the new entrants; (2) cream-skimming: new entrants will want to serve only the more lucrative routes, causing the existing carriers to raise rates in areas not subject to competition, especially local public service; (3) interconnection: if new entrants are kept from interconnecting with the existing system they may be unable to operate economically; and (4) efficient use of radio spectrum: it is possible that cases of interference may arise among new users of the spectrum.

Johnson suggests that the boundary between competition and monopoly be drawn between the "switched" and "unswitched" portions of the national network. The unswitched portion includes mostly private-line services.

59. Kerton, Robert R.   "Price Effects of Market Power in the
     Canadian   Newspaper   Industry."   Canadian Journal of
     Economics 6:4 (November 1973) 602-606.

In G. F. Mathewson's study ("A Note on the Price Effects
of Market Power in the Canadian Newspaper Industry," entry
64), the predicted price effects of monopoly power were not
established   at   the   usual   levels   of   statistical   significance.
Mathewson used national advertising rate per line as his price
variable, but this variable does not allow for the fact that a
small paper has less impact for an advertiser than a paper
with large circulation; Kerton uses the milline rate, which is
the advertising rate per line per thousand of circulation.
Mathewson also failed to allow for differing languages of
publication in Canada; Kerton sets the dummy variable for
competition at one only when a city has a second daily paper
publishing in the same language.
    In contrast to Mathewson's, Kerton's results show the
very strong effects of market power. Prices are particularly
affected by the presence or absence of a second daily newspaper or by a TV outlet. The steady trend towards newspaper takeovers and mergers is not surprising in the light of
these results.

60. Killingsworth, Vivienne. "Corporate Star Wars: AT&T vs.
     IBM." The Atlantic, May 1979, pp. 68-75.

Until very recently AT&T and IBM maintained separate
markets in telecommunications and computer science; now
that the two fields are beginning to merge into data communications, the two corporate giants have become unwilling
competitors. Business communications is the major battle-
ground today, but data communications will become important
in home life too. AT&T is a regulated utility that theoretically
cannot offer data-processing services; IBM is an unregulated
company that cannot offer transmission services and maintain
its unregulated status. Now that the telephone network is
technologically capable of processing information, it is difficult
to define the border between communications and data processing.
    IBM claims that many of AT&T's services and equipment
are of a data-processing nature; meanwhile IBM owns 40
percent of Satellite Business Systems, a satellite communication
firm for which IBM is designing hardware.
    The Justice Department has antitrust suits pending
against both corporations, reflecting America's ambivalent
attitude towards sheer size: the corporations claim their
size permits economic efficiency and innovation, while the
more traditional belief is that competitive industries are more

efficient and innovative.   A crucial question is whether the courts are the best place to solve such a complex issue.   Both companies are central to the U.S. economy and to the country's international position.

61. Knox, Robert L.   "Antitrust Exemptions for Newspapers: An   Economic   Analysis."   Law and the Social Order   3 (1971):   3-21.

In July 1970 the Newspaper Preservation Act was signed into law.   It overturned a U.S. Supreme Court decision that had declared illegal a joint-operating agreement that was the basis for a daily newspaper duopoly in Tucson and was also used in 21 other cities.   Under the typical joint operating agreement, all business operations are combined, to obtain cost economies, but the papers retain separate identities and editorial voices; in Tucson, the agreement included price fixing and profit pooling.   During the congressional hearings for the Preservation Act, proponents of the legislation maintained that the social benefits - presentation of separate editorial voices - outweighed economic issues inherent in a duopoly.   Opponents of the legislation argued that the duopoly would create high entry barriers in the local market.
    Knox provides a close economic analysis of newspaper markets; he defines (1) the market structure and its local nature;   (2) market conduct;   and (3) market performance, emphasizing the high rate of return on revenues that newspapers have enjoyed.   He concludes that since the industry is healthy enough, the newspaper antitrust exemptions are not made on economic grounds but on sociopolitical ones, thereby defeating the purpose of the Sherman Act, which requires sound economic evidence for antitrust exemptions.

62. Lago, Armando M.   "The Price Effects of Joint Mass Communication Media Ownership."   Antitrust Bulletin 16:4 (Winter 1971) 789-813.

Joint mass media ownership is defined as the ownership of more than one local medium.   Lago has studied whether there are differential advertising price effects between jointly owned media and media not subject to joint control.   An earlier study by Bruce Owen (summarized at a later date in "Newspaper and Television Station Joint Ownership," entry 70) showed the existence of higher rates for TV stations and newspapers subject to joint control; however, Owen's study excluded newspaper circulation and TV audience size as variables because of alleged joint dependency between advertising rates and these variables.   Lago discusses this joint dependency problem and then presents three models: (1) Owen's ordinary "least squares" model;   (2) the same model, but including audience size/circulation as variables;   (3) a two-stage "least squares" model which recognizes joint dependency.

Using data from 546 U.S. TV stations and 357 daily newspapers, Lago estimates the three models and presents the results in tabular form.   His study shows no evidence of differential price effects caused by joint ownership; the earlier study was incorrect due to misspecification of the price equation - that is, audience/circulation were excluded.   Policies concerning joint ownership must not be determined on the basis of its alleged differential effects on advertising rates.

63. Long, Stewart.   "Antitrust and the Television Networks: Restructuring Via Cable TV."   Antitrust Law & Economics Review 6:4 (1973) 99-108.

The three U.S. TV networks share a monopoly in both the broadcasting and the selection and preparation of programming.   While the FCC permits each network to own only five stations, these 15 stations and the networks themselves in 1971 accounted for 28.8 percent of all TV employment, 50.4 percent of all TV advertising revenue, and 50.1 percent of all TV broadcasting revenue.   Many of the 673 nonnetwork TV stations are affiliated with a network, which acts as the middleman between national advertisers and TV stations.   The networks, because of their financial resources, supply 84 percent of the costliest TV programming, that shown during prime-time evening hours.   To avoid implications of network monopoly of supply, the networks use a device called the "participation" contract; they participate financially and creatively with suppliers in the production of programs.   This is a very efficient method of vertical integration, since the networks don't have to supply all the costs of production.

The technology of CATV can solve this monopoly problem without the necessity for legal wrangling.   With CATV, each local market can have 40 viable stations, since UHF stations will work as well as VHF.   This would allow the profitable entry of eight to ten new networks.   It would have to be a mandatory rule that all TV broadcasting be done by cable.

64. Mathewson, G.F.   "A Note on the Price Effects of Market Power in the Canadian Newspaper Industry."   The Canadian Journal of Economics,   May   1972,   pp.   298-301.

The effects of monopoly power on the national advertising prices of Canadian daily newspapers are examined using a model developed by B.M. Owen for U.S. newspapers (see entry 70). A price equation is fitted for a set of 97 dailies; the dependent variable is the log of the per-line price of national advertising. Three dummy variables are used in the regression to test three hypotheses on market power. A variable for "TV ownership" is set equal to 1 if a newspaper owns a TV station in the same community; it is set equal to 0 otherwise. The sign on the coefficient was expected to be positive, and the results do show a 24 percent increase in prices with such joint ownership.

A second variable is set equal to 1 if a newspaper is a member of a group or chain; otherwise it is set equal to 0. A positive coefficient was anticipated in this case also, but results show no effects on price.

A third variable is set equal to 1 if a newspaper has competition from another daily in the same community. A negative coefficient was expected in this case; the hypothesis is supported, but rather weakly perhaps due to the presence of regional newspapers from large metropolitan areas which may offer competition in a local market. (See also Kerton, entry 59.)

65. Mayer, Caroline E. "Ma Bell Fights Off Invasion of Her Domain." U.S. News & World Report, 14 August 1978, pp. 55-58.

AT&T's monopoly is under attack on several fronts, although it hasn't been harmed financially yet; earnings in early 1978 were the highest on record. New competition has arisen, especially because of the computer; businesses now require high-speed, digital, and private communications networks for data processing, recording devices, and facsimile machines. The FCC has permitted competitors to provide both "interconnect" and long-distance services. AT&T claims that competitors are cream-skimming, taking the high-volume, low-cost routes only; since AT&T's long-distance profits subsidize local rates, thus keeping them below cost, AT&T maintains that competition will lead to higher local rates. Competitors say there is evidence that residential users are subsidizing business and long-distance services. Since Bell's accounting system doesn't separate costs and returns for individual products and services, it is difficult to prove either charge.

The FCC plans to continue fostering competition in the telecommunications industry. The Justice Department is pushing an antitrust suit that would require AT&T to give up Western Electric and some or all of its long-distance service. State utility commissions are now looking at rate-hike requests much more closely and are often approving amounts lower than requested.

66. Mitchell, Bridger M. New Technologies, Competition, and
    the Postal Service. Santa Monica, CA: Rand Corp.,
    1978.

New communication technologies have created demands
for new services and pressures for price changes; however,
regulated suppliers have used the regulatory process to
block entry of new competitors and maintain existing prices.
Deregulation has opened some portions of the U.S. communications market to competition. The post office is an interesting
case because of the rapid development of electronic communications; costs of electronic alternatives to current postal
services are dropping precipitously. Mitchell describes general
characteristics of a natural monopoly and the potential role
of competition, and then specifically focuses on the postal
service.
     The key question for the post office is whether or not it
should enter the electronic communications market. First-class
mail has been a homogeneous service on the supply side;
electronic communications will offer low-cost alternatives for
segments of first-class mail, especially financial transactions.
The post office is likely to lose a large portion of its market
and will have to raise prices on the remainder. Cream-
skimming, which refers to selective entry by competitive
suppliers into high-margin markets, will occur on a large
scale. The post office has no regulatory commission to protect
its vulnerable markets.

67. "The Mounting Pressure to Break Up 'Ma Bell.' Telephone
    Monopoly: Good or Bad?" U.S. News & World Report,
    22 November 1976, pp. 42-44.

Government regulators and private competitors are challenging the Bell system monopoly. There is a pending lawsuit
to force Bell to divest itself of its equipment manufacturer,
Western Electric; competitors want the right to duplicate
such services as long-distance calls between major cities;
manufacturers of switchboards and other devices want to sell
their products to phone users; AT&T's rates and accounting
practices are being investigated.
     John deButts, Chairman of AT&T, claims that rivals will
be allowed to offer intercity services on the most profitable
routes, while AT&T has to serve everyone. He cites evidence
that outside equipment has impaired phone service. He
predicts that residential phone bills will rise by as much as 70
percent if AT&T's pricing system is undermined; under
present practices, no resident pays the full cost of his phone
service.

Richard Wiley, Chairman of the FCC, points out that AT&Ts' monopoly is not being ended; rather, competition is being permitted in two distinct areas, terminal equipment and private-line services. New equipment must be registered with the FCC. Private competitors will not be able to "skim the cream" of the most profitable routes; the FCC has endorsed AT&T's proposal to establish private-line rates on a deaveraged cost-of-service basis.

68. Nelson, Richard W. "Domestic Satellites, the FCC, and Competition in Domestic Telecommunication." Land Economics 51:3 (August 1975) 235-246.

The potential effects of satellite communication technology on the market structure of the U.S. domestic, long-distance telecommunications industry are analyzed. In 1972 AT&T dominated the industry with 91 percent of the market; competition existed only in private-line services, which constituted 11 percent of industry revenues. Satellite technology will reduce the significance of economies of scale because of such cost characteristics as insensitivity to transmission distance. Therefore more suppliers will be able to operate efficiently, and there will be more intense rivalry among existing suppliers; nationwide service could be established with a smaller total investment, meaning reduced barriers to entry.

FCC regulatory decisions are oriented toward use of satellite technology; in 1972 it was decided that all firms meeting certain financial and technical qualifications would be allowed to estabish satellite systems. The growth of specialized common carriers, using terrestrial technology, had already affected industry structure; satellite technology will enhance their capabilities. Nelson concludes by discussing current competitive activity in the industry.

69. Nixon, Raymond B., and Hahn, Tae-youl. "Concentration of Press Ownership: a Comparison of 32 Countries." Journalism Quarterly 48:1 (Spring 1971) 5-16.

The increasing concentration of newspaper ownership in larger economic units seems to be a world-wide trend. There are many inherent implications for freedom of the press and its consequent social effects. The authors have developed a "press concentration index" to measure and compare the concentration across countries. One of the difficulties is to define concentration: relative concentration refers to the highest x percent of all units in the newspaper industry that control y percent of circulation; absolute concentration refers to the largest x number of firms that hold y percent of circulation. The "concentration index" combines both definitions of concentration; using various statistical methods the authors show graphically and with the numerical index that among 32 economically disparate nations it is the less developed nations that have a more highly concentrated press. Among the more developed nations, the United States showed the lowest amount of national concentration.

70. Owen, Bruce M. "Newspaper and Television Station Joint Ownership." Antitrust Bulletin 18:4 (Winter 1973) 787-807.

Concentration of ownership of communications media is a natural consequence of the economies of scale inherent in the transmission of mass media messages. Owen presents the results of an empirical test of the effects of joint ownership on the prices for U.S. national advertising. National advertising accounts for 10 percent of newspaper revenues and 47 percent of local TV station revenues. Owen's main hypothesis is that a decline in competition will lead to high prices for advertisers. He describes his methodology and then presents and discusses the results of fitting several regression equations to 1966 data for 156 daily newspaper firms and all commercial TV stations.

Major conclusions are: (1) when a newspaper owns a TV station in the same city, the newspaper price for advertising increases by 10 percent (2) chain ownership of newspapers results in a 7 percent price increase; (3) competition from a local newspaper results in a 15 percent decrease; (4) newspaper-owned TV stations charge 15 percent more for national advertising; (5) network-affiliated stations (in reality, a type of chain ownership) charge 42 percent more; (6) stations that compete with newspaper-owned stations charge 7 percent more, due to what Owen describes as an "umbrella effect," that is, the competing station can take advantage of the high prices charged by the newspaper-owned station by charging similar prices itself. (See also Mathewson, entry 64, and Lago, entry 62.)

71. Peterman, John L. "Concentration of Control and the Price of Television Time." American Economic Review 51:2 (May 1971) 74-80.

The FCC believes that concentration of control among U.S. broadcast media adversely affects the price of advertising time. The FCC is concerned with the control of TV licenses by newspapers and radio stations in the same market areas, and with group ownership of stations, especially in the 50 largest markets. Consequently, the FCC has been giving greater weight to diversity of ownership when determining licenses and also has adopted a rule forbidding any party from holding more than one full-time broadcast license in any market. However, the FCC has not examined these assertions about the adverse effects of concentration to see if there is a factual basis.

Peterman investigated rates in various markets to see if ownership does in fact have an effect. For prices, he used the stations' 20-second announcement rates charged national advertisers. These prices were viewed as a function of homes reached and family income, plus a dummy variable representing TV station ownership. Results showed that market prices of TV time do not increase because of concentrated ownership.

72. Posner, Richard A. Cable Television: The Problem of Local Monopoly. Santa Monica, CA: Rand Corp., 1970.

Cable TV is a technical, or natural, monopoly at the local level operating under municipal franchise. The main economic objection to monopoly is possible reduction in output due to monopoly pricing; in the case of CATV, output is the number of subscribers, which would decline if fees were excessively high. Local governments have responded to the problem of potential monopolies with rate regulation and franchise regulation; the latter is the principal method for CATV. Before analyzing the advantages and disadvantages of regulation in detail, Posner considers the consequences of no regulation; he feels that while the concern over monopoly in the cable industry is frequently overstated, it is quite possible that unregulated firms would obtain monopoly returns.

There are two approaches under the franchise method of regulation: (1) the concession approach, which involves extracting concessions from the cable operator via lump-sum auctions, auctions geared to the size of the cable system, or auctions based on service concessions; (2) the bargaining approach, in which the franchising authority uses its leverage to prevent the charging of monopoly prices.

Direct rate regulation has rarely been used for CATV service. Posner concludes that none of the alternatives is free of difficulties and recommends a period of experimentation, during which methods of preventing monopoly prices and methods of capturing them should both be tried.

73. Priest, A.J.G.   "Must AT&T Be Dismembered?" Public
     Utilities Fortnightly 96:1 (3 July 1975) 17-21.

     The antitrust division of the U.S. Department of Justice
is seeking to break up AT&T because it has grown too large to
regulate.   Priest maintains that AT&T has run the best telephone system in the world and that its research arm, the Bell
Laboratories, is a major national asset.   The system is
thoroughly regulated at the federal and state levels, and there
is no indication that pulling it apart will lead to reduced rates
or improved service. Public utilities have generally functioned
as monopolies; the question shouldn't be whether a utility is a
monopoly, but whether it is serving the public interest.
     The goal of regulation is the most efficient allocation of
resources possible in the existing circumstances; the Justice
Department must consider whether the absence of competition
is bad for the public interest. The purpose of the Communications Act of 1934 was to make available to all people a
rapid, efficient service with adequate facilities at reasonable
charges; there is no hint that unrestricted competition should
motivate telephone service. It will be difficult for the antitrust division to demonstrate that antitrust laws override or
take precedence over the Communications Act; all but two of
the 30 charges against AT&T are regulatory matters within the
exclusive jurisdiction of Congress, the FCC, and the state
agencies. Telecommunications rates cannot be fixed by the
laws of supply and demand.

74. Ross, Leonard.   Economic and Legal Foundations of Cable
     Television. Sage Research Papers in the Social Sciences,
     no. 90-012. Beverly Hills, CA: Sage, 1974.

     CATV has the potential to increase the quantity and
quality of television programming. Ross analyzes the economic
and regulatory restraints that threaten this potential diversity
and shows the reasons for them and ways to avoid them. As
background information he discusses theories that explain the
uniformity in American programming, the structure of the TV
industry, and the history of CATV.
     Most programs are sold to networks or stations on the
basis of exclusive contracts, which makes much programming
unavailable to CATV stations.   There are many economic
reasons for the practice of exclusivity, including gains in sales
efficiency, allocation of risk between copyright owners and
broadcast stations, and premiums paid by broadcasters for
exclusive contracts. One way to restrict exclusive contracts
is by imposing time limits. Ross compares restrictions on
exclusivity with other ways to expand program availability,
such as by allowing CATVs to carry distant signals while
compensating copyright owners for use of their programs.

TV networks are based on economies of scale and the enhancement of market power; Ross discusses the effects on networks if CATVs are allowed to import distant signals. CATV operators themselves might be tempted to enter into network-like exclusive agreements to block potential competitors. Current regulatory issues are reviewed, including the proposal that the status of CATV systems be changed from franchised private communications carriers to common carriers.

75. Saliba, Michael T. "Television Programming and the Public Interest: Subscription TV Versus Public Ownership." Antitrust Law and Economics Review 6:4 (1973) 109-117.

A major reason for public dissatisfaction with U.S. TV is the lack of diversity in programming; supposedly competing stations duplicate each other's programming. Saliba proposes Subscription TV (STV) as a solution. "Free" TV is not really free, because viewers pay for receivers, operation, and maintenance and are charged higher prices for advertised products. Program uniformity results from the necessity for a TV station to obtain a certain portion of a viewing market; in a three-station market, for example, a station would want to obtain one-third of 80 percent of the viewers who prefer a "mass"-type program, rather that get all of the 10 percent of viewers who prefer a minority-type program. Minority groups obtain little benefit from mass-type TV and are therefore subsidizing the majority.
Government ownership would not work, because there would be no economic criteria by which the government could make programming choices. Under STV, the viewer agrees to pay for shows on a per-program basis; with STV, broadcasters would count dollars that viewers are willing to pay rather than merely numbers of viewers. Saliba concludes by showing that a larger consumer surplus would result from STV and speculates that pressure from STV would cause quality improvement in mass TV.

76. Spence, Michael, and Owen, Bruce. "Television Programming, Monopolistic Competition, and Welfare." Quarterly Journal of Economics 91:1 (February 1977) 103-126.

Three aspects of advertiser-supported television make it an unusual industry: (1) consumers receive a free product; audiences are sold to advertisers; (2) TV programs have some characteristics of public goods; and (3) there is an artificial scarcity of channels, due to regulatory decisions. These conditions may lead to deficiencies in programming, particularly in terms of numbers and types of programs offered. Using calculus, the authors analyze the forces that influence program selection under four different supply structures: advertiser-supported or pay TV with either limited or unlimited channels. In comparing outcomes, total surplus is used as a measure of welfare.

Advertiser-supported TV is found to be more biased against programs with low price elasticities of demand ("minority taste" programs) and high cost programs than is pay TV. However, with limited channels, advertiser-supported TV is the better solution. If pay TV is introduced with limited channels, consumers must pay for programs without an increase in the number of programs offered; income is shifted from viewers to broadcasters. The authors recommend that cable TV be structured as a common carrier so that there will be open entry into supplying programs, and that suppliers be allowed to charge both advertisers and viewers.

77. Spicer, Michael W. "The Annan Report and the Economics of Broadcasting Reform in the United Kingdom." EBU Review 30 (March 1979) 36-40.

Spicer examines the major findings of the U.K.'s Committee on the Future of Broadcasting (the Annan Committee) from an economist's point of view. The Annan report found that the duopolistic structure of the British broadcasting industry inhibits diversity in programming and recommended that a new TV channel be granted to a new public Open Broadcasting Authority; OBA would not produce its own programs but rather those of other organizations, thus providing an outlet for a variety of contributors. The report also recommended a Local Broadcasting Authority to provide local radio stations for rural areas now doing without any local radio.

Spicer demonstrates why the present structure inhibits diversity, then explains that the Annan proposals won't necessarily increase it. If the fourth channel is at least partially financed by advertising, as the report recommends, then program producers will be forced to compete for mass audiences by duplicating existing program types. Methods of program financing seem to be a major determinant of program type; less emphasis should be placed on financing methods that promote audience maximization, such as advertising and license fees. Spicer recommends pay TV and radio, which allow consumers to express the intensity of their preferences. Diversity would be encouraged, as in the publishing industry where consumers pay for a wide variety of printed materials. The Annan Committee's opposition to pay broadcasting is "excessively negative."

78. Spiegel, John W. "Telex v. IBM: Monopoly Pricing Under
    Section 2 of the Sherman Act." Yale Law Journal 84:3
    (January 1975) 558-583.

In the Telex decision it was held that IBM had violated
the Sherman Act by cutting prices in the face of new entrants
to the computer equipment market. At issue is what pricing
strategies a lawfully acquired monopoly may implement to
maintain its market share against competition. In economic
theory there are three models of pricing strategy for the
profit-maximizing monopoly: umbrella, limit, and "credible
threat" pricing. IBM used a limit-pricing strategy: "The firm
sets its price just below the 'limit price' - the price below
which no potential competitor can enter the market and no
existing competitor can expand." IBM tried to keep its market
share by trading short-run gains for long-term profits.
    Spiegel explains that case law is not clear on whether or
not any of these pricing strategies are illegal; limit pricing has
not previously been considered evidence of specific intent to
monopolize. Telex therefore makes new law, that a monopoly
is not allowed to lower its prices to stop new entrants.
Spiegel demonstrates that in a monopoly market limit pricing
yields the best attainable outcome; prices will be lower than
under umbrella pricing, and some monopoly profits will be
distributed to consumers. The Telex decision should be
reversed.

79. Stewart, David O. "Competition in the Telephone Equip-
    ment Industry: Beyond Telerent." Yale Law Journal
    86:3 (January 1977) 538-560.

The FCC has stimulated competitive entry into the U.S.
telephone equipment industry by requiring the common carriers
to interconnect customer-provided equipment. In North Carolina Utilities Commission v. FCC (Telerent), the Fourth Circuit
Court upheld the FCC against attempts by state regulatory
agencies to block interconnection; the Court said the state
agencies have exclusive control only over matters that don't
affect interstate communications, and that equipment is used
for interstate calls. However, the FCC has no control over
intrastate rates; it is feared that the common carriers will
manipulate intrastate rates and use them to subsidize their own
equipment prices, thus blocking competition.
    State agencies have opposed competition because they
claim the prices of local exchange service have been subsidized
by common carrier earnings from equipment; they fear that
competition in equipment will cause local service prices to rise.
However, there is no evidence to support this view; it is
possible that local prices have been used to subsidize equip-

ment prices. Competition should be encouraged; the FCC should convene a federal-state Joint Board to help the state agencies monitor relationships between costs and pricing. The rates of regulated firms in competitive markets should be based on long-run marginal cost pricing; the Joint Board would provide guidelines to the state agencies based on this type of pricing.

80. Turner, Donald F. "The Role of Antitrust Policy in the Communications Industry." Antitrust Bulletin 13 (Fall 1968) 873-879.

There cannot be a uniform antitrust policy in U.S. communications because it is so diverse an industry. Newspapers and other printed media are not regulated at all. In broadcasting, the FCC cannot fix rates but does have extensive control over entry; broadcasting is not a natural monopoly, and competitive principles should apply in this industry. In the common carrier services the FCC has all the controls associated with public utility regulation; the role of antitrust is harder to determine than in the print and broadcasting sectors, because common carrier markets do have significant elements of natural monopoly. In the area of transmission, for example, substantial economies of scale are available.

Where economies of scale exist, competition won't be efficient. However, monopoly should be strictly confined to the area where scale economies exist. Monopolists must not be permitted to force their way into competitive markets. Nor should a monopolist be assured of a perpetual protected status; technological advances may change the structure of an industry. Regulatory agencies must try to make monopolists at least approximate the behavior of competitive industries.

81. Wiley, Richard E. "The U.S. Communications Consumer and Monopoly Supply: The FCC Position on the Proposed Legislation." Telecommunications Policy 1:2 (March 1977) 99-111.

The background of U.S. telecommunications policy is reviewed to give perspective to present problems: up to the mid-1960s the industry was characterized by a monopoly structure, which was appropriate since it consisted of only three homogeneous markets. By the late 1960s computer and electronics developments had led to such a diversity of potential communication services that the FCC had to make some decisions as to whether competition would now be beneficial in at least some parts of the market. Despite competition in

terminal equipment and private lines, Bell and the independent
telephone companies have had record earnings and revenues
during 1975 and 1976, and have dominated the newer sectors
of the market.

Wiley gives a detailed summary of the FCC's position on
the Consumer Communications Reform Act, which would amend
the Communications Act of 1934. Some of the consequences of
the Act would be: (1) elimination of federal jurisdiction over
terminal equipment; (2) substituting 50 state regulatory programs for a unified national program; (3) permitting the
telephone industry to use incremental pricing policies that have
potential to raise rates of basic services. These steps are
planned becuase of alleged economic and technological harm to
the telephone industry, which has never been proven. The
FCC recommends rejection of the Act because it will do serious
disservice to the public interest.

C. OTHER REGULATORY ASPECTS

82. Besen, Stanley M., and Soligo, Ronald. "The Economics
    of the Network-Affiliate Relationship in the Television
    Broadcasting Industry." American Economic Review 63:3
    (June 1973) 259-268.

Three primary objectives of the FCC in relation to
regulating the U.S. TV broadcasting industry are the encouragement of local programming, the encouragement of program
diversity, and the maintenance of widespread ownership of
facilities. The FCC has established regulations to further
these objectives; the authors' purpose is to analyze the effects
of these regulations via an economic model of the network-
affiliate relationship. First the network-affiliate contract is
examined, particularly the methods by which advertising
revenues are shared by the network and its affiliate. The
model of affiliate behavior is based on the fact that different
hours of the day or week have different values for advertisers; the value of the hours a station will clear for network
programming is a function of the proportion of revenue
returned to a station by advertisers. A "supply" curve of
hours cleared for network programming is diagrammed.

Based on this model, the impact of price discrimination by
networks is considered; networks can charge different prices
for each program cleared or not compensate an affiliate for all
programs cleared. The impact of the Prime Time Access Rule
is discussed in the framework of the model; it appears that
network profits will be reduced when the Rule is implemented.
Regulatory and economic reasons for the failure of a fourth
commercial network to emerge are presented; the Group Owner-

ship Rule, which restricts the number of stations a network can own, has had considerable impact on network profits.

83. Besen, Stanley M., and Mitchell, Bridger M. "Noll, Peck, and McGowan's Economic Aspects of Television Regulation." Bell Journal of Economics and Management Science 5:1 (Spring 1974) 301-319.

    In this detailed review of Noll, Peck and McGowan's (NPM) Economic Aspects of Television Regulation, (entry 95), Besen and Mitchell choose to analyze in depth four of the major issues treated in NPM's comprehensive survey: (1) consumer demand for television, upon which so many policy questions depend; (2) economics of networks, very important because most network affiliates are profitable while most independents are not; (3) financing unremunerative services, such as public TV; and (4) analysis of regulatory behavior.
    Besen and Mitchell conclude that, while this is an excellent introduction to the major issues in U.S. television regulation, it fails as a statement of NPM's views on major policy questions. NPM's conclusions get little support from either their own or others' research. The policy chapter does not follow from all the preceding economic analysis and could have been provided independently. Finally, NPM's call for a new legislative mandate for broadcast regulation would be as difficult to bring about as it would be to get the FCC to change its behavior.

84. Comanor, William S., and Mitchell, Bridger M. "The Costs of Planning: The FCC and Cable Television." Journal of Law and Economics 15:1 (April 1972) 177-206.

    Legislation authorizing various U.S. federal regulatory agencies usually specifies that they regulate "in the public interest." This has been interpreted by the FCC as permitting economic planning by regulation to achieve social ends. The FCC has allowed broadcasting prices to rise above costs so long as the surplus generated is used in the public interest, which the FCC has designated as "diversity" and "localism." Many of the rules constraining CATV have been intended to protect UHF stations, which the FCC views as protecting localism. UHF stations have not grown as rapidly as the FCC hoped. Planning by regulation works best when there is internal subsidization of one part of the system by another; the problem has been deciding who will subsidize UHF.
    If planning by regulation is to be successful, revenues must be sufficient. Where demand is strong, high prices must

be set. The authors estimate the elasticity of demand for various cable prices. Rates of return must be high enough to attract the necessary capital; rates of return earned by large cable systems are estimated to fall between 10 percent and 14 percent. Finally, the authors compare the gains from and the costs of monopoly pricing. The producer's surplus and loss of economic efficiency in the system are calculated for alternate demand elasticities. It is concluded that when demand is highly inelastic, the producer's surplus is high and social costs are small; however, when demand is more elastic the producer's surplus declines and efficiency costs increase rapidly. In the case of broadcasting, even when the producer's surplus is high, it may be used to promote ends - diversity and localism - for which there is little consumer demand, and therefore ultimate benefits will be low.

85. DeVany, Arthur S.; Eckert, Ross D.; Meyers, Charles J.; O'Hara, Donald J.; and Scott, Richard C. "A Property System for Market Allocation of the Electromagnetic Spectrum: A Legal-Economic-Engineering Study." Stanford Law Review 21:6 (June 1969) 1499-1561.

Federal regulation of the allocation and use of the electromagnetic spectrum has been criticized for its inflexibility and lack of adaption to changes in technology and demands that have occurred since World War II. Market allocation of spectrum use is proposed, and solutions to the inherent legal, economic, and engineering problems are discussed by an interdisciplinary team. Three essential elements in such a private property system are: (1) the definition of unambiguous and valuable rights compatible with the physical properties of electromagnetic radiation; (2) a mechanism for legal enforcement of rights; and (3) a means for initial distribution to the public of the spectrum-use rights now owned by the government.

The physical and economic characteristics of electromagnetic energy are described; the proposed system will include the portion of the spectrum between 50 MHz and 1000 MHz, where most electromagnetic communication now takes place. The economic theory of property is applied, and such aspects as exclusivity and externalities are discussed. The proposed system of property rights is then defined in terms of the technical dimensions that give the resource its economic value: time of transmission, geographical area covered, and the particular portion of the spectrum. Legal aspects of the definition, enforcement problems, legal precedents, and methods for disposal of government-owned resources (such as land and water) are presented in detail. The authors suggest an initial experiment with certain portions of the spectrum.

86. Frech, H.E., III.   "Institutions for Allocating the Radio-
    TV Spectrum and the Vested Interests." Journal of
    Economic Issues 4:4 (December 1970) 23-37.

    The radio spectrum has been considered a unique natural
resource because the supply is fixed. Its true value is undetermined because it is not traded in a market; it is allocated
by administrative action of the FCC and is given free to
users.   Frech argues that this method is inefficient and a
threat to freedom of speech. He first gives a brief history of
U.S. spectrum allocation; it was instigated in the 1920s as a
result of a chaotic period of massive interference in radio
broadcast. It was felt that the market had failed, but actually
the interference was caused by a lack of private property
rights.
    The current system is inefficient because the FCC favors
government and educational users at the expense of commercial
interests, transfers of rights are prohibited, innovation and
technical progress are retarded, and there is excess space in
some fields and shortages in others.   As examples of misallocation, Frech cites the excess profits of VHF TV stations and
the unused spectrum rights possessed by the common carriers,
which have large opportunity costs to alternate users.   Most
important, the FCC can refuse to grant or renew licenses,
which means potential restrictions on freedom of speech.
    Frech briefly describes six alternative methods for al-
locating spectrum, including the creation of transferable
private property rights, the renting of rights by the government at market-clearing prices, and cost-benefit analysis to
allocate spectrum to the most efficient uses. He discusses the
effects of these plans on existing vested interests and concludes by examining the question of whether or not monopoly
could become a problem under a system of private rights.

87. Harwood, Kenneth.   "Broadcasting and the Theory of the
    Firm." Law and Contemporary Problems 34:3 (Summer
    1969) 485-504.

    By exploring the theory of the firm, Harwood seeks
answers to such questions about broadcasting as how many
firms should there be, how large should they be, and how
should a broadcasting station be governed. A firm is defined
as an entity broader than an organization that seeks to maximize profits; a firm's members give services, rather than take
services, and they comply with the demands of those who
govern the firm rather than the demands of other persons.
Both the state and the firm are valuable only to the extent to
which they develop the individual; it is in this context that
the fair allocation of inputs to and outputs from broadcasting
must be judged.

Broadcasting serves an entertainment/information function for the individual, an economic function for the firm, and a political function for the state; the firm must, with economic efficiency for itself, satisfy the individual and the state. The state needs criteria to use in decision making to ensure an equitable distribution of broadcasting time among various segments of the population. Perhaps those in remote areas or those with low literacy should be granted the first signals; economics and politics work against such criteria, especially because advertising supports broadcasting. Possible remedies include the use of tax revenues to operate stations in thinly populated areas and the requirement that broadcasters also operate in less profitable areas when they seek licenses for more profitable operations. Broadcasting should be governed by all those who share an interest in its operations.

88. Levin, Harvey J. The Invisible Resource: Use and Regulation of the Radio Spectrum. Baltimore: The Johns Hopkins Press, 1971.

Because of the institutional structure of radio spectrum management, there is currently a crisis of both spectrum congestion and underutilization. The spectrum has been managed by technologists and administrators/lawyers; the economist's viewpoint is long overdue. Economist Levin contends that a regulated market-type system, midway between the current nonprice system and a full-fledged market approach, would go a great way toward alleviating current problems.

Levin first reviews the spectrum system as it exists. He then looks at market incentives that would improve the efficiency of spectrum allocation, the role of market incentives in spectrum development, and finally regulatory policy. Regulation will always be required to keep allocation in line with such social priorities as safety, security, and cultural and educational goals, and because of such economic factors as technical barriers to entry, externalities, and economies of scale. Within this regulatory framework, a major contribution of a market-type system would be that the spectrum manager would have to be very precise in his or her reasons for rejecting market criteria in decision making.

89. Mathison, Stuart L., and Walker, Philip M. <u>Computers</u>
    <u>and Telecommunications: Issues in   Public Policy</u>.
    Prentice-Hall Series in Automatic Computation. Engle-
    wood Cliffs, NJ: Prentice-Hall, 1970.

As the telecommunications and computer industries begin
to converge, many policy questions are being raised. The
authors present a number of policy options and for each provide their own recommendation based on their economic and
technical analysis of the issue. A background description of
the current structure of the U.S. communications common
carrier industry and the computer industry is provided.
    In the computer industry itself, free competition has
produced rapid growth and innovation; the continually decreasing costs to scale characteristic of a natural monopoly are
not evident. Regulation is not required in this industry.
Common carriers wish to offer data-processing services; the
authors recommend that the carriers be required to establish
separate subsidiaries for this purpose, so that a regulated
carrier can offer an unregulated service. The carriers have
restrictions in the use of their lines in regard to foreign
attachments, interconnection, and line sharing; the carriers
feel these restrictions are necessary to protect the integrity
of the national network. The authors find these claims
overstated and unduly restrictive from the data user's point
of view.
    The present network is inadequate for data transmission,
as channels have been designed for voice and teletype; a
service is required in which the user could be charged according to the amount of information sent rather than the
amount of time "holding" the line. Technical safeguards
to insure privacy in the new world of data exchange are
presently quite adequate.

90. Minasian, Jora R. "The Political Economy of Broadcasting
    in the 1920's."   <u>Journal of Law and Economics</u>   12:2
    (October 1969) 391-403.

In the 1920s U.S. radio broadcasting reached a state of
chaos because of the lack of effective and appropriate regulation. A system was needed to keep interference at a minimum,
but little was done; instead, wave lengths were assigned all in
a group, and there was a very liberal policy of granting
licenses to amateurs. In the <u>Intercity</u> case of 1921, it was
declared that anyone had the right to get a license from the
Secretary of Commerce; documents show that license requests
were often refused, based on newly forming notions of benefit
to the radio public, although such refusals were against the
law. The <u>Zenith</u> case of 1926 destroyed this allocation pro-

cess, declaring that the Secretary of Commerce could make no regulations, such as requiring license applicants to show "public interest," but only issue licenses.

In economic terms, radio was treated as if there were no scarcity problem. After the 1921 case, people realized they could obtain a valuable resource free, and license applications rose rapidly. The court decisions were not in accordance with economic principles, as a scarce resource was declared a free good. A legal basis to prevent interference began to emerge (public interest), but the most efficient way to control interference would be to regulate power output rather than the uses of radio.

91. Murphy, Thomas P.   "Federal Regulatory Policy and Communications Satellites: Investing the Social Dividend."   The American Journal of Economics and Sociology 31:4 (October 1972) 337-351.

Even when private enterprise is considered the best vehicle for innovative development of a new technology, the scope of the project may require federal funding. In this case, economic and social benefits flowing from the new technology should be passed along to the taxpayer. The U.S. government became directly involved in competitive enterprise through the creation of Comsat in 1962. During the 1960s it was noted by members of Congress that other countries were progressing in the establishment of satellite communication systems by using American research; it was felt that the government itself had frustrated U. S. progress in the field.

In the early 1970s the White House and the FCC initiated policies to foster more competition in communications; a White House document supported the policy that domestic satellite systems be operated by private interests. At the time, Comsat feared the impact AT&T's entry might have, since AT&T would be able to subsidize a new satellite service with revenues from its profitable telephone monopoly; the significant question would be what effects satellites would have on domestic communication rates.

At the time the article was written, a number of firms had submitted proposals to launch a domestic satellite system; several of the proposals are reviewed, and it is pointed out that, since initially the market will be small, it is possible that competition will prove deadly to weak systems.

If Comsat has failed to implement socially useful programs, can a totally private carrier do any better? The dividend arising from the efficiencies of the new technology could be used for such social purposes as education and health; it could also be used to reduce broadcasting bills or telephone charges.

92. Nelson, Boyd L.   "Costs and Benefits of Regulating
    Communications."   American Economic Review 51:2 (May
    1971) 218-225.   '

    There is a rationale of public utility regulation that can
be demonstrated with benefit-cost analysis. The regulatory
agency must set rates so as to keep total revenue inflow equal
to cost; technological progress, regulatory lag, and monopoly
power make it difficult to bring revenue down to costs.
Nelson studied U.S. common carrier communications as regulated at the federal level between 1951 and 1970. Costs are
defined as the portion of FCC appropriations used for common
carrier regulation; benefits are defined as the effects on
revenue inflow resulting from rate changes. Benefits are
considered positive when revenue inflow decreases. Nelson's
first crude benefit-cost ratio is 7.9:1. Most rate reductions
were for telephones, most rate increases were for telegraphs.
    Various adjustments successively lower the ratio: adding
in legal fees incurred by the carrier brings the ratio down to
7.6; including the time value of money lowers the ratio of 4.1;
considering changes in price level over time yields 2.2.
Nelson considers this last ratio to be quite favorable to communication users.
    Problems with the analysis include aggregation: all
benefits don't actually occur to all people, and many people
don't use all the services available. Discriminatory effects
occur, due to favorable rate treatment accorded to private-line
services. Some nonprice benefits cannot be measured, such as
improvements in quality of service.

93. Nelson, Boyd L.   "Econometrics and Applied Economic
    Analysis in Regulatory Decisions." Law and Contempor-
    ary Problems 34:2 (Spring 1969) 330-339.

    Econometrics is defined as the application of the prin-
ciples of statistical inference to economic quantities; multi-
variate analysis is the usual technique. An example in the
field of telecommunications would be an equation in which the
quantity demanded of a telecommunications service is a function
of the price of the service, the price of substitute services,
and the income of customers.
    The use of econometrics as a tool in U.S. communications
regulatory proceedings is relatively new. In the Bell Rate
case, an economist's model for setting rate of return was
presented before the FCC; his recommendation was not a
major factor in the decision, but the FCC noted it was a
promising technique. For more effective regulation, research
in demand and cost areas is also needed. Demand studies are
particularly complex because of a lack of appropriate data, the

problem of defining a unit of service (length of call or number of calls), and cross-elasticities with substitute services.

For econometric studies to be useful in adversary and rule-making proceedings, an expanded data base going beyond traditional accounting information is needed. Greater exchange of data and more interaction between theory and practice are also required.

94. Nelson, Richard W. "Regulation of Comsat's Financial Structure." New York, 1978. Mimeographed.

In a 1975 decision, the FCC stated that Comsat was operating with an inefficiently low degree of financial leverage (the ratio of long-term debt to total capital). Until that date Comsat had operated with no long-term debt and had used an all-equity financing structure. Comsat appealed the FCC decision, but the FCC was upheld. Comsat then began to take action, moving toward the 45 percent debt level specified by the FCC. This case is a good example of the problem of efficiency of production in regulated firms; the FCC is concerned with leverage because of the traditional financial theory that leverage affects the average cost of capital.

Nelson first presents a theoretical outline of the financial behavior of the firm, with respect to leverage, in competitive, monopolistic, and regulatory equilibria. He then relates this analysis to the Comsat case. A brief review of Comsat's regulatory history shows extreme regulatory lag, raising the questions of the applicability of the pure regulation model to Comsat.

The choice of optimal regulatory technique to promote efficient choice of leverage by public utilities is a major policy issue. Nelson suggests that the firm's managers, basing their decisions on the dynamic operations of their firm, can be expected to make a more efficient determination of leverage than can a regulatory agency, working on the basis of precedent.

95. Noll, Roger G.; Peck, Merton J.; and McGowan, John J. Economic Aspects of Television Regulation. Washington, DC: The Brookings Institution, 1973.

The U.S. television industry has been a very profitable one; in 1969 television earned a 20 percent return on sales - all manufacturing corporations earned about 8 percent. As in other enterprises, the quest for profits shapes television performance, but TV is distinctive in that (1) it gives away its principal product, and (2) its profit seeking is conditioned by regulatory policies. The authors' objective is to provide a comprehensive economic analysis of the regulatory policies that determine the structure of the television industry.

Television is studied from a consumer welfare point of view; the existence of free television substantially augments our real income, especially that of the poor. However, present industry structure incorporates many economic inefficiencies; there is a great deal of unmet consumer demand, including both minority-type programming and additional programs of the most popular type. The possibility of expanding commercial television is the subject of one chapter, in which the economics of program supply and the influence of FCC policy are treated. Subscription TV, cable TV, public TV, and new technologies (satellites, videocassettes) are also analyzed intensively. For example, the key variable determining the economic viability of cable TV is penetration rate, since a high proportion of both fixed and operating costs are set by the number of miles wired.

Television's most essential problem is the lack of viewing options, which restricts consumer choice. The FCC's promotion of UHF will not solve this problem; UHF is technically inferior. The authors propose policies to encourage industry competition through both cable TV and subscription TV to solve the diversity problems. The FCC should have no concern for program quality and content, thus putting broadcasters on the same legal footing as printed media. For licensing purposes, the FCC should primarily consider the technical aspects of spectrum management. (See also Besen and Mitchell, entry 83.)

96. Owen, Bruce M. "The Economic View of Programming."
    Journal of Communication 28:2 (Spring 1978) 43-47.

Owen examines broadcast regulation in America with reference to the goals of diversity and fairness and argues that these goals are irrelevant to the consumer. Diversity in programming is hard to define; there is much diversity within such traditional program types as public affairs shows and westerns. Diversity is also a function of scheduling and the number of program types offered. An economic analysis of costs and benefits of television programs and alternative policies for them becomes difficult because no one knows the exact worth to each consumer; consumers do not pay directly for most programs, so a demand schedule is difficult to derive.

Owen extends the principle of underproduction of special interest products under monopolistic competition to TV programs, to demonstrate that, even under advertiser-supported broadcasts, some special interest programs will be eliminated. He further maintains that diversity of programming has nothing to do with freedom of expression. Public TV and FCC policies in favor of localism are supposed to promote diversity, but demand for public TV and geographically specialized programs is low.

97. Owen, Bruce M. Economics and Freedom of Expression: Media Structure and the First Amendment. Cambridge, MA: Ballinger, 1975.

The economic structure of the American mass media unnecessarily constrains freedom of expression. When access to the means of transmitting messages is concentrated in a few hands, competition and diversity of ideas are reduced. In the first chapter, Owen outlines the major issues he later details in separate chapters on newspapers, radio and TV, and magazines and motion pictures. There are three stages of production in the supply of mass media messages: (1) creation; (2) selection, or the editorial process; and (3) transmission. The first two stages are labor-intensive across the major media; entry into these stages should be completely competitive. Technological changes have made the third stage heavily capital-intensive; heavy capital costs and economies of scale in this stage have raised barriers to entry. In some media, concentration in the transmission stage has encroached on the first two stages, leading to vertical integration. Economies of scale in the media derive from first copy costs and the technology of distribution.
Owen concludes with a list of policy recommendations. Among the more significant are that newspaper printing and delivery systems should be divested from editorial and news-gathering services, that private property rights in the electro-magnetic spectrum should be established and sold, and that FCC rules against pay TV should be eliminated. In general, due primarily to industry structure, there has been in this century a decline in the effective number of independent general mass sources of national political news and ideas.

98. Owen, Bruce M. "The Role of Print in an Electronic Society." In Communications for Tomorrow: Policy Perspectives for the 1980s, pp. 229-244. Edited by Glen O. Robinson. New York: Praeger, 1978.

The use of electronic and computer technologies for the production of print media has important communication policy implications. The electronic media are now regulated; if print uses electronic technology and becomes subject to regulation, there will be inherent dangers to free speech through possible regulation of the message as well as the medium. Owen analyzes the economic structure and trends in print media to show potential changes as new technologies are applied.

Print has definite economic advantages: it is durable, compact, portable, cheap, and supplies a high level of editorial service. Print (books, magazines, and newspapers) revenues have grown despite the appearance of substitutes; however, in 1968, per-household expenditure on nonprint surpassed that on print permanently. There has been a decline in the numbers of individual cities with competing newspapers, and also in mass magazines. It is possible that FCC policies to restrict cable TV have protected the print industry, especially the more specialized magazines and books, because the proliferation of cable promises the possibility of many more specialized TV programs.

If regulations are applied to print in the same manner as to broadcasting, controversial material will be relegated to production by old-fashioned means and eventually virtually eliminated. In regulation, the medium and the message must be kept separated; electronic transmission technologies must be treated as neutral conveyors.

99. Owen, Bruce M.; Beebe, Jack H.; and Manning, Willard G., Jr. Television Economics. Lexington, MA: Lexington Books, 1974.

Television policy makers have ignored the fact that U.S. television is a business whose performance is primarily influenced by economic motivation; the economic motivation of TV stations is fundamental to this book. An economic analysis of television markets will provide a sound basis for policy decisions. Part I deals with economic analysis and theory, covering the program-supply market, the problem of program choice by stations and networks, and the role and behavior of television networks. Television stations are in the business of selling access to audiences, not programs, because they cannot directly charge viewers for the programs.

Part I provides the economic basis for the chapters on policy in Part II; questions raised in Part II include the possibility of improvement in industry performance through utilization of UHF, pay TV, new networks, cable television, and public television.

The authors stress the necessity for maximization of economic efficiency through greater competition and the greatest possible degree of freedom of expression. The FCC's objectives are characterized as compromise and stability rather than maximum diversity, access, and competition; to improve industry performance, structural changes that create incentives to achieve the latter objectives are required.

There is a bibliography containing 619 items.

100. Pelton, Joseph N., and Snow, Marcellus S., eds. Economic and Policy Problems in Satellite Communications. Praeger Special Studies in International Economics and Development. New York: Praeger, 1977.

This book is divided into two sections, one on economic issues and the other on policy issues; the first section, covering economic issues and problems of satellite communications at the domestic and international levels, is described in this abstract.

The first chapter, written by Marcellus Snow, examines the theory of monopolistic price discrimination in its application to public utilities. Snow argues that, given monopoly power, price discrimination is to be preferred to uniform prices on grounds of operational efficiency. Public utilities, however, are required to base prices on marginal costs rather than average costs. Price discrimination helps to cover the consequent deficits.

Intelsat is a commercial system based on a natural monopoly and has practiced price discrimination for political and equity reasons more than for economic efficiency. Long-term pricing in Intelsat is based on the assumption that plant capacity is adjusted to a cost-minimizing level. The U-shaped, long-run average cost curve of conventional theory is rejected.

The next chapter, by Richard W. Nelson, deals with domestic satellite communications and the economic issues that arise from a regulated industry undergoing technical change. Nelson deals with the type of market structure that should be permitted, vertical integration, and the influence of regulation on the use of technology.

The third chapter, by Kenneth B. Stanley, deals with economic issues in international telecommunications. Selected aspects of the economic performance of the international telecommunications industry are examined. The economics of Comsat and submarine cable are analyzed as interrelated technologies. The regulations imposed by the FCC as an effort to promote economic performance are examined, and Stanley suggests some changes in FCC policy that would increase the benefits of satellite technology to the users of international telecommunications services.

101. Snow, Marcellus S. "Problems in Regulating New Informa-
     tion Technology at the National and International Levels:
     The Case of Communications Satellites." In Information
     Societies: Comparing the Japanese and American
     Experiences, pp. 55-67. Edited by Alex S. Edelstein,
     John E. Bowes, and Sheldon M. Harsel. Seattle:
     International Communication Center, 1978.

     Intelsat is the only international organization that is
operational and commercial. Over 100 members jointly own
and use communications satellites; Intelsat has a cooperative
structure. Investment quotas are periodically reviewed and
changed to reflect usage shares. Since the late 1960s, Intelsat's capital and operating expenses have been met from
revenues, and its charges have dropped precipitously.
     Intelsat's unique organizational character has created
two anomalies in the regulatory framework: (1) Intelsat does
not interface with consumers, so there is no "consumer advocate" role for any potential regulator; and (2) no separate
regulatory body is required, since the cooperative financial
structure (members are both investors and users) adjusts
financial motivations - Intelsat regulates itself.
     Snow describes the period when Intelsat was managed by
Comsat and outlines the debate over the creation of Comsat.
Ambiguities in the Comsat Act led to disagreements over such
issues as ownership of earth stations and Comsat's rate structure, which has not reflected the fact that satellite costs are
insensitive to distance. Japan's institutional and regulatory
response to satellite communications technology is described in
some detail. Nelson concludes that Intelsat has performed
well; the fact that satellite communications have not yet yielded
economic benefits to consumers is due to domestic institutions
and legislation in various Intelsat countries.

102. Stanley, Kenneth B. "International Telecommunications
     Industry: Interdependence of Market Structure and
     Performance Under Regulation." Land Economics 49:4
     (November 1973) 391-403.

     It is proposed that the international telecommunications
industry faces a crisis: because of a unique market structure
and certain regulatory decisions, resources are not allocated
with economic efficiency. One important aspect of the market
structure is the conflict between cable and satellite technology:
AT&T has a substantial investment in cables yet is the principal stockholder in the Communications Satellite Corporation
(Comsat). The FCC's Authorized User decision has made
Comsat a carriers' carrier, unable to serve the final market,
thus theoretically allowing the common carriers to protect their
cable investments from satellite competition.

Other regulatory decisions have led to overinvestment in excess satellite and cable capacity by both Comsat and AT&T. The corporations' pricing and depreciation policies have also led to source misallocation. Two suggestions are made to improve industry performance: (1) AT&T should be divested of Comsat stock to remove its influence on Comsat; (2) the Authorized User decision should be rescinded, and Comsat should be allowed to provide satellite service directly to final users.

103. Webbink, Douglas W. "Regulation, Profits and Entry in the Television Broadcasting Industry." Journal of Industrial Economics 21:2 (April 1973) 167-176.

New firms cannot enter a U.S. television broadcasting market without a license from the FCC; nor can existing firms expand output beyond a maximum number of hours per day or outside a certain area. Where there are no legal barriers to entry, high profits in a particular market should lead to new entry since existing firms cannot expand. In this study it was hypothesized that given such variables as income per station, revenue/cost, and audience size per firm, entry would take place in markets where the particular variable was relatively large, while no entry, or exit, would occur where the variable was small. One hundred three markets were divided into four groups, depending on whether (1) two new stations entered (1966-1968), (2) one entered, (3) no change occurred, or (4) one station exited. Results of an analysis of variance strongly supported the hypothesis: for example, income per station had the following mean values in the four groups: (1) $1,501,100; (2) $759,700; (3) $148,900; (4) $37,880.

The FCC has a policy to encourage the entry of television stations in small communities; one way it has tried to accomplish this is by limiting entry in larger, more profitable markets. This policy cannot succeed, since entry is so strongly affected by the economic variables included in the study; today there are many unused station allocations in small markets.

D. DEMAND STUDIES

104. Artle, Roland, and Averous, Christian. "The Telephone
     System as a Public Good: Static and Dynamic Aspects."
     The Bell Journal of Economics and Management Science
     4:1 (Spring 1973) 89-100.

     The telephone system possesses the properties of a public
good through its provision of access to information exchange.
Using calculus, the authors provide a model for determining
the optimal number of telephones in a static resource allocation
framework; this optimal point is also an efficient point. It is
assumed that the planner will allocate resources on the basis of
a social welfare function and will decide on the optimal number
of telephones within a general equilibrium framework. Such
allocation of resources is derived without reference to either
perfect planning or perfect competition. The central analytical
problem is the discreteness associated with access/no access;
many "systems" in modern life have a similar property, particularly other communications systems and transportation
systems. The analysis also shows that new subscribers to the
system provide gains in the form of savings in transaction
costs.
     A growth model of the demand for telephones is then con-
structed; a self-sustaining growth process is deduced, which
is jointly dependent upon income-distribution and public-good
properties of the telephone. It is concluded that social
benefits are vastly greater than economic costs for the
telephone system. (see also Rabenau and Stahl, entry 128.)

105. Barzel, Yoram. "The Market for a Semipublic Good: The
     Case of the American Economic Review." American
     Economic Review 61:4 (September 1971) 665-674.

     The theory of public goods is caught in certain opera-
tional dilemmas. Barzel tries to circumvent these problems by
studying a semipublic good, The American Economic Review.
A semipublic good has a mixture of public- and private-good
characteristics; the ideas in a journal are its public-good
component, and the costs of publishing and distributing these
ideas are its private-good component. A demand function for
a semipublic good can be approximated using quantity and
price information concerning its private-good component. The
objective of Barzel's empirical work is to estimate production
costs of the Review and user benefits deriving from it. Policy
problems concerning quantities and prices of semipublic goods
are similar to those of purely public goods, so information
generated by studying semipublic goods will be quite useful in
both cases.

Barzel uses data from 1930 to 1965 to estimate a cost function and a demand curve. In the regression equations, total cost is a function of number of pages and circulation, and demand is a function of real price, real per capita income, population (defined as total labor force), and number of pages. Barzel uses the regression results to discuss two basic problems: (1) whether to produce the good at all; (2) what quantity of resources to devote to the good. One problem with measuring demand for the Review is that subscribers receive it as part of the membership dues to the American Economic Association; Barzel devotes a final section of his paper to benefits received from the Association in addition to the Review.

106. Berg, Sanford V. "An Economic Analysis of the Demand for Scientific Journals." Journal of the American Society for Information Science 23:1 (January/February 1972) 23-29.

Journal policy decisions should be made on the basis of benefit and cost estimates, particularly in the case of publicly subsidized journals. Since journal costs have been estimated in other research, Berg focuses on demand for scientific journals. The private demand for journal subscriptions can be distinguished from the social demand for journals; research has important externalities, resulting in a social value greater than private value. However, Berg chooses to use private demand as an approximation of social demand.

The most important variables affecting journal demand are listed and discussed: price, number of pages published, journals produced, research pages submitted, researchers working in a given field of study, and institutions that employ the researchers. The most useful variable, price, is not easily defined for journals: many scientific journals are received as part of a society membership; price also involves storage space and time spent reading the journal.

Three pricing policies are illustrated: (1) commercial presses use profit maximization; (2) scientific societies and universities use average cost pricing; (3) some scientific societies use marginal cost pricing.

The Journal of Physical Chemistry is used as an example to measure whether or not a journal has an efficient number of pages in terms of costs and benefits. It is concluded that institutional users need a larger journal for archival purposes, while individual users require a smaller, more specialized journal.

107. Besen, Stanley M., and Mitchell, Bridger M. Watergate
     and Television: An Economic Analysis.   Santa Monica,
     CA: Rand Corporation, 1975.

     It is commonly observed that the size of the total tele-
vision audience does not vary with changes in the available
viewing alternative.   This "constancy" hypothesis suggests
that new programming available through CATV and public TV
will cut into existing network audience sizes.   The authors
describe three models of viewer behavior that are consistent
with the "constancy" hypothesis: (1) the "passive viewer"
first chooses to watch TV, then selects a program from among
the available fare; (2) the "first choice viewer" will watch only
his or her preferred program type; (3) the "second choice
viewer" will watch a mass-audience program if the first choice
is unavailable.
     The models cannot easily be tested because of the difficul-
ty of characterizing programs accurately by type.   However,
the Watergate hearings provided a natural experiment for
measuring the size of audience groups with different program
preferences.   In the experiment, two types of programs,
Watergate and "other," and five types of viewers based on
the three-viewer models were postulated; viewing data from
New York and Los Angeles were analyzed.   It was concluded
that the viewing models failed to describe substantial portions
of the audience; a significant number of households joined the
TV audience that don't usually watch standard programming.
"Constancy" appears to be a result of the usual sort of programming rather than the passive preferences of viewers.
     Rotating coverage of the hearings by the three networks
is also discussed as an example of successful cooperative
economic behavior.

108. Bower, Linda Lee.   "Telecommunications Market Demand
     and Investment Requirements."   Telecommunication
     Journal 39:3 (March 1972) 177-181.

     Input-output analysis is used to estimate the market
demand for telecommunications services in a given country
and the plant in service required to produce the desired
service.   In this type of analysis the sectoral composition
of the economy is a major factor, which is significant in
developing countries where the structure of the economy
may be changing rapidly.   In the model, market demand is
expressed in terms of revenues to the operating entity,
which consist of business and personal expenditures.   Business expenditures are derived directly through input-output
analysis, by applying a telecommunications input coefficient to
the dollar volume of production in each sector, yielding the

dollar volume of telecommunications services demanded by each sector. Personal expenditures are derived indirectly through a correlation between the proportions of business and personal telephones.

Plant in service required is derived from an empirical relationship between plant and annual operating revenue; an optimum level, from observations in the United States and Sweden, is 3:1.

Specific examples are provided in the article. The model can be used to plan and allocate resources for developing a national communications system.

109. Bowman, Gary W. "Demand and Supply of Network Television Advertising." The Bell Journal of Economics 7:1 (Spring 1976) 258-267.

The product that the three U.S. TV networks sell to advertisers is viewers to watch commercial advertising minutes. Bowman has constructed a demand and supply model for this product; his basic model is a two-equation simultaneous system. The demand equation sets price as a function of number of advertising minutes watched, disposable income, unemployment rate, and a seasonal variable; the supply equation sets quantity as a function of price, time (it is assumed that quantity has increased over time), weather, and cost of inputs. The price elasticity of demand was found to be 0.73, not significantly different from 1; price elasticity of supply was close to 0.

These elasticity estimates imply that decreases in the amount of programming offered by the networks because of regulatory policy will not substantially change the aggregate revenues of the networks. Public policies that affect the supply of the product are: (1) the prime-time access rule; (2) rules to decrease advertising on children's program; (3) public service requirements; and (4) prohibition of cigarette advertising.

110. Casper, Cheryl A. "Estimating the Demand for Library Service: Theory and Practice." Journal of the American Society for Information Science 29:5 (September 1978) 232-237.

Casper first presents a theoretical discussion of techniques for deriving a demand function. Demand for library service can be expressed as a function of price of the service, price of related services, income of users, and users' tastes/preferences. Price, income, and cross-price elasticities provide useful information for library administrators; for example, price elasticity indicates how revenues might change if fees change.

The demand of institutional users for services provided by the Cleveland Health Sciences Library was estimated using a stepwise multiple regression. The variables explaining the most variation in items requested were institutional payroll, number of personnel, number of patients admitted, and average number of patients receiving care each day. The expense variables had high explanatory power; an income elasticity coefficient of 2.2 was computed, indicating that demand for service is highly income-elastic.

To estimate relative price elasticities, users were divided into two groups: teaching hospitals with a large volume of requests and nonteaching hospitals with a small, more random number of requests. Results show that the price elasticity of demand of larger users is more elastic than that of small users. The larger users are more sensitive to changes in fees and more likely to use substitute sources.

111. Chaddha, Roshan L., and Chitgopekar, Sharad S. "A 'Generalization' of the Logistic Curves and Long-Range Forecasts (1966-1991) of Residence Telephones." Bell Journal of Economics and Management Science 2:2 (Autumn 1971) 542-560.

The logistic growth function has been used to model telephone growth. This function "implies the concept of a constant saturation level," which the authors call "M"; M equals the maximum telephone market in an area. In this econometric study, the authors first formulate the logistic growth curve model. They then test the hypothesis that M is constant and find that, actually, it varies over time, corresponding with ups and downs in the U.S. economy. It has a particularly strong relationship with changes in per capita disposable income. The authors therefore "generalize" the model by incorporating factors to represent the effects of the economy on telephone growth. The model is fitted to data from 1946 to 1965; the results are compared with long-range forecasts (1967-1991) prepared for AT&T.

112. Corbo, Vittorio, and Munasinghe, Mohan. "The Demand for International Telecommunications Services and Their Policy Implications: The Case of Canada." Telecommunication Journal 45:9 (1978) 493-503.

The authors' purpose is to study the demand for flows of Canadian international telecommunications, specifically telephone, telegraph, and telex. The effect of such key policy variables as price and quality of service is stressed. Six separate demand equations are formulated, three for outgoing and three for incoming flows. The results for incoming flows were not as good as for outgoing, because they depended on the much more heterogeneous preferences of users in many countries. The regressions are based on data from 40 countries for the years 1969 to 1972.

Important results from the outgoing equations include the following: (1) the demand for telephone service is independent of the price of telegraph and telex; (2) telegraph and especially telex have high own-price elasticities; and (3) for telephone and telegraph, trade and tourism are the most important explanatory variables, while for telex trade alone is the most important.

The results have the following policy implications: (1) price changes in telegraph/telex services would not affect telephone service; (2) price reductions in telegraph or telex service could increase revenues in either service; and (3) high cross-price elasticities between telegraph and telex should be considered when setting prices for either service.

113. Cracknell, David. "Econometric Models of Inland Trunk Calls." Telecommunication Journal 45:9 (September 1978) 482-486.

The United Kingdom Post Office uses econometric models to forecast demand for telecommunications services; the models also give estimates of income and price elasticities that have significant implications for rate setting. In this article models for inland trunk calls (calls outside a local charge area) are examined; in 1975 and 1976, such calls accounted for 54 percent of total inland telephone call revenue and 31 percent of total telecommunications revenue.

Five sets of factors influence the demand for telephone calls: (1) system size; (2) technological improvement; (3) level of economic activity; (4) price; and (5) number of working days during the period. Two separate models are presented: (1) full rate trunk calls, 90 percent of which originate from business connections; (2) cheap rate trunk calls, most of which are made from private residences. When the two models are compared, it is demonstrated that quite different factors influence the growth rates of the two types of calls. Greater understanding of the telecommunications market can thus be attained by disaggregating different classes of service.

114. Craver, R. "An Estimate of the Price Elasticity of Demand for International Telecommunications." Tele-communication Journal 43:11 (1976) 671-675.

The volume of overseas voice telecommunications is growing rapidly; at the present rate of increase, U.S. overseas revenues will exceed interstate revenues by the year 2000. Total revenue per message has decreased over time, as average prices have been reduced. For future tariff policy it will be important to know the effect of price changes on demand. Craver's study develops an approach to establishing price elasticity for a given country market in international voice communications; the U.S.-U.K. market from 1960 to 1974 serves as the test case.

The dependent variable is message units billed in the United States. The most significant variables regressed against message minutes were time trend and a price index that was constructed from prices in several rate categories. A trade variable, though not significant, was included in the final equation because it improved the standard error of the estimate. In examining the residuals, Craver found that the largest occurred in periods when the growth of minutes was greater than the growth of circuits; he constructed a "supply constraint" variable, which proved to be very significant and was included in the final demand equation.

While the time trend variable dominates the model, Craver was not concerned with specifying it more closely. He was primarily interested in the price coefficient; after several statistical tests, it is concluded that demand is highly inelastic with respect to price and also that this situation has been quite stable since 1970.

115. Dunn, Douglas M.; Williams, William H.; and Spivey, W. Allen. "Analysis and Prediction of Telephone Demand in Local Geographic Areas." Bell Journal of Economics and Management Science 2:2 (Autumn 1971) 561-576.

It is necessary to forecast the demand for main telephone stations in local areas in order to manage the huge Bell construction program. Much of the construction consists of wire centers, which house the switching equipment for a given geographical area. Forecasting must be done for a period of 12 to 18 months ahead, which is the usual time from design to operation of a wire center. The authors present and discuss several different statistical methods for forecasting demand, using data from three Michigan cities; cities with different economic and demographic characteristics were chosen. The study began with two time series, one for business main telephones and one for residential; observations covered the period 1954-1969. This paper reports the results for the residential analysis; it was concluded early in the study that business and residence demand must be studied separately because they differ so much.

Based on the time series, forecasts are presented for the three cities using adaptive exponential smoothing. Then the analysis is elaborated by adding some exogenous factors; such local occurrences as strikes and welfare policy changes make local forecasting very difficult. The authors chose two variables that reflect new household formation, taking this factor as a prime determinant of new demand for main telephones. A 15 percent gain in accuracy was achieved by the addition of the exogenous data.

116. Ellickson, Bryan. "Hedonic Theory and the Demand for Cable Television." American Economic Review 69:1 (March 1979) 183-189.

The author applies a modified hedonic price theory to estimate demand for cable television; modification is necessary because consumers are not choosing among a wide or continuous spectrum of commodities. The consumer has only two choices, whether to subscribe to the service or not.

Various techniques for modeling demand for CATV have been used for estimating the value consumers attach to additional TV services. The demand equations derived in the first section of this paper are based on the assumption that all consumers have the same income. Each utility function is assumed to be a strictly quasi-concave function of certain variables. Consumer choice is seen as a two-stage process. Subject to budget constraints, the consumer will select the television mode that will maximize utility.

Ellickson acknowledges that even if data for individual households can be obtained, it is market demand that is more relevant to policy-oriented research. He therefore presents an alternative model yielding a market demand, dropping the assumption that all households have the same income.

117. Gellerman, Robert F., and Ling, Suilin. "Linking Electricity with the Telephone Demand Forecast: A Technical Note." IEEE Transactions on Communications COM-24:3 (March 1976) 322-324.

A demand forecast is required for any telecommunications expansion program. Since it is usually impossible to make an in-depth survey, simpler techniques such as waiting list analysis and trend extrapolation are used; these techniques have certain limitations, such as a disregard for income distribution.

In many developing countries sophisticated demand forecasts of electricity consumption are available. Since the factors influencing energy demand often have similar effects on telecommunications demand, it is possible to transform an existing energy forecast into a telecommunications forecast. Historical data and projections of electricity subscribers and consumption per subscriber for several Latin American cities have been used. Results show a ratio of telephone subscribers to electricity subscribers of about 0.4-0.5. The next step will be to study the reasons behind the lead-lag behavior in electricity-telephone development.

118. Greenberg, Edward, and Barnett, Harold J. "TV Program Diversity - New Evidence and Old Theories." American Economic Review 61:2 (May 1971) 89-93.

The authors define "diversity elasticity" as the proportional change in a measure of diversity divided by the proportional change in the number of channels. An elasticity of "1" would result if it were assumed that programs shown on different channels were automatically of different types; "0" would result if it were assumed that all commercial TV is one product with no diversity. Most researchers have taken a middle position, assuming the existence of distinct program types and have demonstrated that diversity doesn't necessarily increase as the number of available channels increases. However, it has been very difficult to define workable categories of program types.

After briefly reviewing several research projects, the authors conclude that viewer behavior must be utilized to construct program types. Using multiple regression techniques, they analyzed share-of-audience data for feature films broadcast in 1968. A significant proportion of the variance in shares can be explained by which month and day of the week the film is shown; the variable for the first TV showing was also highly significant. Film type, based on industry definitions, was not significant except for the coefficient for Westerns. The R^2 of .391 for all variables indicates that there must be other characteristics that explain the variance in shares; it is clear that feature films cannot be considered as one program type.

119. Kuehl, Philip G. "Marketing Perspectives for 'ERIC-Like' Information Systems." Journal of the American Society for Information Science 23:6 (November-December 1972) 359-364.

Marketing, a discipline that focuses on links between products and consumers, can provide valuable insights for managers of "ERIC-Like" information systems (ERIC, which stands for Educational Resources Information Center, is an American system that draws upon educational knowledge to serve users from diverse disciplines). The fundamental goal of marketing is the satisfaction of user needs. Marketing is societal in scope and includes both public and private sectors. Implications for information managers include: (1) a system must be judged on its ability to satisfy needs rather than its professional/technical qualities; and (2) managers must not be passive but should seek out users and form markets.

The "marketing concept," which has a user rather than a product orientation, has four relevant implications: (1) user needs are more basic and general than specific products - this helps a manager define his or her system; (2) new service opportunities are apparent; (3) dissemination patterns are more efficient; and (4) resource allocation is more efficient in the sense that society "profits" from information.

Four marketing techniques helpful to the information manager are: (1) consumer behavior research; (2) channel of distribution technique; (3) organizational theory; (4) market segmentation, or target audience, analysis.

120. Lago, Armando M. "Demand Forecasting Models of International Telecommunications and Their Policy Implications." Journal of Industrial Economics 19:1 (November 1970) 6-21.

The objective of this study is to quantify factors affecting the demand for international telecommunications. The demand model is based on least-squares regression and co-variance analysis of data from 23 countries during the period 1962-1964. The three dependent variables are traffic measures for telephone, telegram, and telex; independent variables include trade, investment, tourism, prices of services, number of telephones, working day hours in common between two countries, and the presence of cable circuits.

The demand functions for telephone service show a price elasticity greater than 1, indicating that if phone rates are reduced both consumers and suppliers will benefit. There is significant demand elasticity of telephone services with respect to operating time; because of their smaller switching times, satellite systems might have greater impact than cables on stimulating demand.

Telegrams have less than unitary elasticity with respect to their own prices. Telephone operating time and the availability of cable facilities have a significant effect on telegram traffic. International trade is another significant factor in the demand for telegrams. Because of inadequate data the telex demand function did not yield meaningful results.

The forecasting accuracy of the various demand models was tested, in comparison with a simple trend projection, by predicting 1965 traffic; the first difference regression model provided the best short-term forecast.

121. Levin, Harvey J. "Program Duplication, Diversity, and Effective Viewer Choices: Some Empirical Findings." American Economic Review 61:2 (May 1971) 81-88.

Television program diversity is used as a standard by which both broadcasting industry and regulatory performance are judged; it is particularly important because the lack of prices for output complicates the regulatory process. Cable and satellite technologies and pay TV may make more diversity possible; Levin wonders how much and how quickly it will happen.

He begins his analysis by looking at three approaches to measuring diversity: (1) prime-time shares of major program types; (2) an index of diversity, defined as the weighted mean rank of program categories in the market, using the number of broadcast hours as weights; (3) his own approach, a coefficient of viewer choice, which takes into consideration the pattern of hourly viewer choices. He ran regressions on the number of viewer choices, including and excluding public TV, using as independent variables the number of quarter-hour units broadcast by commercial, public, independent, network-affiliated, single-owned, group-owned, newspaper-owned, and non-newspaper-owned stations. A number of implications for U.S. broadcast regulatory policy are presented, including serious doubts as to the efficacy of new commercial entry as a method to widen viewer choice and the higher impact of public TV over commercial TV in the regression equations, which indicates underinvestment in public TV from the viewpoint of diversity.

122. Lorenz, Christopher. "Teleconferencing: New Research Shows Unexpectedly Large Demand for Sound-Only Systems." Telecommunication Journal 44:11 (November 1977) 538-544.

Telecommunications prices are gradually decreasing, while transportation prices will increase rapidly due to the surge in oil prices. Teleconferencing possesses valuable potential as a way to substitute communications for travel to business meetings. Lorenz summarizes several recent studies of teleconferencing; a major conclusion is that the greatest potential demand is for sound-only systems. Publication of these studies is causing manufacturers to shift emphasis to sound-only systems.

The studies explored both the economic and the sociopsychological feasibility of substituting for face-to-face meetings. The context of meetings is the most significant factor; it was found that most meetings do not involve "conflict" or "interpersonal relations" but rather are information-oriented and so are not significantly affected by the medium of communication. The level of demand was found to be quite sensitive to the provision of studios on the subscribers' premises.

Mathematical models based on descriptive survey data show that the maximum potential share (ignoring costs) of teleconferencing in the supply of business meeting communications involving travel is about 50 percent. Ten percent would require the use of a video system, and the rest would be adequately taken care of by audio-only systems. When cost considerations are included the demand for video falls away sharply, while audio holds it own.

123. Luke, C. Harvey, and Yatrakis, Pan G. "A Computer-Based Econometric Model of Demand for Telephone Communications Between Hawaii and the United States Mainland." Telecommunication Journal 38:11 (1971) 743-746.

This model is a result of a joint effort between the Hawaiian Telephone Company and the Overseas Operations Group of the AT&T Long Lines Department to explain the volume of telephone messages between their jurisdictions using econometric and computer techniques. The independent variables were: (1) average price of mainland-Hawaii telephone calls; (2) a measure of national employment equal to the number of employees on the payrolls of nonagricultural establishments; (3) number of mainland visitors to Hawaii; and (4) a seasonal adjustment variable. For each variable, 33 observations were recorded covering three-month periods between 1961 and 1969.

The coefficient of determination indicates that 99.4 percent of variations in message volume is explained by the four variables. The regression coefficient of the price variable indicates an almost unitary price elasticity of demand, which contrasts with higher values obtained in earlier studies. The regression equation was tested by "forecasting" messages for the four quarters of 1970; results obtained from the model were accurate to within 3 percent of the actual data. This method seems superior to straight-line projection techniques. The model can also be used to predict the effects of rate changes.

124. Machlup, Fritz. "Publishing Scholarly Books and Journals: Is It Economically Viable?" Journal of Political-Economy 85:1 (February 1977) 217-225.

This article is a progress report on a research project concerning the economic viability of the dissemination of scientific, technological, and scholarly knowledge. Information services such as book reviews and indexes in scholarly journals have recently been cut back dramatically; libraries are in a financial squeeze. Machlup cites trends in publishing that these developments reflect: (1) there has been an increase in the number of authors, subjects, and output per man-year leading to a right-shift of the supply function of publishable material; (2) due to demographic factors and prices, the number of potential readers has leveled off; (3) because of intense competition, the number of copies sold per title has decreased; (4) inflation has led to increases in list prices of scholarly books. Publishers seem to be planning to sell mainly to research libraries, which will presumbly pay any price, rather than to private individuals. This shift to the grants economy from the private sector is dependent on the questionable ability of libraries to increase their budgets at rapid rates.

Machlup presents some statistical evidence of this shift to the grants economy. In the case of a particular journal that raised its subscription rates 33 percent for individuals and 375 percent for institutions, revenues from individuals fell while revenues from institutions rose; there is evidently a large difference in the elasticity of demand between the grants economy and the private sector.

125. Mathewson, G. F. "A Consumer Theory of Demand for the Media." The Journal of Business 45:2 (April 1972) 212-224.

Mathewson develops a complex mathematical model of consumer media use and then tests it for cross-section survey data collected from households in two California communities. Consumers seek information through the media (newspapers, magazines, books, radio, and television) for market use, political and social decisions, and entertainment. Mathewson treats the stock of information as a good and uses an information-production function.

The survey data tested include observations of the amount of time spent using printed media and electronic media; data on media purchases are also included. Empirical results demonstrate the strong influence on demand of age, education, and income. The age variable is significantly negative in all but one regression. The education coefficient is positive for some of the printed media regressions, and not significantly different from zero for electronic media; this implies that more highly educated people tend to reallocate time and media purchases from electronic to print media. The income coefficient is positive for print media and negative for television; as income increases, consumers reallocate time and media purchases from television to print.

126. Munasinghe, Mohan, and Corbo, Vittorio. "The Demand for CATV Services in Canada." Canadian Journal of Economics 11:3 (August 1978) 506-520.

Finding the major determinants of demand for CATV services will help in formulating regulatory policy for this new industry. Data for the study come from the 16 largest CATV companies operating 30 systems. Most of the areas served by these systems could not receive U.S. stations over the air. A summary of the systems' market characteristics shows high penetration ratios (actual/potential subscribers) as compared to U.S. systems.

The demand model is based on the penetration ratio; the dependent variable is an income variable. The regression results show that the most important service provided by CATV is primary Canadian network shows, followed by duplicate U.S. network and U.S. independent stations.

These results confirm the attraction of U.S. TV. Since Canadians seem willing to pay for it, any regulatory constraints may have a negative impact on market penetration. However, unlimited signal importation may be contrary to the national policy of preserving the Canadian character of TV programming.

127. Nelson, Boyd L. "Problems in the Analysis of Tele-communications Demand." In New Dimensions in Public Utility Pricing, pp. 307-320. Edited by Harry M. Trebing. MSU Public Utilities Studies. East Lansing: Michigan State University, 1976.

Nelson outlines several basic difficulties in studying telecommunications demand. Economic relationships don't necessarily hold over time; for example, a coefficient of price elasticity of demand is a theoretical construct existing at one moment in time, while in reality a period of time is needed for prices to change and customers to react. Demand relationships are multicausal, which complicates the analysis; multiple regression techniques do not really explain causality.

Because of flat rate pricing structures, studies of demand for local telephone service are usually reduced to demand for main and extension telephones. Nelson describes the Long Lines Message Generator Model developed at AT&T; in this model messages are classified so minutely, resulting in so many message categories, that the available data are inadequate to the model.

In studying telegraph demand, there is again a lack of data permitting sufficient disaggregation. Telegrams are priced by number of words and length of haul; one study showed that demand was price-elastic for short messages traveling short distances and price-inelastic for longer messages/longer distances. However, the telegraph company has raised prices on short length/short distance telegrams, which have subsequently yielded to various substitutes.

128. Rabenau, Burckhard von, and Stahl, Konrad. "Dynamic Aspects of Public Goods: A Further Analysis of the Telephone System." The Bell Journal of Economics and Management Science 5:2 (Autumn 1974) 651-669.

The authors have enlarged upon and refined a dynamic model of the telephone system developed by Artle and Averous ("The Telephone System as a Public Good: Static and Dynamic Aspects," entry 104). The newer analysis is based strictly on assumptions about individual rather than aggregative behavior, enabling a more extensive analysis of system behavior. Using calculus and graphical analysis, further properties of the telephone system generated by its public good characteristics are shown: variations in price and in population size and income distribution are considered. Some conclusions are that an expansion of demand can be accompanied by a price increase and that to initiate growth a certain threshold must be overcome.

Some alternative dynamics of the model are presented, and the paper concludes with an extension of the model to the urban economy and its growth in time.

129. Rea, John D., and Lage, Gerald M. "Estimates of De-
     mand Elasticities for International Telecommunications
     Services."   The Journal of Industrial Economics   26:4
     (June 1978) 363-381.

     Demand studies are needed by both operating companies
and regulators; price elasticities are particularly important in
determining rates that will give operators a fair return. The
authors cite results of previous demand studies; their purpose
is to present additional elasticity estimates for the period
1964-1973; 1974 data are used to test the predictive power of
their models. Three demand equations (for telephone, telegraph, and telex) are estimated using combined data for 37
major U.S.-originated international routes. Quantity demanded
is set as a function of price indices for each service, trade,
and household disposable income. Two statistical models are
used, covariance and error components.
     It was found that the demand for telephone services is
highly price-elastic and positively related to household income;
telephone calls and telegrams appear to be complements.
Continued growth and inflation should generate substantial
growth in the demand for telephone calls. Demand for international telegrams is negatively related to income and positively
related to trade and telephone prices; no relationship between
telegram demand and telegram prices was found. The results
for telex demand were inconclusive.

130. Reekie, W. Duncan. "The Price Elasticity of Demand for
     Evening Newspapers."   Applied Economics 8:1 (March
     1976) 69-79.

     The price elasticity of demand for evening newspapers
in the United Kingdom is quantified using an experimental
method that avoids some of the inherent difficulties of multiple
regression techniques as applied to newspapers. These difficulties include the facts that: (1) changes in circulation can
be very dramatic, but they are due more to the availability of
alternate media and changing consumer habits than to price
changes; (2) newspaper prices do not change often, so there
are few observations with which to work; and 3) there are
substantial regional variations in propensity to consume newspapers.
     Data were obtained for all 70 evening newspapers, ex-
cluding those published in London.   Each price increase
between any of the 25 six-month periods from January 1, 1957,
to June 30, 1969, was considered an "event."   Circulation
figures were gathered for the time periods preceding and
following an event.   The statistical model is outlined, and
price elasticities for all the newspapers are presented.   A

median value is taken to represent the price elasticity of the industry; the figure is low, indicating a price-insensitive market.

131. Rohlfs, Jeffrey. "A Theory of Interdependent Demand for a Communication Service." The Bell Journal of Economics and Management Science 5:1 (Spring 1974) 16-37.

As others join a communications system, the utility of each subscriber increases. This case of external economies for consumers suggests that marginal cost pricing is not necessarily appropriate for communications services. Since each extra unit adds to total utility, the burden need not be borne by the new subscriber alone.

Rohlfs's analysis of interdependent demand begins from the assumption that there is an "equilibrium user set," which is a set of users consistent with the fact that in equilibrium all users demand the service and all nonusers do not. To move from a static to a dynamic model, a disequilibrium analysis is then made. Forces of disequilibrium in the communications market are isolated from similar forces in the rest of the economy to make the analysis simpler.

The theory is then developed based on a uniform calling model which assumes that incremental utility of telephone service depends on the number of subscribers and not on their relationships. Models characterizing community of interest groups, disjoint groups, and joint groups are also considered. From these a critical mass or initial market penetration is derived.

Implications for supply and pricing conclude the article.

132. Wellenius, Bjôrn. "Estimating Telephone Necessities in Developing Nations." IEEE Transactions on Communication Technology COM-19:3 (June 1971) 333-339.

A development plan for a telecommunications system requires an estimate of demand for subscriber connections and its projection throughout the specified planning period. In a developing nation supply of telephones is typically far less than demand; besides the expressed demand for waiting lists there is a large unexpressed demand, which makes traditional methods of estimating demand unreliable.

It is assumed that the initial goal is to upgrade the telecommunications system until it is compatible with the currently attained socioeconomic situation. This study is concerned only with urban areas. The best way to estimate demand is by direct survey in the field. The telephone market can be

divided into three distinct sectors: (1) residential; (2) business; and (3) public stations.   Each has its own basic consumer unit: (1) a household; (2) a business; and (3) an
individual.   For each sector, the density of demand, which is
the number of telephones per basic unit, must be estimated.
Since satisfied demand can be found in company records,
the purpose of the study is to estimate unsatisfied demand
for each sector.   A statistical approach to the problem is
outlined, and the results of such a survey in Chile are
presented, these results are compared with more traditional
methods for estimating demand.

133. Wellenius, Bjôrn.   "Hidden Residential Telephone Con-
     nections Demand in the Presence of Severe Supply
     Shortage."   IEEE Transactions on Communication Tech-
     nology COM-17:3 (June 1969) 413-414.

     Because of a lack of reliable data it is difficult to estimate
the demand for telephone connections in developing nations.
The results of a survey done in Santiago, Chile, in 1967 show
that the waiting list for telephones represents only a fraction
of the total unsatisfied demand and is therefore a poor indicator of unsatisfied demand when there is a supply shortage.
     Households were classified as real subscribers (satisfied
demand - 14.7 percent), potential subscribers (unsatisfied
demand - 22.4 percent), or households with no demand (62.9
percent).   Potential subscribers were considered as "expressed
demand" if they were on the waiting list, "hidden demand" if
they were not but had indicated a desire for a telephone.   In
the category of unsatisfied demand, only 26.2 percent consisted of "expressed demand."   Hidden demand was due to
such factors an nonownership of homes (no guarantee of
keeping service if a move to a new home is made), excessive
delay in providing new connections, and a conviction that
there were no available lines in a district.

134. Wellenius, Bjôrn.   "A Method for Forecasting the Demand
     for Urban Residential Telephone Connections."   Tele-
     communication Journal 37:6 (1970) 262-267.

     In a previous study by the author it was found that the
telephone waiting list in Santiago, Chile, contained only one-
fourth of the total unsatisfied demand.   Total demand cannot
therefore be projected on the basis of the waiting list because
of the large amount of hidden demand.   Wellenius suggests
that total demand be estimated through a special survey.   He
then describes an econometric method for projecting future
demand.   In analyzing various data, he found that total family

income is the socioeconomic variable most strongly affecting residential telephone demand; in his model, he assumes that demand is based solely on family income.

Wellenius first shows a method for adjusting a lognormal function to the distribution of family incomes. He then presents his model for average demand, applying it to the case of Santiago on the basis of survey data for 1967. The method is particularly useful for countries at an intermediate stage of development, where background data are available for estimating the parameters of family income.

135. Yatrakis, Pan George. "Determinants of the Demand for International Telecommunications." Telecommunication Journal 39:12 (December 1972) 732-746.

Aggregate national demand for international telephone, telegram, and telex may be represented as a function of the price of the service, the price of a substitute, population, income per capita, economic structure, demographic characteristics, and geographic location. Proxy variables are developed for each factor. Countries were selected for the sample that are relatively free of supply restrictions, because with prices being set through regulation a supply shortage may mean the presence of unsatisfied demand.

Twenty variables were tested in the demand equations. Results show that telex demand is price-elastic, telephone demand is marginally so, and telegraph demand is price-inelastic. Telex is most responsive to price changes in competing services, with telegraph being least responsive. The demand for international communications services becomes more elastic with respect to its own price as per capita GDP increases in the sample, showing that such services are not used by the majority of individuals in lower-income countries. Among other variables tested, tourism, per capita GDP, and population were important for telephone; trade, tourism, and population for telegraph; and trade and tourism for telex.

E.   PRICING STUDIES

136. Alden, Raymond M. "Usage-Sensitive Pricing for Exchange Service." In New Dimensions in Public Utility Pricing, pp. 297-306. Edited by Harry M. Trebing. MSU Public Utilities Studies. East Lansing: Michigan State University, 1976.

Telephone rates have been based on value-related pricing; this has contributed to the attainment of an early objective of telephone service, universal availability. Attention must now be directed to newer objectives, usually referred to as equity and efficiency; these objectives require cost-related pricing. An important element in cost-related pricing is usage-sensitive pricing.

Such current rate structures as rate banding and extended area service are applications of value-related pricing; they cater to the "average customer," who does not really exist. With usage-sensitive pricing the needs of potentially all customers could be met; furthermore, the customers themselves could decide what balance of value and cost they prefer. With flat rate pricing, the industry and its regulators are making decisions for the customers.

If freed from regulatory constraints, utility managers could market their products; they would have to learn what people want to buy and set a price for each value. Some "values" are: the ability to call someone in an emergency, the ability to be called, the ability to interrupt. Each service would have its own set of costs and prices. Regulators would simply set the outside limits, such as a price floor for the low user who needs availability, not usage.

137. Baldwin, Thomas F.; Wirth, Michael O.; and Zenaty, Jayne W. "The Economics of Per-Program Pay Cable Television." Journal of Broadcasting 22:2 (Spring 1978) 143-154.

Most pay television is offered on a per-channel basis; per-program pay TV has been discouraged by the cost of installing the required two-way cable technology. However, the authors find a per-program system to be more economically efficient than the per-channel system.

In commercial television, the real consumer is the advertiser; programming decisions are made to maximize audience size for advertising purposes, not to maximize viewer satisfaction. Since viewers of commercial broadcasting have no way to express preferences, there is a great deal of similarity in programming with little available for minority tastes. Per-program pay TV would have more programming efficiency.

There is a flaw in the per-program system due to the public goods nature of TV programs; the authors recommend minimizing this problem by keeping prices low through the encouragement of a competitive market structure in the per-program pay cable industry. They also recommend maintaining the present "free" over-the-air system, and encouraging competition between it and pay TV.

138. Besen, Stanley M.; Manning, Willard G., Jr.; and Mitchell, Bridger M. "Copyright Liability for Cable Television: Compulsory Licensing and the Coase Theorem." Journal of Law and Economics 21:1 (April 1978) 67-95.

The purpose of copyright is to provide financial incentives to authors by granting them control over the use of their work. The U.S. Copyright Act of 1909 can not, of course, deal with such new methods of distributing copyrighted materials as CATV. As background to the economic analysis of pertinent portions of the Copyright Revision Act of 1976, the authors discuss judicial, administrative, and legislative factors.

The 1976 Act "provides a compulsory license that authorizes cable systems to carry those signals currently authorized for retransmission by the FCC upon payment of a specified percentage of revenues." The probable effects of this Act are compared with the economic effects of full copyright liability for distant signals. The arrangement of economic transactions among program suppliers, broadcast stations, and cable systems is analyzed, and the public-good aspects of TV programs are considered.

It is concluded that compulsory licensing will not be a satisfactory solution to the problems associated with distant-signal importation. The fee schedule will provide program suppliers with too little revenue; furthermore, the law provides no mechanism for altering the schedule. There are no financial incentives to create a larger number and a wider variety of TV programs.

139. Besen, Stanley M. "The Value of Television Time." Southern Economic Journal 42:3 (January 1976) 435-441.

FCC policy is to increase the number of TV stations to give U.S. viewers a wider range of choice. To increase understanding of the prospects for new stations, Besen has studied station profitability, network affiliation, and frequency assignment as determinants of the value of station time. He notes that in 1972 only 20.8 percent of independent UHF stations reported profits, as compared to 87.1 percent of network-affiliated VHF stations, 66.7 percent of independent VHF stations, and 55.0 percent of network-affiliated UHF stations. In his model, Besen uses the price that stations quote for use of their time as an estimate of its value. This rate is made a function of presence/absence of network affiliation, VHF/UHF, and potential audience size.

Results show that rates are higher for VHF stations and those with network affiliations; rates are also higher for a station if its competitors operate on UHF or are independent

stations.   The worst handicap is to be an independent UHF
station.   This implies that prospects for new stations will be
improved if all stations in a given market are placed in the
same portion of the frequency spectrum, and/or if a fourth
commercial network can be formed.

140. Blake, Fay M., and Perlmutter, Edith L.   "The Rush to
     User   Fees: Alternative Proposals."   Library Journal
     102:17 (1 October 1977) 2005-2008.

      On-line bibliographic search services provide publicly
funded U.S. libraries with an excellent way to expand information services; however, librarians are charging fees for
these services, contravening the traditional notion of free
public libraries.   A business philosophy seems to be replacing
a socially oriented one.   Also, librarians are viewing data base
services as something entirely new, when in reality they are
simply an expansion of regular reference service.   There will
be many technological advances in information provision; user
fees cannot be initiated to pay for them.   Librarians must plan
to include innovations in their service programs and budgets.
      User fees impose inequities on library users; access to
information is restricted to those who can afford it.   As more
paying customers are attracted, library resources begin to
shift to meet the needs of those users.   Fees also impose social
inefficiencies; the private data base companies will begin to
produce only what the fee-paying customers want, and the
social benefits of education and information will be disre-
garded.   Information services are a collective good; costs must
be borne by regular library budgets and federal funds.
Society requires balanced growth between the public and
private sectors; the authors propose a tax-transfer policy from
the private to the public sector to ensure balanced growth.

141. Blau, Robert T.; Johnson, Rolland C.; and Ksobiech,
     Kenneth J.   "Determinants of TV Station Economic
     Value."   Journal of Broadcasting 20:2 (Spring 1976)
     197-207.

      Data from 34 U.S. television stations sold between 1968
and 1973 were used to determine what variables affect the
selling price of a station.   Variables were classified as internal, over which the broadcaster has some control, such as
net broadcast revenue, size of average daily audience, and
amount of station revenues spent on local programming, or
external, such as type of ownership, network affiliate status,
and number of homes in the market.   A stepwise regression
analysis was used to estimate the interrelationships among

internal and external variables. As anticipated, net broadcast revenue is the most important determinant of sales price, and size of average daily audience is the major determinant of net broadcast revenue. The most interesting result is that higher program expenditures correlate with higher profits.

142. Caramancion, Manuel I. "Pricing Strategies Based on Price and Cross-Price Elasticities from Telecommunication Demand Models." In Pacific Telecommunications Conference Papers and Proceedings, pp. 1E-24 - 1E34. Edited by Dan J. Wedemeyer and David L. Jones. Honolulu: Pacific Telecommunications Conference, 1979.

Caramancion uses a step-by-step approach to show how pricing strategies can be determined based on demand for telephone, telegraph, and telex services. The rate of inflation is included as a major variable. The price elasticity and cross-price elasticity of a telecommunications service are defined in mathematical terms; real price is defined as nominal price deflated by an inflation index. Multiple regression demand models were fitted to aggregate traffic data of the three services; besides price, other explanatory variables included number of immigrants, number of telephones, GNP, and a trade variable. Results of the analysis showed telex and telephone price elasticities to be higher than one, while telegraph is price-inelastic; there were no meaningful cross-price elasticities between the services.
The objective of pricing strategies is taken to be the increase of real revenues. Since there were no cross-price elasticities, prices for each service can be set independently. Elasticities indicate whether prices should be increased or decreased to generate additional revenues; Caramancion presents a table showing appropriate pricing strategies for each service; an important factor is the state of inflation, and each strategy depends on whether inflation is increasing, decreasing, or stable. Numerical examples for each service illustrate the operation of the table.

143. Cooper, Michael D. "Charging Users for Library Service." Information Processing & Management 14:6 (1978) 419-427.

The question of whether or not libraries should charge for services is examined; the specific service used as an example is on-line bibliographic searching. Information in its formless state is a public good, but in the form in which it is available for consumption it has private good characteristics. Information can be defined as a merit good, which is a private good that society thinks should be supplied publicly. Based on evidence from an experimental free on-line search service, Cooper concludes that the merit-good nature of information is not a good argument for public provision of services because the externalities of information were negligible in the experiment.

Actually, libraries do not supply free services but rather charge indirectly through property and income taxes. The key decision, then, is whether people should pay directly or indirectly, and it depends on social equity. Arguments for direct charges are that property taxes are regressive, that with direct charges revenues can be raised to support other services, and that pricing policies more efficiently allocate scarce resources. Arguments against direct charges are that they discriminate against the poor, that such charges mean double taxation, and that a socially optimal allocation of resources won't result.

Libraries will probably continue to rely on indirect charges for most services because to change would have major social/political consequences. However, direct charges to cover costs of more expensive services seem reasonable.

144. Crandall, Robert W. "The Profitability of Cable Television: An Examination of Acquisition Prices." The Journal of Business 47:4 (October 1974) 543-563.

Cable TV has the attributes of a natural monopoly. To keep subscriber fees close to costs, some form of control is required. If the local franchising system is to function effectively in keeping fees down, local authorities need information concerning the appropriate terms for granting cable franchises. If competitive bidding for local franchises is unseccessful, regulation with its attendant costs will be required. Crandall has studied prices paid for existing systems in recent mergers and acquisitions to shed light on U.S. cable owners' expectations of future costs and revenues. He compares his results with the "pessimistic" literature sponsored by the National Cable Television Association (NCTA) on the future profitability of CATV.

Crandall's econometric model of the value of a CATV system is based on discounted anticipated cash flows less total outlays; he estimates the equation by ordinary least squares from a sample of 17 sales. The value of a typical system is estimated to be $321 per subscriber at maturity, much higher than the NCTA estimates. The analysis reveals no evidence that investors will pay more per subscriber for large systems than for smaller ones, thus rejecting the NCTA hypothesis of the existence of significant scale economies in the operation of a CATV system.

145. Currier, Fred.   "Economic Theory and its Application to
     Newspapers."   Journalism Quarterly 37:2 (Spring 1960)
     255-260.

     Currier takes issue with Landau and Davenport's "Price
Anomalies of the Mass Media (entry 153)." He argues that
economists do have a structure for dealing with newspaper
pricing; newspapers are a joint product, which refers to a
situation in which two products are made from a single process.   The two products are advertising and circulation, and
costs and revenues of both products must be considered;
naturally circulation revenue will not cover costs of both
products.   Currier also points out that U.S. newspaper prices
have climbed steadily as various costs have increased, while
Landau and Davenport maintained that newspaper prices have
been rigid.
     Replies from Landau and Davenport argue that news-
papers cannot be defined as joint products.   They also stress
again that the newspaper pricing picture simply cannot be
viewed as a dynamic one.

146. Engelbardt, Robert M.   "The Elimination of Inconsis-
     tencies in International Telephone Services and Rates."
     In Pacific Telecommunications Conference Papers and
     Proceedings, pp. 1E-18 - 1E-23.   Edited by Dan J.
     Wedemeyer and David L. Jones.   Honolulu: Pacific
     Telecommunications Conference, 1979.

     Technical compatibility in the world-wide telephone net-
work has been achieved through the efforts of the ITU and
the UN.   However, there are still wide disparities in types of
service offered and rates.   For example, some countries still
accept only person-to-person international calls at a single,
high rate.   International telecommunications arrangements are
handled through bilateral agreements among originating and
terminating locations.   Facilities are jointly owned or leased,
and revenues are divided equally; a third country providing
transit facilities may receive a portion of revenues.
     The international rate structure is extremely complex.
U.S. rates have been declining, but many other nations will
not lower rates because they don't want to stimulate additional
traffic.   Such countries may not be able to afford the additional investment required to keep up with new demand.
Variable accounting and billing methods, surcharges on calls
made from hotels, and currency fluctuations further complicate
rates.   U.S. carriers are seeking greater consistency of
service offerings and rates throughout the world.

147. "First-Class Mess." The Economist, 27 May 1978, p. 48.

In May 1978 the U.S. Postal Service raised prices for a first-class letter from 13¢ to 15¢, the fifth increase in a decade. It seems a fruitless exercise, as the service has not paid for itself for years; the previous year's deficit was $700 million. It is thought that rate increases in other parts of the service, as high as 37 percent for fourth-class mail, will lower total revenues and drive business away to such competitors as private delivery services and telephones.

A major problem seems to be lack of agreement as to what a postal service is supposed to provide. The postal service and President Carter had agreed on a 13¢ "citizen's stamp" for individuals, while business would be charged 16¢, but the postal rate commission decided that was discriminatory. As a public service, the postal service is supposed to provide identical service for all, irrespective of distance. Since 1970 the postal service has adopted a private enterprise approach; according to business standards, it is foolish to fix charges at a flat rate without allowing for cost variations. At present, there seems to be wide support for allowing the service to become completely private and open to competition.

148. Gell, Marilyn Killebrew. "User Fees I: The Economic
     Argument." "User Fees II: The Library Response."
     Library Journal 104:1 (1 January 1979) 19-23; 104:2 (15
     January 1979) 170-173.

In the first part of this two-part article, Gell sets the economic framework for a discussion of the controversial issue of the installation of user fees for computerized data base services in U.S. public libraries. The property tax is the biggest generator of local tax revenues, but it is under increasing attack; the budgets of many public agencies will shrink. Public provision of certain goods/services is justified on the grounds of efficiency in joint consumption, difficulty of excluding consumers, and externalities. In the face of shrinking budgets, however, public pricing is possible when goods are divisible, capable of exclusion, and their benefits accrue more to individuals than to society at large; this is the case with library materials.

In the second part of the article, Gell shows that although libraries are considered essential to American democracy, they have been very unsuccessful in attracting financial support; in 1974 public library revenues were less than .2 percent of total U.S. information revenues. Most adult library users are middle class people seeking recreational reading; there is no reason for the whole population to be taxed to support this service. It would be more equitable and efficient to use marginal cost pricing and let such services as recreational reading and computerized information search support themselves. Librarians must distinguish among essential and merely derived services; the institution of user fees for the latter is an excellent short-run solution to budget constraints.

149. Herring, Conyers. Letter published in Information Hotline 11:5 (May 1979) 12-13.

    Herring has written a letter in response to a proposed U.S. federal policy on the dissemination of technical information resulting from federally funded research; he is particularly concerned with a statement that information made available by the federal government should be priced to recover the full costs of printing, publicity, and dissemination. Herring states that the total benefits of such publication will be optimized in a free market by pricing equal to the incremental cost of provision; for a publication, then, the market price need represent only the cost of printing and mailing one additional copy.
    Herring includes an earlier, more lengthy letter in which he made the following statements: (1) most information services give a greater net benefit to society if they are subsidized; (2) services that cannot survive in a free market can give a net benefit to society if they are subsidized; (3) a self-supporting service can provide disbenefits to society. Herring explains when these statements hold true and demonstrates with cost equations and demand curve analysis. He concludes that "it is ridiculous to look on a free-market economy as an ideal system capable of ensuring optimal response to the information needs of users." Subsidies may be necessary to provide information users with freedom of choice.

150. Jackson, Lionel S. "Determining the Value of a New Subscription." Editor & Publisher, 4 November 1978, pp. 14-15.

    Newspaper managers may spend a great deal on promoting circulation but often don't know the dollar value of a new subscription. To figure the actual return on investment in promotions, it is not enough simply to compare this year's promotion budget or circulation figures with last year's. Circulation alone is used less and less in figuring a newspaper's market value; circulation gains and losses don't seem to affect the value of newspaper stocks, for example. In Jackson's formula, circulation and advertising are both factored in, since increased circulation attracts additional advertising. His simple arithmetical formula yields a value of $254.80 for a new order of a typical daily newspaper. When promoting circulation, the value of a subscription should first be determined; then management should decide how much it is willing to spend to gain each new subscription.

151. Kahn, Alfred E., and Zielinski, Charles A. "New Rate Structures in Communications." Public Utilities Fortnightly 97:7 (25 March 1976) 19-24.

In the U.S. telephone industry there have been monopoly conditions that have permitted a rather loose relationship between rates and costs; the pricing of services has been heavily influenced by value of service considerations and also a social component, that of trying to make phone service as close to universal as possible by subsidizing the basic charge.

New competition, especially in terminal equipment, will force revolutionary changes in this pricing structure. Inflation has sent capital costs soaring in this highly capital-intensive industry. It is becoming recognized that rates must be differentiated for different kinds of services to bring rates into line with their respective incremental costs. This article treats new concepts in telephone rate structures, especially emphasizing the idea that to be more cost-efficient rates must be "usage-sensitive." It is also pointed out that NARUC, the National Association of Regulatory Utility Commissioners, has taken a stand against increased competition because of their interest in holding down basic service charges. (See also entry 152.)

152. Kahn, Alfred E., and Zielinski, Charles A. "Proper Objectives in Telephone Rate Structuring." Public Utilities Fortnightly 97:8 (8 April 1976) 20-23.

This article is a sequel to the authors' "New Rate Structures in Communications," entry 151). The theme that economic efficiency must play a larger role in the U.S. telephone rate structure is continued. The authors point out the many ways that internal subsidies in rates have been permitted to detract from economic efficiency. For example, usage costs have been allowed to partially subsidize the purchase of terminal equipment. Vintaged rates, which are lower rates for existing subscribers and higher rates for new subscribers, are discriminatory and inefficient. The authors feel that in trying to match incremental costs and rates, it is the more price-elastic services, such as long-distance service, that should be priced more closely to incremental costs. It is concluded that, under present economic conditions of inflation and increased competition, it is dangerous to allow subsidization of rates and the promotion of monopoly for some vaguely defined social purpose.

153. Landau, Edmund, and Davenport, John Scott. "Price
     Anomalies of the Mass Media." Journalism Quarterly
     36:3 (Summer 1959) 291-294.

    Standard economic theories in the field of price deter-
mination do not work for the mass media; no medium follows
the laws of supply and demand or utilizes cost factors in
setting prices. For newspapers, prices do not come close to
covering costs, and prices remain rigid while variable costs
reflect fluctuations in the economy; newspaper prices are
arbitrary, and have evolved historically rather than from
economic theory. The price of a book is also arbitrary, and
once it is set it remains unchanged despite the volume of
sales. Motion pictures are analogous to books; the price of
admission bears no relationship to the cost of producing the
film or the size of the audience. Both books and movies are a
speculation on the mass market. The chief anomaly in the
broadcasting industry is that consumers receive radio and
television free; it is between the advertiser and the medium
that economic laws function, yet consumers are still a crucial
factor in that they indirectly generate revenues for advertisers
and the broadcasting industry.
    More theory development in mass communication economics
is called for; explanations are needed for the economic relationship between consumers, advertisers, and media. (See
also Currier, entry 145.)

154. Larkin, Edward P. "Babes in Phoneland." Public
     Utilities Fortnightly 93:8 (11 April 1974) 15-20.

    Since the U.S. telephone system has evolved as a natural
monopoly, regulatory commissions have been established to set
prices and profits. From the beginning, telephone pricing has
been based on a "value of service" philosophy; this is a
demand-oriented approach, with the primary consideration
being that the telephone will be of more value to one user than
another. Telephony is a two-way process; this pricing approach encourages people to have telephones and use them
often, thus raising the value of the service to everyone.
Those who have only a limited need for service need not be
excluded. Pricing is thus not merely a matter of recapturing
costs and providing earnings.
    There is currently a concerted attack on value-of-service
pricing. Scholars and academicians are advocating pricing

based on costs for the sake of competition and economic efficiency. The FCC has also contributed through decisions creating selective competition. Larkin feels that the residence customer would be adversely affected by such a policy through higher prices and poorer service. Costs are not compatible with value of service pricing. Cost advocates say that if service cannot be economically viable, it shouldn't be provided, but what about customers in rural areas, and low-income customers? Rate making is an art, with flexibility to meet the changing needs of a changing society.

155. Lerner, Norman C. "Economic Policy and Pricing Alternatives for Telecommunications in Indonesia." In Pacific Telecommunications Conference Papers and Proceedings, pp. 1E-1 - 1E-7. Edited by Dan J. Wedemeyer and David L. Jones. Honolulu: Pacific Telecommunications Conference, 1979.

Lerner reports results of an evaluation of telecommunications tariffs carried out for PERUMTEL, the national telecommunications carrier of Indonesia. Telecommunications prices in many LDCs are based on cost-of-service principles utilized in developed nations; a value-of-service orientation may be more appropriate to the achievement of certain social, economic, and financial objectives. Currently the government sets rates and service charges while PERUMTEL establishes installation fees; the two units appear to be working at cross-purposes, with rates very low and installation very high.
Alternatives include the following suggestions: (1) making a distinction between residential and business rates - currently, there is no distinction, but more revenue could be obtained from businesses, which can typically pay more; also, very high installation fees deter most residential customers from owning phones; (2) in areas where the use of some exchanges exceeds desired operating levels to the detriment of service quality, surcharges could be initiated to discourage excessive use; (3) tariff distinctions could be made between peak and off-peak hours; when peak hour rates are increased, many calls are discouraged and increased revenues are obtained from the remaining less elastic demand.

156. Linford, John. "To Charge or Not to Charge: A Rationale." Library Journal 102:17 (1 October 1977) 2009-2010.

The controversy over whether to charge user fees for computer-produced library services has consisted primarily of discussions of ideals and discrimination. Other new services may arise that cannot be worked into existing budgets.

Linford proposes a concrete rationale for deciding whether to charge for new services. Libraries are places where materials and the tools to use them are brought together; patrons are expected to supply the time and/or money to use them. An example is photocopying: patrons can spend their time copying by hand, or they can pay for photocopies. Libraries should not charge for materials/facilities/services made available for general use, or for which patron-specific costs cannot be identified; libraries could charge for services used exclusively by an individual for which patron-specific costs are incurred by the library.

Discrimination against low-income patrons can be avoided by providing printed forms of computerized data bases for manual searching. If no printed forms exist, the library might extend its rationale to define a "reasonable level" of service to be provided at no charge. A library may also choose not to provide the service at all.

157. Littlechild, S. C. "A Note on Telephone Rentals." Applied Economics 2:1 (May 1970) 73-74.

A principle often utilized for setting the annual rental or fixed charge for a telephone is that it be set equal to marginal customer cost, which is "the marginal cost of maintaining a subscriber in the telephone system." However, the value of a telephone to an individual subscriber increases as the number of other subscribers increases, because there are more potential connections. Therefore, subscribers, especially businesses, may be willing to subsidize others to subscribe. Using econometric analysis, Littlechild demonstrates that telephone rental should be set below marginal cost. The article is concluded with a discussion of current rental charges in the United Kingdom.

158. McSweeny, A. John. "Effects of Response Cost on the Behavior of a Million Persons: Charging for Directory Assistance in Cincinnati." Journal of Applied Behavior Analysis 11:1 (Spring 1978) 47-51.

Directory assistance is typically provided free, which means that it must be subsidized by higher charges for other telephone services. In 1974, in an attempt to reduce the frequency of such calls, Cincinnati Bell Telephone Company instituted a system allowing three free local directory-assistance calls per telephone line per month, after which each such call would cost 20¢.

The purpose of this study was to see if the 20¢ charge would reduce the number of calls. Ample data were available through 1976, since Cincinnati Bell has recorded all directory-assistance calls since 1962. No charges were instituted for long-distance directory-assistance calls, so a comparison series was available as a control group. It was found that at the point of intervention, 1974, the frequency of local directory-assistance calls dropped by about 60,000 per day; in contrast, the frequency of long-distance directory-assistance calls did not change. Cincinnati Bell has saved money since the introduction of this charge, and the savings have been passed on to customers in lower phone bills.

159. Marchand, M.G. "The Economic Principles of Telephone Rates Under a Budgetary Constraint." The Review of Economic Studies 40:4 (October 1973) 507-515.

The demand for telephone service shows both random and periodic patterns. Telephone utilities are typically required to cover costs with revenues. Marchand has formulated an econometric model to derive second-best pricing and investment rules for a utility with these demand characteristics and this particular financial constraint. Certain simplifying assumptions are made: there are only two kinds of consumption, telephone service and other, and there is only one exchange. A consumer's expenditure function, a supply function, and the resultant price are derived; the budgetary constraint is formulated in mathematical terms, included with the previous functions, and a market-clearing equation is derived. Practical implications of the model for the policy-maker are discussed; the purpose of the study is to investigate methods for structuring telephone rates that will minimize resource misallocation caused by a constraint on the telephone company's budget.

160. Matarazzo, James M. "Scientific Journals: Page or Price Explosion?" Special Libraries 63:2 (February 1972) 53-58.

Dramatic increases in subscription rates for scientific journals have presented problems for U.S. libraries. In this investigation it is shown that growth in the size of journals has accounted for much of the price increases. Data for 20 physics journals are presented for 1959 and 1969, including number of pages and issues and subscription rates. For the 20 journals there was a 202 percent increase in price and a 147 percent increase in pages.
    Eight of the journals are published by the American Institute of Physics, six by other societies, and six are commercial journals. AIP journals have actually increased more in

pagination than in price, while the other two groups show much greater price than page increases.

These data have implications for library operations in several areas besides budgeting: work load for checking in journals, binding, and shelving space. Scientific management in libraries depends on the availability and utilization of these data.

161. Mitchell, Bridger M. Optimal Pricing of Local Telephone Service. Santa Monica, CA: Rand Corp., 1976.

Implementation of usage-sensitive pricing (USP), with customers being charged for the number and duration of local calls, is under consideration by AT&T and the independent carriers. In this study the effects of USP are analyzed in relation to economic efficiency and equity; comparisons are made with the current system of flat rate tariffs for local calls.

A theory of demand for residential telephone service is developed. An important distinction is specified between the demand for calls and the demand for connections; for a single consumer, the demand for calls depends only on the per-call price, while the demand for a connection depends on both per-call price and the monthly charge. A surprising conclusion of the demand analysis is that under flat rate tariffs lower-income users have the highest calling rates.

The central chapter, on setting optimal prices, involves calculating total benefits to be derived from changing the tariff structure. Information about the demand function and costs is used in calculating consumers' surplus and producers' surplus. Flat rate, two-part, and peak-load tariffs are considered, and optimal tariffs in each case are determined. Quantitative analysis of the benefits and costs of shifting from a flat rate to a two-part tariff, under which there would be a basic charge plus a per-call charge, indicates that total benefits of telephone service would increase by as much as 9 percent. Larger gains are likely if USP is applied to business users, and if peak-load pricing is included. A major effect is that service would be made available to low-income, low-volume users who previously couldn't affort it.

162. Mitchell, Bridger M. Pricing Policies in Selected European Telephone Systems. Santa Monica, CA: Rand Corp., 1978.

Telephone pricing policies in Norway, Sweden, Switzerland, the United Kingdom, and West Germany are described and compared with U.S. policies. There are four categories of charges in European countries: (1) installation fee; (2) subscription fee, for connection to the network; (3) local usage charges, increasingly often based on length of call and time of day; and (4) trunk usage charges. In most countries the same rates apply to business and residential customers, a sharp contrast with U.S. practice; also in Europe, a periodic pulse method of metering and charging for calls contrasts with U.S. flat rates for local calls.

Mitchell has gathered and presented what evidence he could find of changes in traffic patterns resulting from institution of peak/off-peak rates for trunk calls. In Norway, for example, there was found to be a sharp increase in the volume of calls during the first off-peak hour. Mitchell suggests that such data be used to construct a quantitative model of demand for calls under peak-load rates; he discussed factors that would characterize the model, such as price elasticities and externalities inherent in telephone networks. The crux of the peak-load pricing problem is that there must be only a limited number of distinct prices for customer satisfaction, yet a more complex pricing system would have greater economic efficiency.

163. Ohls, James C. "Marginal Cost Pricing, Investment Theory and CATV." Journal of Law and Economics 13:2 (October 1970) 439-460.

The use of marginal cost pricing in the CATV industry is investigated; a corollary subject, optimal investment in the industry, is also discussed. The analysis is based on the following welfare function: welfare equals total revenues plus consumer's surplus minus total costs. For defining costs, the relevant unit of output is one consumer month of CATV service. Four types of costs implicit in CATV technology are defined; the optimal price is a two-part price that includes a hook-up fee to cover the installation costs and a monthly service charge to cover variable costs. The problem with this optimal price is that it doesn't cover other costs of the system; Ohls demonstrates that the monthly charge must be raised to cover all costs, but also that there must be some form of regulation to prevent monopoly profits.

The decision to invest in a CATV system depends on a determination of net welfare. To his basic model Ohls adds such factors as an uncertain number of channels and a revenue constraint; he shows with demand curves how the investment decision can be made.

Ohls also discusses the pricing of common carrier service on CATV, local originations with and without advertising, and pay TV.

164. Ordover, Janusz A., and Willig, Robert D. "On the Optimal Provision of Journals Qua Sometimes Shared Goods." American Economic Review 68:3 (June 1978) 324-338.

A good is shared when its services are used by more than one agent. Journals are "sometimes shared goods": they are private goods to personal subscribers and shared goods when provided through libraries. Policy issues resulting from the "shared good" characteristic include reprography of library journals and copyright problems, dual pricing structures (high rates for library subscriptions, low rates for personal ones), and library usage fees. The authors provide a mathematical analysis of the provision of technical journals; the theoretical framework is based on the existence of separate but linked markets. Consumers who subscribe to a journal value the good above its price; some consumers who use the library journals would not subscribe even if the library option were not available. A second group of library users would subscribe if the sharing option were unavailable; these consumers provide the link between the private and shared markets.

Under the assumption that libraries charge no fees, the authors study subscription prices that are optimal for publisher's profits and user's welfare. These methods are then applied to the 1975 prices of five economics journals, and it is concluded that for four of the journals welfare can be improved by raising library subscription rates and lowering personal rates. When library usage fees are introduced, it is found that total welfare is increased due to decreased subscription prices, increased private subscriptions, and consequent increased publishers' profits.

165. Passell, Peter, and Ross, Leonard. Communication Satellite Tariffs for Television. London: International Broadcast Institute, 1972.

Economic and policy issues that affect the prices for transmission of TV programs over international communications satellite systems are examined. First the organization of satellite TV transmission is described; satellites are owned by Intelsat, while earth stations and land lines are owned by domestic telecommunications entities. Other organizations involved include the UN, ITU, and regional broadcasting unions such as EBU.

An overview of the current pricing system is presented, stressing its complexity. The various transmission links have their own tariff structures and policies; in general, average cost pricing is used, but there are many exceptions. There are vast differences in prices around the world. A theoretical discussion of average cost and marginal cost pricing follows, in the context of the special cost characteristics of communications services, where marginal cost is always less than average cost. There is currently a high level of excess capacity in the satellite system; average cost pricing deters some potential use, but marginal cost pricing might be too low for the financial viability of the ownership organizations.

The authors propose a pricing alternative to suit the situation where marginal cost is less than average cost. The transmission service owners could agree on an annual revenue requirement and set annual system "entry fees" on a basis independent of transmission hours; for example, the fee could be proportional to the number of sets served. After paying this fee, a customer could buy time based on marginal cost pricing. There would be substantial redistribution effects, since most sets are concentrated in the wealthier nations.

166. "Pricing/Value of Service." Telecommunication Journal 44:3 (March 1977) 116-117.

This article is part of a special issue on "Telecommunications in Canada." The Canadian telephone industry is a regulated utility. The many complicating factors in setting telephone rates are described: (1) to satisfy customers; (2) to provide adequate, stable, and improving revenues; (3) to achieve economic operation; (4) to achieve equitable distribution of charges. In developing rates, the overall aim is to achieve a reasonable balance among these objectives.

Several pricing principles are described: (1) the company-wide principle establishes that companies should be treated as a single unit; (2) the cost recognition principle, taking into account such factors as the nature of the demand relationships and the existence of wide fluctuatons in usage, establishes that the cost of individual services can only be approximately determined; (3) the value-of-service principle involves the selection of rates that give consideration to such social factors as customer perceptions and acceptance.

167. Sherman, Roger, and George, Anthony. "Second-Best Pricing for the U.S. Postal Service." Southern Economic Journal 45:3 (January 1979) 685-695.

In 1970 Congress passed an act that changed the Post Office Department into an autonomous public corporation called the U.S. Postal Service (USPS); it was directed to break even except on some specified Congressionally subsidized operations. The USPS operates under the following three conditions: (1) economies of scale exist, so marginal cost pricing would yield deficits; (2) deficits are constrained by the necessity to break even; (3) the USPS does not have a monopoly in all its operations; there are substitute services such as the telephone, the private United Parcel Service, and advertising media that compete with direct mail advertising. Therefore the USPS must choose from a set of second-best prices that exceed marginal costs; the objective of this study is to derive an optimal second-best pricing rule.

The authors first review some relevant models, but none reflects all three of the conditions under which the USPS operates. They then drive a model using econometric analysis. Implications of the model for rate making are discussed. Finally, the model is made more practical by allowing simultaneous determination of a set of prices.

168. Shute, John V.   "Further Reductions in Satellite Rates."
      EBU Review 30 (March 1979) 54-59.

European and American broadcasters have been striving since the late 1960s to obtain reduced rates for bulk or contract service for regular news exchanges via satellite. The first special rate for a daily TV news exchange was initiated in 1971 between Spain and several Latin American countries; the rate consisted of a ten-minute minimum and a per-minute charge thereafter. By 1974 the U.S. joint carriers had on file with the FCC an experimental tariff for bulk nighttime TV service; the EBU was trying to persuade the European Conference of Postal and Telecommunications Administrations to adopt similar tariffs but with no success. Shute describes in detail the tortuous administrative and legislative negotiations and proceedings that resulted in large rate reductions on the American side in 1978; he urges telecommunications administrations in other countries to implement corresponding reductions.

169. Squire, Lyn.   "Some Aspects of Optimal Pricing for
      Telecommunications." Bell Journal of Economics and
      Management Science 4:2 (Autumn 1973) 515-525.

Among public utilities, telecommunications may offer the most external economies. The recipients of calls get benefits for which they don't pay, and all subscribers realize a benefit when a new subscriber joins the system, because they can call the new subscriber. Using econometric methods, Squire derives optimal pricing equations for telecommunications, allowing for these externalities. In order to stress the externalities, he chooses to simplify the cost analysis by assuming that demand doesn't fluctuate, the life of the telephone is very short (thereby avoiding the need for a discount rate), and long-run marginal costs are constant.

Equations describing benefits derived by a subscriber from outgoing and incoming calls are combined into a total benefits equation. An equation governing system size describes the condition that the marginal subscriber will equate the private benefit and cost of phone ownership. An optimal price for each system size can be derived, and the optimal price and system size will determine optimal benefits through the total benefits equation.

Squire concludes that pricing according to marginal cost isn't economically efficient; the price of calls should be less than marginal cost by an amount equal to the external benefit obtained by the recipient of the call.

170. Stanley, Kenneth B. "Pricing of Satellite Services in the International Telecommunications Industry." In New Dimensions in Public Utility Pricing, pp. 403-422. Edited by Harry M. Trebing. MSU Public Utilities Studies. East Lansing: Michigan State University, 1976.

Stanley analyzes Comsat's pricing structure to show how it may lead to widespread resource misallocation in international telecommunications. He first reviews the industry market structure and relevant FCC decisions. Comsat is in the position of a wholesaler, because it can only lease satellite circuits to the other common carriers; the purpose of this FCC decision was to protect the record carriers from Comsat competition. Technological characteristics of the satellite system are compared with those of its chief competition, cable, to show comparative cost advantages and disadvantages: (1) cable costs are a function of distance, while satellite costs are insensitive to distance; (2) new satellites replace existing satellites, meaning a marked decline in unit costs of service; new cables are operated together with older ones; (3) satellites have a much shorter operational life; (4) satellites have enormous capacity.

The key determinant of Comsat's pricing structure is the cost of submarine cables; Comsat rates are based on mileage bands. This distance-sensitive pricing ignores the outstanding cost characteristic of satellites. Efficient utilization and resource allocation indicate that satellites should be the major transmission mode for long distances and cables for shorter distances, but Comsat's policy of competitive pricing against cables does not yield the necessary incentives for economic efficiency.

171. Stern, Carl. "Usage-Sensitive Pricing for Telephone Service." Public Utilities Fornightly 92:8 (11 October 1973) 53-56.

U.S. telephone companies need additional revenues both to meet the present level of demand, which is increasingly costly due to inflation, and to recover the capital costs of plant expansion required by increases in call volume. Rate increases are usually spread among all subscribers, but it would be more equitable to allocate extra costs to high-use subscribers. Flat rates are easy to understand, easy to bill, and seem equitable, but actually subscribers making few calls are subsidizing those who make many; also, the length of calls is ignored.

Monthly flat rates are based on demand, or value of service, which is difficult to measure; cost is a better basis. Monthly flat rates serve to recover fixed costs but do not allow for the variable costs of volume of calls. It is proposed that a system of marginal cost pricing be used in preference to the prevailing system based on average cost pricing. There should be no "free" call allowance combined with the basic rate; the minimum bill would recover the fixed costs, and marginal cost pricing would apply with the first call made.

Measured telephone services might lead to a leveling off in call volume; less new telephone plant would be required. This might serve national priorities better than further expansion would.

172. Stevenson, Rodney E. "The Pricing of Postal Services." In New Dimensions in Public Utility Pricing, pp. 427-452. Edited by Harry M. Trebing. MSU Public Utilities Studies. East Lansing: Michigan State University, 1976.

The United States Postal Service (USPS) provides over 30 distinguishable classes of service. The USPS and the Postal Rate Commission share the authority to establish rates and define service classes. According to the Postal Reorganization Act (1970) each type of service is required to bear its attributed direct and indirect costs. The USPS used a short-run marginal cost pricing approach; the rates for each class are expected to recoup its short-run incremental costs. Stevenson explains how USPS pricing rules are derived from economic theory and then shows how they work in practice. Costs are separated into attributable and institutional categories; attributable costs are those that vary in direct proportion to mail volume on a year-to-year basis. Institutional costs are allocated on a judgmental basis, depending on certain demand factors.

Stevenson finds that the criteria for separating costs and the reliance on subjective judgment distort any possible meaningful application of pricing theory. He suggests that for both revenue allocation and fair competition, prices should be equated to long-run marginal costs. Current postal prices function as a discriminatory strategy to limit competition and favor certain customers.

173. Takahashi, Hirofumi. "Usage Sensitive Pricing - Japanese Experience." In Pacific Telecommunications Conference Papers and Proceedings, pp. 1E-8 - 1E-17. Edited by Dan J. Wedemeyer and David L. Jones. Honolulu: Pacific Telecommunications Conference, 1979.

In Japan, local telephone service was first offered on a flat rate basis, but in 1920 untimed message rate pricing was introduced in the six largest cities; by 1970, 95 percent of subscribers were on the message rate system. There was some initial opposition, but eventually it was seen as promoting equity in sharing the cost burden among subscribers. There was a 50 percent reduction in traffic during the first year after implementation. In a 1954 Supreme Court decision, Nippon Telegraph and Telephone's (NTT) authority to charge by message rate was approved; the Court cited equity, improved efficiency, and cost reduction as advantages of the system.
As city boundaries expanded, areas were created within cities that couldn't be reached by local calls. NTT merged concerned exchange areas, but cities were expanding too rapidly and commuters were moving farther out. To cope with the difference between local call and short-haul toll charges, NTT in 1972 began to time local calls and expand local call areas. Takahashi makes the following concluding recommendations: (1) introduce usage-sensitive pricing as early as possible; (2) use ample public relations activities to introduce such pricing; (3) plan rate structures in anticipation of city growth.

174. "A Whole New Way to Figure AT&T's Rates." Business Week, 14 February 1977, pp. 86-88, 91.

In June 1977 AT&T filed a new rate structure, which was ordered by the FCC the previous October. Rates for various services will be tied much more closely to the costs of providing them than ever before. The first step has been the development of a system called "fully distributed costs." In the past AT&T has relied heavily on incremental costing for pricing new services; Bell's competitors have argued that this

is unfair because Bell's ordinary telephone service, a monopoly, bears most of the company's costs and thus subsidizes the
newer services.

Eventually AT&T's entire accounting system will have to
be revised. Regulated utilities and transportation companies
have used the Uniform System of Accounts, which classifies
data in such a way that costs can't be related to revenues for
any specific service.

In the short term, a likely result of the new price structure will be quickly shifting rates. The long-term impact of
strict costing techniques is likely to be fewer tariff disputes
and accusations against Bell of "predatory" pricing. These
changes should take the mysticism and emotion out of rate
regulation.

175. Zachry, Charles C., Jr. "Usage-Sensitive Pricing for
      Directory   Assistance."   Public Utilities Fortnightly
      100:12 (8 December 1977) 23-27.

U.S. telephone customers have viewed directory assistance (DA) as a free service, but actually it has always been
paid for by general revenues; low- and high-usage customers
therefore pay the same. The use of DA has been growing
much faster that the number of customers, at great expense to
the telephone companies. Telephone rate policies have always
been based on rate averaging and value of service pricing,
but now there is a trend towards usage-sensitive pricing
(USP); telephone companies want to apply USP to DA to slow
the rapid growth of this very expensive service.

It has been found that 20 percent of customers make 80
percent of DA calls. "Free" DA operates for the benefit of a
few, and therefore current pricing is inequitable. Plans to
reprice DA include five parameters, such as a "free" allowance
and selectivity (charging customers for DA only if the numbers requested were in the directory); Zachry outlines five
repricing plans and describes the results of implementing one
plan at a Bell system company. DA calls from residences
dropped from 3.4 to .7 per billing period; revenues increased
by $19,000 per month, and expenses declined by $74,000. The
result was reduced prices of telephone service to the average
customer. In general, the main effect of USP for DA is
expected to be drastically reduced expenses for the telephone
companies; increased revenues will be a minor effect.

176. Zais, Harriet W. "Economic Modeling: An Aid to the
Pricing of Information Services." Journal of the American Society for Information Science 28:2 (March 1977)
89-95.

Because of limited budgets, information centers and
libraries are turning to user fees. There are few precedents
for pricing bibliographic information; Zais presents this overview of pricing theory and techniques to aid the administrator
of an information center. Illustrative data were drawn from
studies of computer-assisted selective dissemination of information (SDI) services.

There are typically several pricing objectives that must
be balanced, such as recovering costs and charging a socially
optimal price; pricing practices must be related to these
objectives. Cost-based, demand-based, and competition-based
practices are outlined and related to SDI services; demand-
based pricing is difficult because of lack of knowledge of the
market value of information. Cost-oriented practices are
considered in detail, cost concepts are defined, and three
pricing techniques appropriate for information services are
discussed: (1) average cost pricing, (2) price discrimination,
(3) marginal cost pricing. Under the first technique, prices
may be set too high from a welfare point of view. Price
discrimination is useful because the information market is easily
segmented, as between institutional and individual users.
Under the third technique, the price of an SDI profile would
be set equal to its marginal cost; this is a problem if cost
recovery is a goal, since survey results show marginal costs
below average costs for SDI services.

F. FINANCING

177. "A Better Way to Pay for Television?" The Economist, 27
January 1979, p. 22.

The BBC is entirely supported by license fees, but
inflation is requiring constant price increases. The BBC has
traditionally insisted on the license fee to maintain independence from government, and yet it may soon have to ask for a
government loan. The only two other means of support are
advertising and direct subsidy from general taxation. The
BBC has correctly rejected advertising, as competition for
advertising would make BBC and commercial programs indis-
tinguishable.

The main objection of the license fee is that it is regressive. Yet Britain's fee is rather low in comparison with other
countries. Exemptions are not granted to pensioners and

other low-income groups in Britain; it is shown that the
license fee has taken proportionately less from old-age pensions over the years.

It is recommended that there be exemptions for pensions
and that more flexible collection arrangements be made. If the
license fee fails to work, advertising is a better solution than
a direct grant. If a direct grant becomes necessary, it does
not have to mean government control of broadcasting.

178. Blonstein, J.L.   "Finance for Telecommunications in the
        Space Age."   Intermedia 5:6 (December 1977) 31-33.

Eurospace, whose 100 members represent most of the
aerospace and telecommunications businesses in Europe,
together with the European Space Agency and ITU, organized
a major conference held in May 1977.   The objectives were to
explain to the financial world the trends and needs of telecommunications and to explain to the telecommunications sector
the availability and constraints of financing.   Telecommunications users, manufacturers, and financers from Europe, the
United States, Africa, and Australia attended.   Blonstein, of
Eurospace, summarizes in this article some of the major papers
and discussions.

European bankers agreed that loan terms are often not
geared to long-term projects nor to the high level of funding
required by telecommunications.   British banks are not prepared to invest in technology.   Bankers stressed that customers must provide sufficient guarantees and suggested that
intercountry collaboration is needed in Europe to prevent
fragmented financing.   The concept of satellite insurance was
discussed; some forms are now available, such as launch
liability insurance.

In developing countries, investment in telecommunications
must compete with projects offering immediate relief or returns.   An OECD representative confirmed that telecommunications shares a very small proportion of aid to LDCs, and
that the aid is often tied to equipment supply.   Aid liaison
between Africa and the Arab world was described.

Participants agreed that bankers profited most from the
conference through a new awareness of telecommunications
needs; manufacturers and users realized that bankers would
still require guarantees.

179. "The Boom in Media Financing."   Business Week, 22
        January 1979, p. 90.

U.S. broadcast industry profits have hit record levels,
and the value of properties has increased by as much as 50

percent in less than a year. Every bank wants to get in on the booming broadcast financing business. Because of the complexities and dangers of the business, it has typically been handled by media specialists from very large banks; however, smaller banks are now showing interest.

It is difficult to project success or failure of an investment in media because fixed assets count for so little; it is such intangibles as cost flow and quality of management that are significant. Another problem is that the purchaser is buying a license to use the airways, and the right to broadcast can be lost through regulatory proceedings. Also, competition from a station that suddenly switches to the same format can cut into market share. Finally, management changes will often drive down ratings.

180. Callahan, Francis X. "Does Advertising Subsidize Information?" Journal of Advertising Research 18:4 (August 1978) 19-22.

The advertising media include newspapers, magazines, television, radio, and direct mail. In each medium, the advertiser buys space or time; the consumer contributes to information dissemination by buying a stamp, a magazine, a newspaper, or a radio or TV set. In each medium, advertising revenues and circulation revenues and/or costs were compared with the amount of advertising and other content. In U.S. newspapers, advertising contributes 77 percent of revenues and takes 62 percent of space; advertising clearly subsidizes information. If consumer revenues were total revenue and advertising was in the paper, under the assumption that newspapers are bought just as much for advertising content as for editorial content, the consumer would have to pay 43¢ for what is now a 10¢ paper.

The analysis of magazines shows a slight tendency for consumers to subsidize advertisers. In radio and television, the advertiser clearly supports information/entertainment. It is pointed out that in the electronic media, total advertising time is limited by broadcasting codes. In postal operations, the consumer, who uses first class and air mail, subsidizes third-class mail which is primarily used by business for advertising purposes.

181. Campbell, David C., and Campbell, Joyce B. "Public Television as a Public Good." Journal of Communication 28:1 (Winter 1978) 52-62.

In contrast to U.S. commercial television, where profit is the primary goal, public television's goals include education of viewers and satisfaction of minority tastes; there has been little consumer sovereignty in public TV, as producers and exeuctives have chosen the programs. The Station Program Cooperative (SPC) was initiated in 1974 to give local station managers some autonomy in program choice by allowing them to vote through the SPC for part of the national programming offered by the Public Broadcasting System. The SPC also provides a method for financing public TV, since the costs for each series purchased by PBS are shared by each station wanting the series.

A major problem with the SPC system is that programs are mistakenly viewed as private goods rather than public goods with a social value. If a station doesn't buy a program, then it isn't allowed to show the program, even though the marginal cost to the system would be 0. Pricing for public goods isn't determined by market supply and demand forces. Characteristics of public goods are discussed, and a proposal for program selection is presented in which public goods effects are taken into account. The proposal is based on "willingness to pay" as an indication of consumer preferences.

182. Carnegie Commission on the Future of Public Broadcast-
     ing. A Public Trust. New York: Carnegie Corpor-
     ation, 1979.

The Carnegie Commission was established in 1977 to "reappraise the condition of public broadcasting in the United States." This report contains the Commission's recommen-dations, plus extensive explanatory, supplementary, and background information. The commission acknowledged that underfinancing has been at the root of public broadcasting difficulties and made the following recommendations: (1) the level of support should reach $1.2 billion annually by 1985; (2) funds should be made available from a diversity of sources, about half each from federal and nonfederal sources; (3) federal funds should come principally from general reve-nues and be nearly automatic in nature, to prevent political interference; (4) specific amounts to come from such non-federal sources as state and local governments, viewers, listeners, and the business community are recommended; (5) a fee for use of the electromagnetic spectrum is suggested. The national structure of public broadcasting must be completely reorganized; the Corporation for Public Broad-casting must be replaced by a new institution, the Public Telecommunications Trust. Other major recommendations include; (1) the bulk of new funds should be spent on programming; (2) 250 to 300 new radio stations must be added to the public system; (3) public broadcasting should be made available to at least 90 percent of the population;

(4) $15 million per year should be allocated for the development of educational programming; (5) public broadcasting must be noncommercial and independent.

183. Carreon, Ceferino S. "The Requirements of Developing Countries." Telecommunication Journal 43:2 (1976) 124-129.

Telecommunications is an essential requirement in developing nations, but it has been difficult to obtain sufficient capital to finance this sector's growth. Current investment as a percentage of GDP is inadequate; it has been recommended that investment should be 0.5 percent of GDP, which amounts to 15 to 20 percent of the resources devoted to economic development.

As background, Carreon presents a series of tables with data on the growth in number of telephones in Asia, from 1963 to 1974, comparisons with other continental areas, telephone growth in specific Asian nations, the amount invested in telecommunications in various Asian nations, and investment as a percentage of GDP.

He then goes on to discuss methods of generating capital. The most common approach has been the use of automatic compulsory subscriber financing. If this is insufficient to cover total capital requirements, long-term indebtedness may be sought through bilateral loans, World Bank financing, and supplier or local financing. Some problems with bilateral loans are current high interest rates and the risk of current devaluation; also, lenders may require that their own suppliers be used. World Bank financing has been considered "the most suitable," but it often involves lengthy delays.

Carreon, who is Chairman of the Board of Communications in the Philippines, closes with three recommendations: (1) priority must be placed on telecommunications investment; (2) U.S. AID financing may be efficacious (Carreon describes a rural electrification project in the Philippines financed by AID); (3) regional cooperation in the manufacture of telecommunications equipment may ease financial constraints.

184. Crum, John K. "Financing a Multijournal System in the 1970's." IEEE Transactions on Professional Communication PC-16:3 (September 1973) 71-72, 173.

The publication operations of scientific societies are increasingly constrained by the rising costs of printing and distribution. The publishing objectives of a nonprofit group such as the American Chemical Society include audience maximization and stimulation of the subject field rather than profit maximization. Various sources of income must be assessed carefully in light of these objectives; Crum reviews advertising, page charges, reprints, back issues, microfilms and microfiche, and subscriptions.

Advertising is hard to sell in scientific publications, except for journal-magazine hybrids and medical magazines; the page rate is proportional to the circulation of the journal. The fairness of page charges is always at issue, but they can be a dependable source of income. Reprint sales and back issues provide substantial income; authors typically buy 100 to 300 copies of their articles. Microforms provide incredible cost savings over paper and have the greatest promise as a future source of income. Subscriptions provide the largest revenues. However, when member rates or dues are raised to cover increased costs, subscribers are lost; this is contrary to the objective of maximum exposure to new information. In 1972, these six income sources for American Chemical Society journals ranked as follows: subscriptions, page charges, advertising, reprints, microforms, back issues.

185. de Tarlé, Antoine. "Financing French TV/Radio." Intermedia 5:5 (October 1977) 29-32.

French public radio/TV (RTF) has two main sources of finance; in 1977, fees on sets accounted for 65.7 percent of RTF income, and advertising 26.4 percent. There are different fees for radios and black-and-white and color TV sets. The fee is a special levy, not a tax, and is therefore fixed by government decision; Parliament, however, has the right to authorize its collection. Brand advertising was introduced on TV in 1968; by law, it should not exceed 25 percent of total RTF income.

In 1974 the national corporation that had administered public broadcasting was broken up and replaced by seven new entities. This created administrative difficulties; resources must be allocated by the Ministry of Finance among the seven entities. The basic distribution principle is that the income is first allocated to the four program corporations (three TV, one radio), which then reassign resources to the other three bodies. Distribution to the program corporations is based on quality of programs and size of audience; the author describes how a quality index is constructed from audience polls and a quality control commission.

De Tarlé characterizes the financing process as complex; two years were required after the 1974 reorganization to make it operational. So far, variations in resources caused by quality and audience indices have been limited. RTF's current financial condition is excellent, particularly because of the rapid increase in purchase of color TV sets; there may be problems when this market is saturated.

186. Dirlam, Joel B., and Kahn, Alfred E. "The Merits of Reserving the Cost-Savings from Domestic Communications Satellites for Support of Educational Television." Yale Law Journal 77:3 (January 1968) 494-519.

A proposed method of financing U.S. educational television (ETV) is to utilize the cost savings made possible by the use of communications satellites to provide interconnections, withholding these savings from the networks. In this paper, the economic appropriateness of the proposal is investigated in terms of whether it would produce an improved allocation of resources to and within the television industry. First, the authors consider five possible consequences of passing the savings on to the networks in lower interconnection rates: (1) an increase in network profits; (2) increased expenditures on programs, giving better quality and diversity; (3) reduced rates to advertisers; (4) increased distribution of revenues to affiliated stations; (5) entry of a new network. Given the current industry sturcture, none of the five is likely to result.
ETV is a public good that is not produced in sufficient quantities by the competitive market; ETV will provide benefits to individual viewers and the public at large without sacrificing present commercial interests. It is concluded that the costs of this proposal are slight in terms of the potential benefits. Commercial network profits are already very high; on distributional grounds, cost-savings should be passed on to consumers. Increased diversity of programming would have a large social benefit.

187. Ferejohn, John A., and Noll, Roger G. "An Experimental Market for Public Goods: The PBS Station Program Cooperative." American Economic Review 66:2 (May 1976) 267-276.

The Station Program Cooperative (SPC) is intended to decentralize the selection of U.S. public television network programs. The 150 participating stations bid for the programs they prefer through an artificial market structure. In this paper, the authors take an early look (the program began with the 1974-75 season) at the workability of this type of market for a public good. A television broadcast is a public good because the cost of transmission is independent of the number of viewers.
The mechanics of the SPC are described; the process centers around a formula that is used to calculate the price of a given program to a given station. The economics of the SPC is discussed within the framework of general equilibrium theory extended to include the pricing of public goods. For each

station, a price vector and a vector of selections is generated, and for programs, a cost vector; a trial set of prices is generated through an initialization procedure, and then prices are changed until a stable equilibrium is reached. The first two SPCs were allowed to run for 12 rounds of bidding and seem to have reached an equilibrium. The authors conclude by stating that since research into this type of market has just begun, they can only suggest further areas of study, such as the equilibrium properties of the SPC.

188. Goldin, Hyman H. "Financing Public Broadcasting." Law and Contemporary Problems 34:3 (Summer 1969) 650-670.

At the time this article was written, the most pressing need for U.S. public broadcasting was to obtain substantial annual federal funding. The 1967 Carnegie Commission's (CC) model of the costs of a fully developed ETV system shows that a quantum leap in funding would be required to give public television the opportunity to develop into an innovative, first-rate entity. Because public and business support is so low, Goldin feels that federal tax power is the only realistic alternative. The CC recommended that funds for plant and operating expenses be provided through a manufacturer's tax on television sets. While the federal government has in the past aided non-governmental organizations and has earmarked federal funds for specified purposes, the CC proposal is innovative in that it welds the two precedents. An earmarked tax would protect public television from political control and assure stable year-to-year funds.

Goldin lists and analyzes new taxes, or taxlike revenue devices, that could be utilized. He prefers the tax on sets, which would be passed along to consumers, or a tax on broadcast revenues. Other possibilities include a tax on all long-distance communication, a spectrum-use tax, and pay TV.

189. Himsworth, Winston E. "Finding Cash for Communications." Datamation 21:3 (March 1975) 49-52.

Himsworth reviews the impact on the U.S. communications industry of four interrelated factors. The first, which provides the theme for the article, is the demand for and availability of investment capital. Communications is a very capital-intensive industry; two to three dollars of capital are required for each dollar of annual revenue. Himsworth cites current limitations on debt and equity financing, especially for new ventures; as long as inflation continues, capital markets will be under pressure. About $50 billion will be required by the entire industry (1975 to 1980), which is 15 to 20 percent of total corporate demand. The telephone companies are and will continue to be the industry's dominant demanders of capital.

Trends in competition, communications technology, and legal and regulatory requirements are also reviewed. Competition should stimulate technological development, but changeovers to new equipment are often slow. This is because of the industry's capital-intensive nature, which produces long depreciation schedules for equipment. Also, common carriers do not traditionally provide new services until they can be made widely available, to prevent discrimination among users.

Because of capital constraints, participation in this industry will be generally limited to the large, well-financed companies.

190. Metzner, A.W. Kenneth. "Integrating Primary and Secondary Journals: A Model for the Immediate Future." IEEE Transactions on Professional Communication PC-16:3 (September 1973) 84-91, 175-176.

A revolution is taking place in the dissemination of research information because of phenomenal growth in the amount of information, more urgent demands for such information, and the impact of new technologies on the dissemination process. The number of pages published by the American Institute of Physics has doubled every eight years since 1940. Metzner describes present costs and methods of producing AIP journals and then outlines a future production model.

A unit record in the primary data base is the text of an article plus its keywords and classification numbers. Page charges cover the cost of creating the primary data base; the costs of products derived from the data base - journals, reprints, microforms - are covered by subscription revenues. Institutional subscribers pay more than individuals, because they cover the costs of authors who cannot pay page charges. The costs of an average article are partly proportional to its length and partly fixed. In 1966 AIP began developing its secondary data base; a unit record contains information about the corresponding record in the primary base. Services derived from the secondary base are tools for accessing, searching, and organizing the primary base.

Presently, some integration of production of the two bases is achieved by keyboarding secondary base information directly from manuscripts submitted by the authors. However, the method of composition is expensive, and costs are 4.5 percent higher than for the primary data base alone. Metzner described a fully integrated system for producing the two data bases, relying heavily on advanced computer processing techniques. The secondary data base will be entirely a by-product of the primary, and costs will be much lower for both.

191. Ragsdale, Warner, Jr. "Why Even More Rate Increases Won't Solve the Postal Mess." U.S. News & World Report, 29 December 1975, 32-33.

In 1975, the U.S. Postal Service (USPS) was in a crisis due to rising costs and deficits. People are more likely to use the telephone than to write a letter, and businesses and government are turning to electronic communications systems; in 1974, these factors caused the first decline in volume of mail in postal history. Yet the number of addresses to be served continues to increase, meaning increased costs to handle each piece of mail. When rates are hiked to cover costs, less use of the mails results; it is apparent that rate hikes cannot solve the postal crisis. A basic decision must be made: what kind of mail service will Americans pay for, and how will they pay for it?

One of the goals of the postal corporation, which was created in 1971, is to become self-sufficient by 1984; tax subsidies would be used to pay only for public-service types of mail delivery. Yet in 1975 the Postmaster General had to ask Congress for a doubling of the annual subsidy. While the subsidy question was being debated, the USPS was trying to economize by restricting the hiring of new employees, cutting down on overtime work, and reassigning unneeded employees to new locations.

192. Schramm, Wilbur, and Nelson, Lyle. "Financing Public TV." Columbia Journalism Review 11:5 (January/February 1973) 31-38.

Despite a high rate of growth during the 1960s, U.S. noncommercial television faced financial difficulties in the early 1970s. By 1971, the increase in mean expenditure per station was insufficient to pay for technical improvements or expanded programming. The article describes ownership patterns and funding sources for public television. There are four distinct types of ownership: (1) community; (2) school system; (3) state and municipal; (4) university stations. Two-thirds of all support comes from taxes; only the community stations receive a substantial portion of their income from private sources, through lists of subscribers they have built up.

In the television business, a high proportion of costs are fixed, making cost reductions very difficult. Also, there is today a general public demand for higher quality programming.

It becomes obvious that an entirely new and higher level of funding will be required to give the nation even a minimum public television service. The authors suggest that the only real possibility for meeting the support needs of public television will be direct appropriations from Congress.

193. Simon, Kathryn, and Bishop, Robert L. "Trends in the Newspaper Budget." Journalism Quarterly 54:4 (Winter 1977) 750-755, 764.

U.S. newspaper budgets from 1947-1974 were analyzed for trends in revenue sources, expense items, and profits. A "composite newspaper" was constructed from available reports; for this "newspaper," advertising contributed two-thirds of the revenue in 1947 and nearly three-quarters in 1974. Local advertisements accounted for more than half of total revenue in 1974; during the time period under consideration, national ads declined while classifieds grew. The proportion of revenue accounted for by circulation declined from one-third in 1947 to one-quarter in 1974; circulation cannot grow because it faces a saturated market, and circulation is lost when prices are increased. Local advertising, on the other hand, is relatively inelastic with respect to price; publishers have been able to raise ad rates and increase revenues. In 1947 larger newspapers obtained proportionately more revenue from circulation, but by 1974 newspaper size made little difference.
Various expense items are listed with proportion of total expenses by date and newspaper size. Newsprint, ink, and handling have together always been the largest single expense item; this item had been shrinking in proportion to newspaper budgets until recent large increases in newsprint prices.
Newspaper profit margins have shrunk, but rates of return are still better than for median American industries. As circulation size increases, the rate of return seems to increase.

G. APPROACHES TO RESOURCE ALLOCATION

194. Barnett, H.J., and Greenberg, E. "On the Economics of Wired City Television." American Economic Review 58:3 (Part I) (June 1968) 503-508.

The costs of wired city TV are compared with the costs of over-the-air TV. Wired city TV uses no spectrum; stations do not require a transmitter and tower; a home antenna is not needed; some elements in TV sets could be eliminated. Wired city TV would require wires and individual droplines to homes.

It is estimated that this initial investment would be about $60 per home.

Benefits of wired city TV include: (1) a much larger number of channels; (2) a much lower cost to carry a signal to the home, overcoming a major financial barrier to entry - high marginal cost for transmission on an additional channel; (3) improved picture quality; (4) cost savings for homes and broadcasters; (5) spectrum saving; and (6) flexibility for communication innovations.

Some objections to wired city TV are: (1) per-home costs in rural areas may be quite high; (2) in very large, densely populated areas an over-the-air system is cheaper than wire, up to the limit of available spectrum; (3) programming costs may be too high to fully utilize a 20-channel system; and (4) networks and stations will be very unwilling to surrender their present oligopoly positions.

195. Bebee, E.L., and Gilling, E.J.W. "Telecommunications and Economic Development: A Model for Planning and Policy Making." Telecommunication Journal 43:8 (August 1976) 537-543.

The authors have developed a model for planning purposes that describes the relationships among economic performance, telecommunications use and availability, and socioeconomic factors, referred to as "development support factors." Since the secondary and tertiary sectors of the economy derive the most benefit from telecommunications inputs, the variable used for economic performance is the value of secondary and tertiary GDP on a per capita basis in the form of an index. A development support index was developed from variables indicating capital expansion and quality of manpower; a telephone index resulted from variables indicating telephones per 100 literate population, business telephones per 100 nonagricultural population, and annual calls per total telephones.

Data for 1970 were collected from 29 countries at various stages of development. Multiple regression analysis was applied to the data; regression equations for the following relationships are presented: (1) performance as a function of development support and telephones; and (2) telephones as a function of development support.

It is concluded that telephone use and availability are policy variables that should depend on the level of development support factors. Graphical analysis of relationships among the three indexes shows probable development paths for telephone expansion and also indicates priorities between telephone expansion and development support factors.

196. Berg, Sanford V. "Increasing the Efficiency of the Economics Journal Market." The Journal of Economic Literature 9:3 (September 1971) 798-813.

The development of a journal system for dissemination of research results and new ideas in economics has been haphazard. More attention must be paid to efficient resource allocation in this market; besides economic efficiency, openness and responsiveness to new methodologies are also needed. Because of the peculiar characteristics of information, certain nonmarket elements have led to institutional involvement in the production and distribution of journals: (1) dissemination of information has externalities; workers can utilize the research of others; (2) there are economies of scale in journal production; (3) information cannot be used up; and (4) because the evaluation of new information is difficult, libraries tend to be comprehensive rather than selective; market entry is thus easy for new journals.

Berg gives a brief history of the economics journal market, which reflects the above characteristics. The quantity of research output has increased so greatly that it is now necessary to study whether new entry, the coverage of new journals, and prices are efficient from the standpoint of meeting the communication needs of economists. Berg reviews the innovative efficiency of communication efforts in such disciplines as physics and chemistry; he makes several recommendations to improve efficiency in economics: (1) a divisional structure for the American Economic Association, to prevent needless duplication and fragmentation; (2) experimental joint ventures by journals; (3) creation of a council of economics editors; (4) analysis of communication patterns in economics as a prerequisite for the establishment of a modern computer-based system.

197. Blackstone, Erwin A., and Ware, Harold. "The Cost of Systems at 900 MHz." In Communications for a Mobile Society: An Assessment of New Technology, pp. 96-116. Edited by Raymond Bowers, Alfred M. Lee, and Cary Hershey. Beverly Hills, CA: Sage, 1978.

Most growth in land mobile communication systems is expected to occur within the spectrum allocation near 900 MHz. Nine hundred MHz systems will have a cost disadvantage compared to lower-frequency systems, because they will require transmitters of higher power and receivers of higher sensitivity. In this paper, the authors analyze the direct costs to the user of various 900 MHz systems. Prices are computed based on data published from 1969 to 1972. It is found that costs depend on the following factors: (1) values of such service parameters as message length, range, and waiting time; (2) type of service provided; (3) technological complexity; (4) spectral efficiency; (5) economies of scale; (6) depreciation rates and accounting practices.

The systems analyzed include one-way paging, conventional, trunked, and cellular. One-way paging requires the least investment per user; at the time the paper was written prices could have been lower and still yielded a profit, but demand exceeded supply. Conventional systems are the least costly of the two-way systems; dispatch services are analyzed. Trunked systems have additional costs for computers and a greater number of channels; the monthly charge for a trunked telephone service is estimated to be from $50 to $70. Various cost estimates are presented for a combined dispatch-mobile telephone service cellular system.

In a concluding section, capital requirements for each system are estimated for low-, medium-, and high-deployment scenarios. Key factors are overall level of penetration, market shares of each system, and cost per unit.

198. Burgess, Eric. "Public Service Satellite System: The Development of an Independent Public Interest Satellite System. Part I." "A First Step to a Public Interest Capability: The Hybrid Satellite System. Part II." Satellite Communications 2:10 (October 1978) 16-17, 20, 34; 2:1 (November 1978) 26-29.

It is now conceivable to plan for and develop a nation-wide U.S. public service satellite system. Burgess reviews the economic, technical and regulatory constraints, and shows how these may be overcome. A chief factor is costs, which must be kept low for all public services. Satellite communications has surprisingly low costs, from which the public has not benefitted because satellites have been lumped together and priced with the older communications methods.

Instructional Television Fixed Service (ITFS), which is now being used in schools and hospitals across the country, has broadcast and interactive capabilities; it is financially independent of the traditional communications system and has proven cost-effective to its users. Burgess suggests the development of a hybrid system using a large-antenna, multi-beam satellite together with the existing ITFS network; the use of cost-effective parts should yield a cost-effective system. Potential uses include education of the handicapped, job training, and nuclear medicine; demand must be forecast for user groups. An important regulatory aspect will be obtaining the necessary frequency band; Burgess provides some technical detail and concludes by laying out a ten-year plan to create an affordable hybrid satellite service.

199. Butman, Robert C.; Rathjens, George W.; and Warren, Colin J. Technical-Economic Considerations in Public Service Broadcast Communications for Developing Countries. Academy for Educational Development, Report no. 9. Washington, D.C.: AED, 1973.

Alternative systems for the distribution of educational materials are compared and evaluated. The report consists of five separate studies. The first is "Communications for Education in Developing Countries." Cost-effectiveness comparisons are made for three systems of TV distribution: (1) netting of conventional TV stations by microwave relay; (2) the use of satellite to relay signals to TV stations that rebroadcast them; and (3) direct transmission of signals from a satellite to individual TV sets. A system preference chart is developed; factors include size of area to be served, number of receivers, and distribution of population.

The second study covers "Satellite Television for India." In India, instructional TV for children and adults is a major objective; another is the promotion of national unity. The costs of major systems components are reviewed: (1) TV transmitters; (2) satellites; (3) TV receivers; (4) microwave relays. These cost estimates are used to compare three basic systems; the cheapest and most versatile is a TV broadcast system that uses ground transmitters and a satellite relay for networking.

The third study is concerned with "Education and Telecommunications in Brazil." A systems analysis of four TV program distribution systems is presented. Cost analysis shows that the major expenses lie in reception facilities. Educational system deficiencies are described, which lead up to a major educational reform implemented in 1971.

A fourth brief study is titled "Comments on Expanding Radio and TV Broadcasting Services in Ethiopia." The most realistic technology for Ethiopia would be an expanded radio broadcast system based on the use of low-cost, battery-powered transistor receivers.

The final study is an "Introductory Assessment of the Technical Aspects of Educational Communication Technologies." It is a listing and evaluation of technologies relevant to the educational needs of developing countries.

200. Carnoy, Martin. "The Economic Costs and Returns to Educational Television." Economic Development and Cultural Change 23:2 (January 1975) 207-248.

The use of classroom educational TV (ETV) is evaluated using data assembled from several ongoing projects in the United States, Latin America, and Africa. Carnoy finds he can only make an analytical beginning, since few ETV projects have defined their objectives clearly or evaluated their effectiveness in terms of the objectives. In many studies the effectiveness of ETV is compared with that in classrooms where no changes have been made; Carnoy prefers to compare ETV with teacher retraining and other educational improvements to find out what increased effectiveness actually costs.

His cost analysis shows that ETV is not cheaper, since it requires teacher retraining anyway, but it is a more rapid way to expand a system. The data from cost-effectiveness and cost-benefit analyses are not persuasive in favor of ETV; many studies show no significant differences in test scores in classrooms where ETV has been used. The analysis of educational benefits is made very complex by such issues as the hidden curriculum of ETV and its impact on traditional societies, the effects of a capital-intensive industry on unemployment, and the benefits of teacher training in societies where leadership is needed desperately. None of the ETV projects reviewed were implemented in a way that would redistribute education or the income derived from it.

201. Carpenter, Margaret B.; Chesler, L.G.; Dordick, H.S.; and Haggart, Sue A. Analyzing the Use of Technology to Upgrade Education in a Developing Country. Santa Monica, CA: Rand Corp., 1970.

Systems analysis is applied to educational planning in a developing country, with emphasis placed on the potential usefulness of educational TV. Colombia was chosen for the analysis because of its ongoing ETV project and the large quantity of available data. Colombia has a severe shortage of school facilities and teachers; the low quality of its educational system has led to high drop-out and repeat rates. In light of both qualitative and quantitative objectives, four alternative programs for primary and four for secondary education were compared in terms of cost and effectiveness. Programs utilizing ETV proved comparable to more conventional approaches, such as providing more teachers; ETV seems the preferable alternative because it requires many fewer trained teachers, which is more realistic in terms of available manpower in Colombia.

Additional research is needed to determine the causes of the high drop-out rate; if it is due to the nature of the curriculum, then technology may lower the rates. Appendices include estimates of school-consolidation potential for the rural population, to achieve economies of scale in education, and the supporting mathematical detail for the cost-effectiveness analysis.

202. Carpenter, Polly. Cost-Effectiveness as an Aid to Making
Decisions in Education.   Santa   Monica,   CA: Rand
Corp., 1970.

Cost-effectiveness analysis is explained and illustrated
with data from a Rand study of an educational TV project in
Colombia.   It is stressed that cost-effectiveness is an aid to
decision making, not a substitute for it.   The essence of
cost-effectiveness is comparison; the effectiveness and cost of
one program must be compared to those of another program or
to variants of the same program.   In the Colombian example,
two alternatives were compared: conventional educational
improvements versus educational TV.   There was no significant
difference between costs for the two programs.   Conventional
improvements would require an additional 71,000 trained
teachers, while ETV would require only 29,000.   There was
very little difference in the number of students to be reached
by the two alternatives (it was assumed that ETV would not be
used in remote areas).   Other measures of effectiveness, such
as whether ETV would reduce the high drop-out rate, had not
been researched.   In this example, the choice turned not on
relative effectiveness but on resource requirements; the fact
that ETV required many fewer trained teachers made it the
preferable alternative.

203. Cooper, Michael D.   "The Economics of Information."   In
Annual Review of Information Science and Technology,
1973, pp. 5-40.   Washington, DC: American Society for
Information Science, 1973.

In this survey of the literature, economics of information
is defined as the economic analysis of the creation, dissemination, and processing/use of information.   The theme is the
optimal allocation of scarce resources, with emphasis placed
on information services and libraries.   Economic studies in
the following areas are reviewed: the information-processing
behavior of individuals, information producers and dissemin-
ators, including education, research and development, the
communications industry, computing equipment, and information
services; funding, tax regulations; and patent and copyright
systems.   Decision-making methods for resource allocation are
discussed in detail, including welfare economics, cost-benefit
analysis, demand analysis, operations research models, cost-
effectiveness analysis, and cost analysis.   Cooper points out
that there is little analysis of costing as a continuing process
in which data collection is integrated with regular routines.
Cooper concludes by recommending the following areas for
research: information-processing by individuals; demand
analysis, to justify the development of information products

and services; and measurement of the benefits and externalities of information services. An extensive bibliography is
included.

204. "The Cost of Communicating." Intermedia 4:4 (August
      1976) 5.

     The economics of mass communications is gaining new
attention from communication specialists; it is to be hoped that
economic analysis will be integrated with the more traditional
technical, legal, social, and political analyses on a permanent
basis. Policy makers and the public need to know how to
allocate their resources among the various media. A good
starting point would be the study of the cost of each medium,
which can be very difficult to determine. For example, ad-
vertiser-financed TV is often considered "free" to the public,
but one study has shown that viewers pay the largest share of
TV costs through maintenance of their sets. Two new Swedish
studies that analyze information on mass media costs in Sweden
are briefly described; one finding was that during the period
1965-1974 Swedes spent a declining proportion of their income
on radio, TV, and books, and an increasing proportion on
newspapers and magazines. The authors of this study point
out that such information could be very useful to government
decision makers.

205. Dammers, H.F. "The Economics of Computer-Based
      Information Systems: A Review." Journal of Docu-
      mentation 31:1 (March 1975) 38-45.

     In this review of literature published in the 1960s and
early 1970s on computer-based information systems, it is
apparent that cost is a primary determinant of the use of
such systems. In the 1960s the literature reflected great
expectations for computerized systems because of the rapidly
improving cost performance of computers coupled with rising
costs in traditional library/information systems. However, by
the late 1960s problems had arisen: (1) the difficulty of
applying automation to the intellectual aspects of information
search; (2) failure of large time-sharing systems to live up to
low-cost expectations; (3) avoidance by users, who typically
prefer to be self-sufficient rather than use remote systems.
To many writers, the cost penalty of system failure appeared
much greater than potential rewards.
     Encouraging factors that appeared in the late 1960s/early
1970s included: (1) the continuing decline in computer processing costs relative to labor costs; (2) the realization that
users don't care as much about stringent recall and precision

factors as information scientists had thought, therefore searches could be run at lower cost levels; (3) the cost-effectiveness of computerized search, in terms of cost per relevant hit, is much better than for manual search.

Dammers, writing from a British perspective, explains that U.S. system costs are much lower than in Europe because of larger scale of operations and cheaper data transmission costs. He predicts that because of decreasing costs computerized systems will shape the library of the future.

206. David, B.E.; Caccappolo, G.J.; and Chaudry, M.A. "An Econometric Planning Model for American Telephone and Telegraph Company." Bell Journal of Economics 4:1 (Spring 1973) 29-56.

A planning tool called FORECYT (Econometric FOREcasting model for Corporate PoliCY Analysis for T - (the ticker symbol for AT&T) is described and demonstrated with examples. The model is based on the idea that the national economy determines demand for a firm's output, and the firm's supply capability responds to this externally derived demand. The demand forecast is therefore derived from a forecast of the U.S. economy.

The model consists of three submodels, which contain a number of modules: (1) environment model - national economy, regulatory, and price-wage review modules; (2) corporate model - demand, price, capital market, financial, revenue, and production modules; (3) management model - input (policy variables for control) and output (performance indicators) modules. Each submodel is presented mathematically with a set of behavioral equations and interacting econometric relationships. The model was used for a forecast in January 1972; results of the forecast show acceptable precision when compared with actual Bell System performance during the forecast period.

207. Dei Rossi, J.A.: Heiser, R.S.; and King, N.S. A Cost Analysis of Minimum Distance TV Networking For Broadcasting Medical Information. Santa Monica, CA: Rand Corp., 1970.

A methodology for estimating the cost of networking the TV broadcasting of scientific information to a particular scientific community is described. Minimum distance networks were calculated using a computer program; such a network is known as a "minimal weighted spanning tree." The methodology was applied to the broadcasting of biomedical information on a national basis to physicians and to accredited medical schools in the United States.

In broadcasting to physicians, costs were estimated on the basis of networking ETV stations with at least one Standard Metropolitan Statistical Area (SMSA) within range; it was found that 96.7 percent of the SMSA physician population could be reached by 106 ETV stations. Because of the very uneven distribution of doctors, it was found that 52 percent of the largest stations could reach 90 percent of the doctors at half the cost of the 106-station network; it is most cost-effective not to try to attain 100 percent coverage.

Costs for networking the 97 medical schools were based on continuous-use charges of a closed circuit TV network. Again, the costs highlight the uneven distribution of the subject population. Detailed cost estimates are presented for both applications, and aspects of the computer work are presented in extensive appendices.

208. Dei Rossi, J.A.; Lindholm, C.R.; Mills, G.F.; and Sumner, G.C. A Telephone Access Biomedical Information Center. Santa Monica, CA: Rand Corp., 1970.

The costs of telephone access information centers are analyzed, using as a base case a center at the University of Wisconsin that offers recorded messages concerning biomedical subjects. Demand, or utilization of the center, is estimated as a function of library size (as measured by the number of messages available), physician population, and the frequency with which the service is publicized. Operating costs are then estimated for various levels of utilization at the single center and also for two-, three-, and four-center configurations. The major portion of operating costs is incurred by telephone line rental charges; the necessary number of available lines, to prevent too-frequent busy signals, is estimated with the statistical method of queuing theory. Also, the best mix of flat-rate and metered-rate lines is calculated.

Including noncommunications costs, cost per call for a national center is estimated to range from $1.06 to $1.45. A single center is found to have a distinct cost advantage over a multiple-center configuration. Utilization is very sensitive to the frequency of promotional advertising. A technical appendix describing the automated voice message store is included.

209. Dhawan, B.D. Economics of Television in India. New Delhi: S. Chand, 1974.

The author focuses on the capital and operational costs of developing a nation-wide educational TV service for India. The necessary foreign-exchange component of the costs is an important issue. Dhawan examines the opportunity cost of satellite versus terrestrial TV and then analyzes the marginal opportunity cost in order to improve the allocative efficiency of scarce resources. He believes that the magnitude of TV benefits in a developing country are variable and indeterminate, and he suggests that cost-benefit analysis is not a good tool of evaluation when used for a single project in isolation. To substantiate his analysis, the author cites several studies on TV in India done in the 1960s by Schramm and Nelson, by Rosenberg, and by Stanford University (the ASCEND study) (not in this bibliography).

The estimated capital costs for terrestrial microwave relays for TV are analyzed and compared with the capital cost of coaxial cables. According to Dhawan, both costs are approximately the same. The cost of reception for community viewing is estimated at $420 million, while operational and ancillary costs of reception are calculated at $682 million. The foreign exchange component of all costs is estimated at 50 percent. The author seems undecided on the economic viability of a nation-wide TV network. Extensive appendices contain details of cost estimates of various TV systems.

210. Elchesen, Dennis R. "Cost-Effectiveness Comparison of Manual and On-line Retrospective Bibliographic Searching." Journal of the American Society for Information Science 29:2 (March 1978) 56-66.

The basic objective of the study was to determine whether a manual or on-line search mode is faster, less costly, and more effective for the type of bibliographic searches performed in scientific/technical organizations. The cost components were labor, information, reproduction, equipment, space, and telecommunications; the performance criteria were the average number of relevant citations retrieved per search, recall ratio, precision ratio, and cost per relevant citation retrieved. Forty topics were searched in both modes by experienced workers at the Lawrence Livermore Laboratory, University of California.

Using the most important cost-effectiveness measure, cost per relevant citations retrieved, on-line searches were found to be cheaper: $0.65 per search as compared with $0.86. Five on-line searches were performed in the time taken to perform one manual search. A typical on-line search cost $26, while the corresponding manual search cost over $30.

The cost of conducting an on-line search has steadily decreased during the past decade. The time and cost advantages of on-line searching should continue to improve as the cost of telecommunications declines.

211. Elldin, A. "Traffic Engineering in Developing Countries. Some Observations from the ESCAP Region." Telecommunication Journal 44:9 (September 1977) 427-436.

Traffic engineering concerns the following activities in a telecommunications administration: subscriber and traffic forecasting; dimensioning; traffic measurements; network planning. A developing country is one in which the demand for telecommunications far exceeds the supply. Elldin compares conditions in developed and developing countries to improve understanding of the specific traffic problems existing in LDCs and shows how planning and skillful engineering can ameliorate difficult problems of scarce resources and ever-increasing demand. A crucial problem for LDCs is the shortage of foreign currency with which to purchase telecommunications equipment from abroad.
Elldin uses a mathematical analysis to model the quality/ quantity trade-off; in situations of excess demand, the question is whether to provide good quality for a few or less quality for many. Typical overloading/congestion problems are discussed. Conditions for the successful introduction of subscriber trunk dialing (STD) are outlined; factors for choosing the best order of introducing STD route by route include a cost/benefit criterion. Modern methods of network planning and optimization, including computer programs, will contribute to a more efficient use of scarce resources.

212. Engvall, Lars. "International Network Planning - Two Case Studies: the Pan-African Telecommunication Network and the Middle East and Mediterranean Telecommunication Network." Telecommunication Journal 44:7 (July 1977) 331-337.

In planning the Pan-African Telecommunication Network, computer calculations were used to analyze the cost effectiveness of various hierarchical network layouts. Engvall explains the principal input data for the calculations and the method used. Extensions of this method were used for a study of a Middle East and Mediterranean network involving 27 nations. Input data included international telephone traffic, hourly traffic distribution, permissible routings, and systems' cost figures. The possibility of future satellite links was included in the calculations, along with the constraining factor that earth stations would also be intended to receive/transmit television programs. A map of the results, showing the most economical routing pattern for the region, is included in the article.

213. Feenaghty, B.J., and Jessop, C.W.A. "Evaluating Network Costs in Choosing a New Telephone Switching System." Telecommunication Journal 45:1 (January 1978) 13-19.

Telecom Australia has completed a study evaluating technical and economic aspects of several stored program control (SPC) switching systems; the results had a significant influence on the choice of the most suitable SPC system for Australian urban networks. In this paper one aspect of the study is stressed: the effect of the switching equipment on the costs of the overall network in which the equipment is to be installed. Cost variations in this one factor were found to have a significant effect on the final selection of the SPC exchange system. Computer programs were used to generate a set of models to establish network costs for various switching and traffic levels; the methodology is described, and data and results are given. It is concluded that large capacity systems will effect considerable network cost savings over a period of ten years, offsetting possible equipment cost advantages of small capacity systems.

214. Gimpelson, Lester A. "Communications Planning for Developing Countries." Electrical Communication 48:4 (1973) 359-363.

Communication systems in developing countries are often characterized by high growth rates. Constraints include restrictions on investment capital, lack of clear goals and priorities, and substantial unsatisfied demand; such constraints mean that developing countries may need to utilize planning techniques differently from the methods of advanced countries. Forecasting is the first stage of planning, but where there is no accurate historical data and much unsatisfied demand, accurate forecasting is impossible; too much time should not be wasted on it. Underestimation has been typical of voice communications forecasting. A concept of service is required, which includes priorities for types of services, geographical apportionment, business versus residential priorities, and response times.

In the area of planning technology, it is suggested that developing nations use standard techniques; trying to be unique can be costly; standard computer techniques are useful. Equipment must be appropriate to the level of engineering and maintenance staffs and to the availability of capital for investment. Finally, flexibility must be planned for to accommodate major technological developments.

215. Goddard, Haynes C.   "An Economic Analysis of Library
    Benefits." Library Quarterly 41:3 (July 1971) 244-255.

    Public library managers find themselves with increasingly
limited resources; these scarce resources should be allocated
to those activities that yield the greatest benefits to society.
Goddard utilizes the notions of social benefits and private
benefits from welfare economics to analyze library benefits.
The traditional functions of U.S. public libraries are education, information, and recreation; most library externalities,
or social benefits, are in the form of the education that
libraries distribute. Much less is known about the externalities of information and recreations.
    The amount of effects of private and social benefits vary
as a function of the group of users receiving the benefits.
Users are classified into the following seven groups, and
benefits are discussed for each: (1) school-age children and
others involved in education; (2) disadvantaged minority
groups; (3) the business community; (4) civic and cultural
organizations; (5) governmental officials and staff; (6) those
in leisure pursuits; (7) the elderly and the infirm. Resources
would be most efficiently allocated in a social sense by concentrating on educational functions at all ages and on service to
government; free service for business and purely recreational
uses are not justified.

216. Grooms, David W.   Telecommunication - Economic Studies:
    A Bibliography with Abstracts.   Springfield,   VA:
    National Technical Information Service, 1976.

    Ninety-four research reports contained in the National
Technical Information Service Collection concerning the economics of telecommunications are cited, with abstracts. The
NTISearch information collection contains federally funded
research reports dating from 1964. NTIS produces published
searches, such as this one, in addition to custom-produced,
on-line searches. Order and price information for each document cited in the bibliography is included.

217. Gushee, David E.   "Factors Affecting Dissemination of
    Chemical Information."   Journal of Chemical Documen-
    tation 11:4 (November 1971) 201-204.

    The structure of chemical information systems is being
changed by the rapidly expanding volume of scientific publication and stringent budget constraints on purchasers.
Library acquisitions budgets have been just holding their own
against inflation, while publishers' prices have been increasing

by 20 percent a year. Gushee predicts that acquisitions budgets will level off; federal funding of science and industrial profitability are both leveling off, and there has been a consistent relationship among these variables for many years.

Acquisition librarians typically implement two cost-saving steps: (1) they reduce the number of multiple subscriptions to individual journals; and 2) they stop subscriptions to high cost publications with low-use frequency. The latter step is especially tricky because of the high social cost of not learning or delayed learning. In addition to the decline in the number of institutional subscriptions, the number of individual subscribers is also declining. Gushee sees great opportunities ahead for marketers of scientific information; joint efforts between institutions and information suppliers are required to compensate for the decline in public subsidy of scientific information.

218. Hindle, Anthony, and Raper, Diane. "The Economics of Information." In Annual Review of Information Science and Technology, 1976, pp. 27-54. Washington, DC: American Society for Information Science, 1976.

The authors survey literature published primarily in 1975 on the economics of formal information services; an extensive bibliography is included. A major theme is the decline in resources available for information services; managers of information systems must use economic analysis in their decision-making processes. Yet the authors find a disappointing lack of studies utilizing economic methods apart from simple costing exercises. Managers lack motivation to use economic analysis, perhaps as a result of past abundance of resources for information services.

The three stages of analysis for economic evaluation are (1) definition of the problem: (2) measurement of costs and benefits; (3) modeling. The literature reveals that studies have been concentrated in four areas: (1) specialized information services; (2) systems of libraries; (3) the library as a system; (4) collection control within libraries. Under the first stage of analysis, problem definition, studies concerning the economic environment, the setting of objectives, and methodology are reviewed. Under the second two stages, studies in each of the four areas are discussed. The advantages/disadvantages of automation is a subject treated extensively under all categories.

219. Horley, Albert L.   "An Approach to Planning Investment in Telecommunications for Development."   Stanford Journal of International Studies 5(1970) 114-137.

Horley outlines a systems planning approach for telecommunications that focuses on the investment decision. Benefit-cost ratios serve as the criteria for selecting among alternative systems.   It is difficult to estimate the benefits of such collective goods as communications systems; Horley uses indifference curves to translate subjective evaluations of system performance into benefits that are quantifiable on a relative basis.   To illustrate his technique he generates a set of indifference curves showing the trade-offs between classroom lecture time and TV instruction.

Given similar benefits offered by several alternative systems, the basis for selection will be cost.   Typical capital and operating costs are listed.   Characteristics and costs of the following systems are provided: line-of-sight microwave, tropospheric scatter, coaxial cable, high frequency radio, and satellites.   A chart depicts the best system for various configurations of distance and traffic.

Horley applies his benefit-cost technique to a proposed satellite educational TV project for rural Brazil, where there is massive illiteracy.   His results show a large dollar benefit to be obtained from substituting satellite-distributed TV programs for some of the additional formal training of rural teachers required for Brazil to meet its educational objectives.

220. Hu, Teh-wei; Booms, Bernard H.; and Kaltreider, Lynne Warfield.   A Benefit-Cost Analysis of Alternative Library Delivery Systems.   Contributions in Librarianship and Information Science, no. 13.   Westport, CT: Greenwood Press, 1975.

Bookmobiles and an experimental books-by-mail program (MOD, or Mail-Order Delivery) are analyzed as alternatives to the usual fixed-site public library.   The purpose of such systems is to make library service available to those who are unable to reach a public library, or to make service more convenient for those who can get to a library but don't bother.   The objectives of the study are: (1) to determine the costs of bookmobile/MOD service; (2) to determine demand for such services; (3) to compare the costs and benefits of the two services.   Data were collected in 1972 by mail questionnaire from users and nonusers of the two services in Pennsylvania.   A profile of users is presented, including information about the type of materials borrowed.

Survey data show that average cost per book circulated for bookmobiles is $.34, and for MOD $.60.   Regression analysis was used to estimate the relationship between cost and circulation; it was found that both systems are operating under a decreasing cost condition; an expansion of service would therefore further reduce average cost per book circulated.

To quantify benefits, the costs of the following alternatives were considered: (1) monetary value of time saved as a result of using the services; (2) books purchased if the services had not been available; (3) the amount survey respondents would be willing to pay per book borrowed to assure continuation of the service. Per book borrowed, benefits were $.29 for bookmobiles and $.47 for MOD.

Benefits, costs, and benefit-cost ratios are lower for bookmobiles than for MOD, and benefit-cost ratios are considerably lower than 1 (one) for both services. The study concludes with a discussion of policy implications and suggestions based on the economic findings.

221. Indian & Eastern Newspaper Society. Newspaper Distribution Costs: Case Study of a Delhi Newspaper. IENS Studies, no. 3. New Delhi: IENS, 1974.

To be useful, a newspaper must be available when and where the reader wants it. Since newspapers have a very short life span, speed and cost of transporting them are crucial factors in the efficiency of distribution. Preliminary to an extensive study of distribution costs, the authors analyzed a New Delhi daily paper as a test case. Distribution costs for this case can be divided into four categories: (1) commissions given to distribution agents; (2) transport; (3) packing; (4) administrative costs of the distribution department. Transport constitutes 34.1 percent of the total. Transport costs per copy are compared for distribution by bus, air, rail, and taxi. Air transport is the fastest and by far the most expensive at 17 paise per copy; it is recommended that Indian Airlines give newspapers a greater freight discount than the 25 percent now allowed, as newspapers are of national importance. Railways are the cheapest way to transport newspapers, at 1.3 paise per copy. Some newspaper distribution should be shifted from other modes to rail.

222. Jamison, Dean T.; Klees, Steven J.; and Wells, Stuart J. The Costs of Educational Media: Guidelines for Planning and Evaluation. Beverly Hills, CA: Sage, 1978.

The authors have developed a cost evaluation methodology for educational media projects and have applied it to several ongoing instructional radio (IR) and TV (ITV) projects.

Essential cost concepts and methods are presented in a general chapter, and it is stressed that the necessity to buy now but realize utilities later is a key factor in project decision making. In the following chapter, relevant special problems are raised; a key concept is shadow pricing, which refers to the true cost of a resource to society. Shadow prices can be estimated using an appropriate social rate of discount.

For several projects, a cost function is derived of the form "total cost = fixed cost + variable cost per student + variable cost per programming hour." Costs are then specified in greater detail as being central, production, transmission, and reception costs. Detailed case studies of two IR projects, in Nicaragua and Mexico, and five ITV projects, in El Salvador, the United States (2), Korea, and Mexico, are included, with the cost analysis presented as much as possible in a comparable format across projects.

Concluding tables summarize the annualized cost information at a social discount rate of 7.5 percent. IR costs per student per hour range from $.01 to $.04, about one-third to one-fifth of ITV costs.

223. Jamison, Dean T., and McAnany, Emile G. Radio for Education and Development. Beverly Hills, CA: Sage, 1978.

From case studies and other sources, the authors provide a synthesis of what is known about the potential of radio for education and development communication. Radio is the most pervasive means of communication now available to most of the world. For formal education, radio has the potential to improve quality and relevance, lower costs, and improve access, especially in rural areas. Teacher costs are continually rising relative to capital-intensive radio technology, and, consequently, use of radio can reduce educational costs. Radio is used in development communication to motivate, inform, teach, and change behavior through three strategies: open broadcasting, campaigns, and regular listening groups.

The cost elements of a radio system include administration/planning/evaluation, program conceptualization and production, transmission, reception, and such complementary inputs as printed materials and training. Costs are given for various types of transmitters and receivers. Costs should be thought of as functions; the total cost of financing instructional radio is a function of the number of students to be reached. Average and marginal cost, fixed and variable costs, and capital and recurrent costs are defined. The costs of several projects are reviewed.

In conclusion the authors assess the potential of various strategies of radio use to meet educational and developmental goals. The appendixes contain authors/titles of the case studies on which the book is based, information on radio transmission and reception capabilities in various countries, and an annotated bibliography.

224. Jowett, J.K.S. "Technology, Economic Constraints and Possible Solutions for Providing Wide-Coverage Educational Systems by Means of Satellites." Proceedings of the Royal Society of London 345:1643 (7 October 1975) 511-529.

The technology and costs of a satellite communications system for distribution of educational TV in a developing country are examined. In the Intelsat system, the earth segments have cost three times as much as the space segments; space sector charges are low because most countries use large, expensive earth stations that make minimal demands on satellite power. If the diameter of earth stations is cut, satellite costs must increase to obtain the same transmission capabilities.

In this model satellite TV distribution system, Jowett assumes the need for six transponders; one each for four TV transmissions, one for accompanying sound channels, and a spare. He estimates satellite costs for a 15-year period and earth costs for 1,000, 10,000 and 100,000 schools; the variable part of the earth sector costs is a function of aerial diameter. He adds the space and earth sector costs to get total system costs; for 10,000 schools the optimal cost is given with aerials of just over four meters diameter, while for 100,000 schools the optimal cost is given with aerials of fewer than three meters diameter.

Jowett briefly considers other cost factors including software, teachers, orbital space, and a feedback system. He also lists and compares costs of several cheaper methods of transmitting visual material over distance.

225. Karunaratne, N.D.; Lamberton, D. McL; Murnane, P.F.; and Stayner, R.A. Cost Analysis of Public Libraries in Australia. Australia: University of Queensland, 1977.

To study current operating efficiency of public library systems, the relationship between total costs and level of service is determined using circulation as an output measure. Linear, quadratic, cubic, and logarithmic total cost functions are specified; the linear and logarithmic forms provided the best "fit" to the collected data, so results are reported for those two forms only. In most regions of Australia decreasing average costs prevail, and average cost exceeds marginal cost. In this basic analysis circulation is the sole output measure.

To investigate the relationship between costs and other factors, a multivariat function with eight explanatory variables
was used.

To compute a benefit-cost ratio for library services, a
method of imputing monetary value to benefits is required; the
authors used the amount of money users saved as a result of
the existence of library facilities. The benefit-cost formula
was then modified to take into consideration nonuser benefits
due to the externalities of library service. Benefit-cost ratios
for various systems and regions are presented and ranked.

Average costs for such library operations as acquisitions,
cataloging, end-processing, circulation, and interlibrary loan
are compared across systems and regions. One general conclusion is that larger systems are more efficient and have
lower unit costs; also, regional systems incur lower unit costs
than comparable independent libraries.

226. King, D.W., and Brown, R.N. "An Economic Model of
     Interactive Information Services." In Information Sys-
     tems and Networks: Eleventh Annual Symposium, March
     27-29, 1974, pp. 105-114. Edited by John Sherrod;
     produced by Informatics Inc. Westport, CT: Greenwood
     Press, 1975.

This model has been created for administrators who must
make decisions on implementing or modifying interactive information services. The demand for use of such systems
depends on: (1) volume of need for information; (2) awareness of systems; (3) accessibility and ease of use; and
(4) price. There are several modes of interaction between the
user and the system; the users may interact directly, they
may formulate their queries with intermediaries who perform the
search, or they may mail or telephone requests to a central
site. Each mode has substantially different cost and price
curves.

The authors discuss the large number of factors involved
in determining cost and then formulate a cost/demand curve;
cost per search is plotted on the vertical axis against searches
per day. Ideal levels of system attributes vary from user to
user; information on user "trade-offs" is needed to formulate
the price/demand curve. When a typical cost/demand curve
and price/demand curve are superposed, a point of optimum
profit can be readily seen.

Important factors in using the decision model include
whether a system is addressed to the final user or an intermediary, the distance from a terminal, and the degree of
communication between the user and the intermediary.

227. Klees, Steven J., and Wells, Stuart J. Costs and Satellites: Implications of the ATS-6 Health/Education Telecommunications Demonstration. Washington, DC: Agency
or International Development, 1977.

The costs of satellite systems designed for the delivery of
health and education services are examined from an economics
perspective. The results of six demonstration projects utilizing the sixth in a series of Applications Technology Satellites
(ATS-6) provide much of the data analyzed in this paper.
In the first section the authors provide a framework for
the specific discussion of the demonstration projects by out-
lining the concepts of competitive market theory. Prices are
seen as measures of social value. Unit cost comparisons as a
guide to efficiency are only useful when the outputs compared
are identical. After discussing the issues underlying the
economic concept of cost, the authors go on to discuss costs
as functions of input and output, fixed and variable costs,
marginal and sunk costs, capital and recurrent costs, opportunity costs, and nonmonetary costs.
In the second section satellite system costs are analyzed;
the transmission system hardware and its operation, instructional programming costs, and other monetary costs are
considered separately; data and charts accompany the text.
The authors conclude that for a number of reasons very little
specific information can be learned from the ATX-6 projects.
The projects lasted less than a year, so long-run costs and
impacts cannot be assessed. Since the projects took place in
the United States, the technology cannot be directly transferred to developing nations; there may be many hidden costs
in such transfer, because of lack of appropriate technical and
human infrastructure. It was learned that high-powered
satellites can be used to relay signals to lower cost ground
terminals than had been previously used.

228. Kressley, Konrad M. "EUROVISION: Distributing Costs
and Benefits in an International Broadcasting Union."
Journal of Broadcasting 22:2 (Spring 1978) 179-193.

EUROVISION, the television network of the European
Broadcasting Union, currently links some 25 national TV
systems in Western Europe, North Africa, and the Middle East.
Its principal activities are the sharing and exchanging of live
sports and news broadcasts. The basic idea of the cooperative
scheme is to capitalize on the economies of scale inherent in
broadcasting. Kressley describes the various methods that
have been used to calculate and share costs and benefits; the
system rests basically on members' ability to contribute,
determined by annual license revenues. Through accounting

methods attempts have been made to resolve the problem of larger, wealthier nations subsidizing smaller members; in 1969, several wealthy networks were ready to leave EUROVISION. This issue seems to have been settled in 1974 with the invention of the Basic Sharing Scale, under which the larger members only partially subsidize the less affluent networks.

229. Kuehn, Richard A. Cost-Effective Telecommunications. New York: Amacom, 1975.

Kuehn has written a handbook for the manager of a communications department in an American business. Cost control of telecommunications systems is stressed. The cost of information transmission is the fastest growing expenditure in the typical corporation, increasing by 13.2 percent per year. Effective control should reduce costs by 16 to 20 percent per year.
Kuehn shows how to identify costs, to inventory equipment, and to select and evaluate equipment and services for voice, written-record, and data communications. Methods are analyzed in detail and accompanied by extensive charts, tables, and pictures. While equipment costs are relatively stable, costs of service can vary widely depending on the service plan chosen; Kuehn shows how to read, analyze, and interpret telephone tariffs. With increasing competition among suppliers, there are now many rival services to evaluate. Communications managers must be able to select the equipment and services that best meet their organization's long-term goals.

230. Leyland, George. "Cost-Benefit Analysis of Urban Information Systems." In Urban and Regional Information Systems: Service Systems for Cities, pp. 92-117. Edited by John E. Rickert. Kent, OH: Kent State University, 1969.

A computerized information system is needed to sift, process, edit, and display the enormous amount of data available to urban administrators and planners. Eight major information-processing systems are listed, together with method of processing, output, and examples for each: bibliographic reporting systems, social reporting systems, management information systems, computer modeling systems, data series reporting systems, program planning and budgeting systems, planning information systems, and research information systems. A cost-benefit analysis is presented to help in choosing the most appropriate system; the analysis concentrates on relative rather than actual costs and benefits, to show clearly differences among the alternatives.

To quantify costs, an extensive list of technical/opera-
tional elements and political/business elements are assigned
relative weights, which are then totaled to give relative costs
for each system; a similar method is used to calculate benefits.
In Leyland's analysis, a program planning and budgeting
system has the highest benefit-cost ratio; if costs must be
kept low, a social reporting system for producing reports that
describe the community by significant indicators is a good
alternative.

231. Marchant, Maurice P.   "University Libraries as Economic
     Systems."   College and Research Libraries 36:6 (Nov-
     ember 1975) 449-457.

If libraries can be viewed as economic systems, exhibiting
generalizable interrelationships among economic variables over
time, then library planning and budgeting could be improved.
Marchant reviews studies, including his own doctoral work,
which give evidence to support this view in academic libraries
with more than 500,000 volumes.   In a limited study, it was
found that collection size and decentralization (number of
branches divided by number of volumes) explain 80 percent of
the variance in size of the professional staff.
     A more general attempt was made to identify a set of
mutually complementary inputs that are stable over time.
Regression analysis was performed on two sets of data, including three funding measures and five measures of basic
library resources.   It was found that expenditures are best
predicted by the size of the professional staff and the number
of acquisitions.   A very encouraging result was that when data
were analyzed over a twenty-year period, a similar pattern
emerged from year to year; this consistency is promising for a
theory of library economy.

232. Mayo, John K.; McAnany, Emile G.; and Klees, Steven J.
     The Mexican Telesecundaria: A Cost-Effectiveness Anal-
     ysis.   A.I.D.   Studies in Educational Technology.
     Washington, DC: Academy for Educational Development,
     1973.

To alleviate pressures of high demand on the traditional
educational system (in 1965, 37% of sixth graders couldn't
enter a secondary school), Mexico instituted the telesecundaria
(TS), which uses TV lessons to provide a full three-year
secondary education for those who don't have access to
secondary schools.   For evaluatory purposes, the authors
decided to use cost-effectiveness analysis in order to examine
the efficiencies of alternative methods for using educational

resources; the report is intended, therefore, to be directly relevant to educational decision makers.

Inputs and outputs of the traditional secondary system and the TS are compared. Inputs include school and community, student and teacher characteristics, and costs. Across the four traditional categories of administration, classroom teachers, facilities, and student expenses, TS expenses per student in 1972 were $125, while in the traditional system the figure was $200. ETV components added $26 to the TS costs. It was also found that if the regular schools were expanded to the rural areas served by TS, the costs would be 50 percent higher than TS costs.

Outputs analyzed include learning and attitudes. Achievement tests showed no striking differences between student learning gains in the two systems. Considering that TS students are generally poorer and are from rural areas, this is an important finding. It is concluded that the TS is a cost-effective educational strategy. Criticisms of the TS, and some alternatives for the future, are included.

233. Middleton, John M., ed. Approaches to Communication Planning. Paris: Unesco, 1980 (forthcoming).

Communication planning is a new field that has emerged from a number of traditions and trends; five different approaches to the subject are presented, including process, systems, technology, economics, and evaluation. For the purposes of this bibliography, two chapters in the economic section and one chapter in the technological section are especially pertinent. Steven Klees and Stuart Wells co-authored "Economic Analysis and Communication Decision-Making," and "Financing and Control of Capital-Intensive Broadcasting Systems: Efficiency and Equity Considerations." In the first paper, the authors examine economic concepts and techniques useful for communication decision making; they apply both neoclassical and Marxist economic concepts to four aspects of communications systems: the products of communications activities, the structure of the industry, the role of communications in national development, and the measurement of benefits.

In their second paper, the authors examine three types of communications system control (private nonregulated ownership, publicly regulated private ownership, and public ownership) and three ways to finance these systems (user charges, tax revenues, and advertising). Alternative patterns are analyzed in terms of economic efficiency and equity criteria.

John A. Spence wrote "Short- and Long-Term Forecasting for Communication Technology Planning." He outlines methodologies, which were applied to telecommunications in Australia, for both short- and long-term forecasting. As a long-term technique, the examination of alternative possible futures seems a more practical strategy than relying on the application of a single future forecast.

234. Mili, M. "Economics and Telecommunications." Telecom-
     munication Journal 45:1 (January 1978) 2.

The multiplicity of telecommunications systems is of serious concern to authorities and led the ITU in 1964 to create a special study group devoted to macroeconomic re-search in telecommunications at the country level. This group, the CCITT (International Telegraph and Telephone Consultative Committee), has issued a series of "economic studies" handbooks, which are compilations of many diverse and fragmentary studies. Some important findings include: (1) the correlation between telephone density and GNP per person; (2) the utilization factor, which links the number of telephones to a value of $100,000 U.S. of GNP; (3) the average investment necessary per telephone line ($1,500); and (4) the average investment necessary for a telex station ($3,000).

The CCITT's work has also resulted in the publication of a "Yearbook of Common Carrier Telecommunication Statistics," which gives chronological series covering the last ten years for many basic data. The Yearbook is used by administrators and also serves as the basis for many macroeconomic studies; one such study revealed a key ratio, known as Huntley's Law, between the capital invested in telecommunications equipment and the annual financial revenue of the operating agency. The ratio is 3:1, which is just the reverse of ordinary in-dustrial undertakings, and reveals the large amount of capital investment required by telecommunications.

235. Netzer, Norbert. "Production Costs of Film and Tele-
     vision Programmes: the Myth and Reality." Media Asia
     5:1 (1978) 23-26.

Film and TV are the most powerful visual media, but when planners compare them to other visual media for con-veying information/education their apparent high costs seem to put them at a disadvantage. Netzer demonstrates that actually neither medium is very expensive when size of audience reached is calculated. He compares a 25-to-28-minute TV show, a film of the same length, a dia-slide-show of the same length, and a printed pamphlet that conveys the same message. In terms of average production cost, film is the most expensive and the pamphlet is the cheapest; however, distribution costs escalate very sharply for the pamphlet and the dia-show as the audience size increases. For an audience of 200,000, TV is the cheapest medium while the pamphlet is the most expensive.

Of course, choice of medium cannot be determined by cost alone. Netzer reviews artistic and psychological factors that must also be taken into consideration.

236. Newhouse, Joseph P., and Alexander, Arthur J. An Economic Analysis of Public Library Services. Lexington, MA: Lexington Books, 1972.

The primary subject of this study is the development of a tool to help public libraries determine which books to buy. The model is based on the "user-oriented" rationale of book selection, which means the library provides the books the public wishes to read. The "supplier-oriented" view maintains that the librarian should select "quality" books. A demand curve for books is developed, based on the willingness of consumers to pay for books; both a nontechnical and a technical discussion of the demand curve analysis are given. It is assumed that the library should buy that mix of books for which its users would pay the most money; that mix provides them the greatest benefits.

The model was applied at the Beverly Hills Public Library. Books were divided into 49 subject classes; to establish demand for each class, circulation of a systematic sample of books was tabulated for one year. Benefit/cost ratios for each class were established; the highest ratios occurred in the following classes: Mysteries, Preschool and Young Adult Fiction, Psychology, Art Techniques, and Business Skills. In terms of total community benefit, significant gains can be realized from reallocating a book budget among the various classes of books.

Other topics include who uses the library, budgeting, circulation control, and the effects of varying the length of the loan period.

237. Oettinger, Anthony G., and Zapol, Nikki. "Will Information Technologies Help Learning?" The Annals of the American Academy of Political and Social Science 412 (March 1974) 116-126.

Educational technology has been advocated as a way to meet the varied learning needs of people of all ages. However, research has shown that technology has made no significant differences in learning achieved through formal schooling. The authors feel that these findings point up the limitations of research rather than technology; they point out that significant differences have been found in such areas as attitudes, pace of learning, stability of schools, and costs.

Media discussed include computers, telephones, movies, videotape, broadcast and cable TV, radio, and print. These media can substitute for one another, however imperfectly, and can be dispensed in a variety of ways. A more fundamental factor is the preference of economy versus the preference for individual choice. Several diagrams are used to illustrate that for a given technology unit costs go down as the degree of aggregation increases; "aggregation" includes whether devices are custom-built or mass-produced, whether goals are particular or universal, whether processes are custom-tailored or standardized, and whether learners are alone or grouped. A fundamental question is how to get from a high unit cost prototype to economies of scale. For the short term the crucial decision is between custom-tailored and standardized learning situations; a technology should be selected only after this primary decision is made.

238. "Optical Fibres: Economic Take-Off." The Economist 24 February 1979, p. 88.

Optical fibers are very expensive: strictly in terms of length, they cost 100 times as much as copper. Taking account of fiber's high capacity, the cost falls to three times that of copper. Fiber costs will fall for three reasons: (1) the price of copper is rising; (2) the capacity of fiber can be increased; and (3) there will be learning and production economies of scale.

An optical cable as thick as a finger can replace several much thicker copper cables; optical cables are therefore most attractive where existing ducts are too full for any additional copper cables.

How telephone companies choose to invest in optical fibers is of crucial importance, as it will determine which companies become the major world suppliers.

239. Park, Rolla Edward. Television Station Performance and Revenues. Santa Monica, CA: Rand Corp., 1971.

Broadcasters have claimed there is a positive relationship between the quantity and quality of public service and local programming offered and broadcasting revenues. Park has tested this claim by estimating relationships between programming and revenues using data obtained from 567 U.S. stations in 1968. Public service programming is defined as consisting of news, public affairs, and other programs that are specifically not sports or entertainment. An ordinary least squares regression is used to estimate hours of public service and local programming as functions of revenue. A statistically significant positive relationship is found, although revenues account for less than one-fifth of the variance in quantity.

Expenditure per hour of local programming is used as a measure of quality, under the assumption that higher cost programming is better programming. Expenditures are found to be highly correlated with revenues.

240. Peck, Merton J. "The Single-Entity Proposal for International Telecommunications." American Economic Review 60:2 (May 1970) 199-203.

A Task Force on Communications established by President Johnson recommended that a "single entity" operate the long-distance portion of international telecommunications. This would bring together the overseas functions of Comsat, AT&T, Western Union, RCA, and IT&T. Among the five reasons offered for this proposal, this paper focuses on the first: the promotion of system optimization and the realization of economies of scale. System optimization primarily concerns the division of investment between satellites and cable.

A study authorized by the Task Force showed that, to achieve a 10 percent annual growth in demand, a strategy of putting all new investment into satellites is by far the cheapest. Furthermore, satellites have a shorter life than cables, so innovations can be incorporated into the system more quickly; satellites also attain economies of scale more easily because they collect signals over a wide area.

However, cost minimization is not the only criterion. Satellite telephone conversations sometimes have a delay factor; also, cables provide insurance against interruption of satellite service. Peck suggests that since the Department of Defense is the major customer valuing protection against interruptions, the DOD should finance any new cable construction: the "single entity" would maintain existing cables and place incremental investment in satellites.

Existing FCC regulations unfortunately promote the parallel expansion of cable and satellites. The carriers can own cable, but can only lease satellite circuits from Comsat. Since their allowed profits are determined by their capital investment (rate base), they will prefer to expand their cable facilities.

241. Perraton, Hilary, ed. "Distance Teaching for Formal
     Education: What the Projects Tell Us About Costs and
     Benefits." Washington, DC: World Bank, 1978.
     (Draft, mimeographed.)

Distance teaching is defined as "an educational process in
which a significant proportion of the teaching is conducted by
someone removed in space and/or time from the learner" (p.
7). A combination of media is utilized. Its economic appeal
lies in its use of mass production methods that yield economies
of scale; the costs of traditional education rise in proportion to
the number of students, while with distance teaching the
marginal cost of each additional student is negligible. The
purpose of this book is to analyze several projects to see if
cost economies have been realized in practice, and also to see
if educational quality has been maintained.

Three overview chapters concern the scope, cost-
effectiveness, and methods of distance teaching. Seven case
studies cover projects in Brazil, Korea, Malawi, Kenya,
Mauritius, and Israel. In the chapter on cost-effectiveness,
cost analysis methods are discussed and cost information for a
number of projects is summarized; where available, evidence of
project impacts on pedagogical quality, access, cost per
enrollment, and cost per graduate is presented. Most of the
projects appear to be cheaper than traditional educational
methods, but the complexity of cost-effectiveness comparisons
is stressed.

242. Pitroda, Satyan G. "Telecommunication Development –
     The Third Way." IEEE Transactions on Communications
     COM-24:7 (July 1976) 736-742.

Telecommunications development in third world countries has been based on patterns in industrialized nations.
Telecommunications has been planned for business and governmental uses and for urban consumption, and prices have
been kept high to discourage demand. Rural areas have not
been sufficiently served. Third world countries have imported
equipment and technology designed for more developed
countries; Pitroda describes two cases illustrating the inappro-
priateness of some imported equipment. Telecommunications
growth in industrialized countries is based on increasing the
private telephone density; this is not possible in resource-poor
countries.

Pitroda suggests that the third world way must stress
three primary goals: (1) rural communications, to be consistent with other national programs; (2) accessibility;
(3) reliability. Planners must design systems in keeping with
these three goals plus three secondary objectives: (1) labor-

intensive programs, to provide jobs; (2) sensitivity to the shortage of capital; (3) self-reliance.

He recommends the creation of an autonomous, nonprofit Telecommunication Technology Center to develop appropriate technologies. It would be product-oriented, perhaps based on a structure similar to that of Intelsat. The community telephone is an example of an appropriate third world technology. Services for a small community would be provided through one telephone line.

243. Queen's University Interdisciplinary Study of Telecommunications. "The Application of Dynamic Modelling to the Study of Telecommunications Development in Canada: Final Report." Kingston, Ontario, Canada: Queen's University, 1976.

A multidisciplinary team consisting of researchers from electrical engineering, political science, psychology, business, sociology, and biology spent four years (1972-1976) studying the use of socioeconomic dynamic modeling as an evaluation tool for planning telecommunications development. Northwest Ontario was studied as a representative developing region; the whole region, plus two small communities within the region, were modeled. The models were based on a technique known as "System Dynamics"; variables and equations for this technique, plus a review of other applications, are presented in Section 2 of the report.

In Section 3, the conceptualization of the model for Northwest Ontario is described from its beginning stages. The model was broken down into four components: demography, health/education, the economy, and communications. The economic component, which includes tourism, mining, forestry, and other industries, is considered to be the main driving force of the model; this is because of the influence of the economy on income and migration, which are key factors in determining communications requirements.

Extensive charts, graphs, tables, and other illustrations are included. Additional detailed discussions, data, and a bibliography are supplied in 15 appendixes.

244. Rouse, William B. "Optimal Resource Allocation in Library Systems." Journal of the American Society for Information Science 23:3 (May-June 1975) 157-165.

A library consists of a large number of services; resources must be allocated within each service (how many librarians should be at the reference desk during each period of the day?), among services (should more books be purchased

or more staff hired?), and among the library and other institutions. Rouse uses the mathematical models of operations
research to demonstrate a method to optimize resource allocation at all three levels. He is concerned with the quantity
of service - how much to provide - rather than the quality.
Two performance measures are chosen: the average time
necessary to receive a service, including waiting, and the
probability of not receiving the service. These measures can
be predicted using queuing processes, which depend on three
parameters: average arrival rate, average service rate, and
number of servers. To illustrate, Rouse models two library
services, the circulation desk of the reserve book room and
the general circulation desk at Tufts University. Man-hours is
used as the measure of resources. The optimal allocation of
resources within and between these services is defined as that
which "maximizes the expected value of the decision-maker's
utility function." Specific results for the two services are
presented in tables and charts.

245. Sankar, U. "Investment Behavior in the U.S. Telephone
     Industry - 1949 to 1968." Bell Journal of Economics
     and Management Science 4:2 (Autumn 1973) 665-678.

     In an earlier paper Sankar had applied an econometric
model of investment behavior to the U.S. electric utility industry; he now applies the same model to the U.S. telephone
industry and compares and discusses the results of the two
analyses. He first reviews investment models formulated by
Clark, Hickman, and Jorgenson and Handel; these models
have three components: (1) determination of desired capital:
(2) characterization of the time structure of the investment
process; (3) replacement investment. Sankar uses a modified
version of the Jorgenson-Handel model. He estimates his model
equation with annual telephone industry data for the period
1949-1968.
     Estimates of long-run elasticities of capital with respect to
relative price and output are 0.51119 and 1.18225. The peak
response of investment to price and output changes occurs in
the second year; the average lag in investment time is 2.9
years. The average lag in the electric utility industry was
more than a year longer than this; differences in both technology and the time structure of investment show that public
utilities cannot be lumped together for purposes of analysis.

246. Saunders, Robert J., and Warford, Jeremy J. "Evaluation of Telephone Projects in Less Developed Countries." Telecommunication Journal 46:1 (January 1979) 22-28.

Methods for determining the appropriate amount and type of investment in telecommunications for LDCs are described and discussed. Special reference is made to the objective of supplying telephone service to remote and economically deprived areas. Because the ability to pay for service is often absent in such areas, other ways to justify project investment must be found; investment must often be based on unquantifiable social objectives. In financial terms, investment in telecommunications has usually been very successful, showing high rates of return. However, only a privileged sector of an LDC's population may receive any direct benefits.

The authors describe two methods for measuring benefits and the problems inherent in each: (1) conventional demand analysis, and (2) direct benefit measurement. Three actual cases of benefit estimation using these methods are outlined; the estimates are seen to vary widely depending on the assumptions made. Implications for pricing policy are discussed; there are four typical approaches to pricing, and the narrowest, in which the objective is to assure the financial viability of the utility, is too frequently used in LDCs. The authors suggest a much broader approach that takes into consideration national development objectives: high connection fees and high busy-hour call charges in urban areas would yield increased revenues that could be used to provide public call offices in unserved areas.

247. Schkolnick, Raul. "Costa Rica: A Case Study of the Telephone Cost Structure on a Service-Related Basis." IEEE Transactions on Communications COM-24:3 (March 1976) 311-321.

Costa Rica has one of the highest quality telephone networks in Latin America; in this paper, results of a case study of the cost structure of this network are reported. A physical description of the network is supplied, along with its metering and tariff structure. The following costs are formulated mathematically: (1) connecting a subscriber; (2) keeping a subscriber connected; (3) providing urban and long-distance and busy and off-busy calls. Due to the existence of joint costs in the network, it is not possible to determine average costs of various services; therefore, marginal costs are determined in the study.

Pricing studies would be a natural follow-up to this discussion of costs. However, prices cannot be determined solely by marginal costs for the following reasons: (1) information on the demand structure is also needed; (2) there are externalities in the telephone system; (3) tariffs should be simpler than marginal cost pricing would require.

248. Schramm, Wilbur. Big Media, Little Media: Tools and Technologies for Instruction. People and Communication, no. 2. Beverly Hills, CA: Sage Publications, 1977.

Information helpful in the choice of instructional media is assembled and reviewed in this survey. Particular attention is paid to the contrasts between big media and little media: big media are more complex and expensive, such as TV, sound films, and computer-assisted instruction; little media are simpler and cheaper, such as radio, slides and transparencies.
The chapter most pertinent to the economics of communication concerns relative media costs. Cost, cost-effectiveness, and cost-benefit analysis are discussed, and results of economic studies of media systems and data from field projects are presented. Costs of the various media tend to cluster in two broad bands, corresponding to big and little media; one study concludes that the big media cost 3 to 15 times as much as the little, depending on number of users. Size of coverage is thus a crucial factor in determining media choice; radio and TV are especially responsive to economies of scale. Another major cost factor is the level of quality to be expected from media teaching materials.
Other chapters include the results of experiments on the effectiveness of various media for instruction, guidelines from pedagogy and instructional technology, and an extensive presentation of data from the field, including media use in national educational reform projects, media to supplement instruction, and use of media for distant teaching and nonformal education.

249. Snow, Marcellus S. "Investment Cost Minimization for Communications Satellite Capacity: Refinement and Application of the Chenery-Manne-Srinivasan Model." Bell Journal of Economics 6:2 (Autumn 1975) 621-643.

An econometric model of cost-minimizing investment in new capacity is described as a function of the rate of demand growth, economies of scale, and a discount rate. Snow modifies this basic model, first developed by Chenery, Manne, and Srinivasan, by making provision for depreciation and technological progress; the Manne-Srinivasan assumption that capital equipment doesn't depreciate is too simplistic, and when Snow augments the model with a factor for depreciation the original model's "cost-minimizing optimality of equally-spaced regeneration points" still holds.

The revised model is applied to investment policy for Intelsat, the global commercial satellite organization. Optimal investment behavior for Intelsat from 1975 to 1989 is derived, assuming that 1975 is a regeneration point at which demand and capacity are equal. Implications of the study include the need for more flexibility in satellite design so that capacities could be easily varied and the requirement that satellite capacity be matched to demand in each region, probably resulting in different-sized satellites. Furthermore, cost-minimization may not be the major goal of Intelsat managers; such objectives as traffic growth and technological sophistication might conflict with cost minimization.

250. Standera, Oldrich R. "Costs and Effectiveness in the Evolution of an Information System: A Case Study." Journal of the American Society for Information Science 25:3 (May-June 1974) 203-207.

Budget constraints make it essential for information system managers to perform cost-effectiveness analyses at regular intervals. Cost-effectiveness analysis should be included in a system from its beginning. In this case study, user needs were first analyzed by questionnaire and discussions with potential users; objectives and additional benefits of the system were formulated. Since this system was being designed for a university library, priorities were assigned to subject areas depending on such factors as number of faculty members and graduate students and availability of an information service in a particular discipline.

A key objective of the information system was formulated as "high precision and reasonable recall." User feedback forms were designed to report on relevance (precision). The dimension of synonymity (use of synonyms and antonyms) was added to searching to promote recall. The indicators of cost-effectiveness are cost per relevant hit and cost per question. A format for the monthly compilation of a cost-effectiveness account sheet is presented.

251. Summers, F. William. "The Use of Formulae in Resource Allocation." Library Trends 23:4 (April 1975) 631-642.

Formula budgeting is defined as "the allocation of resources based upon some known or assumed relationship between two or more variables which are pertinent to the service to be rendered." It has been common in U.S. librarianship to appropriate funds based on the size of the population to be served. Summers discusses the implications for library service of the use of formulae in allocating state funds for public higher education.

Problems with formula allocation include the following: (1) formulae rely on past experience; current conditions are no guide to what ought to be; (2) if formulae are based on what ought to be, political problems result; growing libraries will favor recognition of growth factors in formulae, libraries at universities with large graduate programs will favor measures of graduate students; (3) the use of formulae began in an era of growth in public funding; this is no longer the case, and today the same formulae yield static or even declining budgets.

Formulae have been used for library services because of a lack of viable alternatives; empirically based performance measures that can be applied to the problem of resource allocation are needed.

252. Todorov, P.M., and Mirski, K.I. "General Factors Governing the Plans for the Development of National Telephone Networks." Telecommunication Journal 44:4 (April 1977) 185-188.

Based on an analysis of statistical data for various countries covering the period 1955-1970, the authors have formulated some general statistical rules and relationships to be used in planning the development of a national telephone network. There is a fairly constant ratio of telephone density to per capita income in a given country; once the national density is determined, it can be distributed among five categories of population centers, from villages to capital cities. Functions relating density for each category to national density are specified and diagrammed.

A regression formula is given for the relationship between the number of main stations and the number of extensions; for the countries studied, the ratio was 62.3:37.7. Functions are also derived relating business stations to private stations. Finally, the volume of trunk traffic is analyzed; trunk traffic as a percentage of total traffic is quite stable for a given country; the percentage increases with economic development, automation of the trunk network, and the relative decrease of rates as living standards improve.

253. Unesco. "Revised Guidelines for the Economic Evaluation of National Communication Systems." Paris, 1974. COM/WS/366 (Mimeographed).

This annotated questionnaire is intended to be used for the evaluation of national mass media systems in developed and developing countries; it covers radio, TV, film and film facilities, the press, and books. The communications sector in most countries consists of three distinct systems: (1) broadcasting; (2) film; (3) the press. The following topics are stressed as areas in which the economic analyst can make the greatest contribution to national planning efforts: (1) resource allocation to mass media development; (2) costs of alternative choices; (3) resource allocation within the communication sector; (4) operational efficiency of the sector.

The questionnaire is divided into six sections; for each, an outline is followed by more detailed comments: (1) the purpose of "Priority Objectives" is to determine a country's goal structure for communications activities; (2) in "Media Coverage and Status" the size and complexity of each industry are described; (3) in "Media Use of Resources," investment, costs, employment, and other inputs are estimated; (4) "Media Output and Consumption" concerns production and distribution aspects; (5) in "Media Finance" the principal resources for each medium are described; (6) "World Communication" is concerned with international exchange and trade of media output and personnel.

254. Waldron, Helen J. Book Catalogs: A Survey of the Literature on Costs. Santa Monica, CA: Rand Corp., 1971.

A library's catalog is a communication device that serves as the major point of access to a library's collection. The traditional card catalog is increasingly often being replaced by a book catalog. Waldron has performed a literature survey on book catalogs to determine whether a book catalog would be an economically feasible replacement for the card catalog at Rand Corp. She first summarized the advantages and disadvantages of the two types of catalogs, cost considerations aside: book catalogs have such important advantages as mobility, capability for multiple copies and wide dissemination, and suitability for photocopying.

The major cost question for book catalogs is how many copies will be reproduced and bound. Book catalogs provide economic benefits only when there is a reasonably wide distribution, which causes the per-copy costs to drop. In some cases, high per-copy costs for a limited distribution have been justified on the basis of noneconomic criteria.

Costs are compared for two methods of producing a book catalog, a phototypeset output approach and a printout approach; phototypesetting seems to be cheaper.

Rand Corp. made no changes in its catalog because of a budget reduction in 1970.

255. Walsham, Geoffrey. "Models for Telecommunications Strategy in the LDCs." Telecommunications Policy 3:2 (June 1979) 105-115.

Planning procedures used in LDCs for telecommunications development are inadequate; they lack strategic analysis of alternatives, show a tendency to copy the policies of industrialized nations, and are too static. Walsham suggests that corporate planning models would provide a more sophisticated approach, in which all options and uncertainties would be explored. He describes a prototype computer model and fits it to actual data for a Latin American country. Internal telephone demand is divided into three parts: urban, rural, and public call offices. For each service the model goes through a sequence of calculations: tariff setting, demand for connections, connections achieved, traffic, income statement, equipment cost, and performance indicators. The model closely matched past and predicted future data.

Two illustrations are given to demonstrate the model's ability to evaluate strategic options. In the first, a strategy is adopted to utilize extra revenues generated by high urban tariffs to subsidize rural services; the model showed that the extra urban revenue exceeds the loss in rural revenues and that by 1987 rural traffic would be 30 percent higher than in 1978. The second example shows that by a modest increase in the growth rate of rural public call offices, the access performance indicator can be improved significantly.

256. Weinberg, Charles B. "The University Library: Analysis and Proposals." Management Science 21:2 (October 1974) 130-140.

The resources of university libraries have grown rapidly, but service has declined for the following reasons: (1) the increase in published and unpublished information and number of users; (2) increase specialization in subject fields, requiring more books per user; (3) growth of interdisciplinary studies, increasing the difficulty of selection and location of books. Libraries must change their strategy from one of storing and providing access to materials to one of supplying information. Weinberg shows how this new strategy will require changes in library operations and allocation of resources.

A library should deal with a commodity called the "in-formation message unit" (IMU). The value of an IMU is subjective, since it can only be defined in terms of its worth to the user, and probabilistic, since libraries acquire IMUs in anticipation of their future use. Weinberg describes a system for defining the value of an IMU through user evaluations; funds for storage and retention of IMUs will be based on these evaluations. IMUs that have lost all value over time can be disposed of, thus freeing funds for new acquisitions. A flowchart of the system shows how user evaluations are utilized for purchasing, deciding proper storage, and periodic re-evaluation of the IMUs; it will be to the user's advantage to participate in the evaluation system.

257. Wellenius, Björn. "Some Recurrent Problems of Tele-
        communications in Developing Countries." IEEE
        Transactions on Communications COM-24:7 (July 1976)
        723-728.

Developing countries face many problems in expanding their telecommunications services. Many of these difficulties can be classified as problems of implementation, for most of which there are well-established solutions. However, there are more complex problems of method for which solutions may be based more on intuition, and for which research and field work will be required before solutions can be found. Wellenius discusses four classes of such problems: (1) the most serious problem is forecasting, particularly the determination of demand; (2) because of the difficulty of ascertaining costs and benefits, the evaluation of alternative projects is a problem; too often, for example, telephone projects are selected for high rate of return to capital rather than contribution to rural development; (3) pricing problems; (4) technological dependence problems. Wellenius concludes that only an interdisciplinary research approach will be able to handle all the factors involving telecommunications and development.

258. White, Herbert S. "Cost-Effectiveness and Cost-Benefit
        Determinations in Special Libraries." Special Libraries
        70:4 (April 1979) 163-169.

Academic, public, and school libraries are assumed to have an inherent educational value; special libraries in or-ganizations in the "for-profit" sector of the economy may have to justify their value in cost-benefit terms. Libraries in businesses are generally considered to be an overhead operation; therefore it is difficult to analyze their specific contributions to organizational goals. However, cost-benefit analysis can be applied to internal library operations if the library's objectives are established in terms of their impact on the performance of various operating groups within the organization. Traditional library objectives are inwardly directed: a certain number of volumes will be added to the collection, a certain percentage increase in circulation will be achieved. These objectives are unimportant to organizational managers, who are concerned with meeting business objectives.

The librarian must analyze the extent to which library support can benefit programs and activities within the organization. Two particular types of projects should be emphasized: (1) new projects, which are most in need of timely information; (2) projects run by personnel who can affect library funding.

259. Wills, Gordon, and Christopher, Martin. "Cost/Benefit Analysis of Company Information Needs." Unesco Bulletin for Libraries 24:1 (January-February 1970) 9-22.

Improved methods of handling information, such as computers, microforms, and indexing techniques, frequently have higher costs; these costs have been justified in terms of the value of possessing information sooner. The authors' objective is to evaluate formally this notion by assessing the costs and benefits of information sets; the difference is the net value of information.

They first show how a company may determine its information budget. The purpose of collecting information is to reduce the risk inherent in the conduct of a business. For example, a firm planning to launch a product in new markets needs to know how much to spend on information to assess the likely outcomes. An example is worked through in which market shares and the probabilities of achieving them are postulated; the maximum sum it would be worth spending on information to avoid an unfavorable outcome can be determined from these probabilities.

To determine the optimal level of information, the authors postulate a cost function, consisting of fixed and variable costs, for the collection of information sets. An S-shaped value function is postulated, based on the notion that when a library is very small the marginal value of an extra book is low; as the library increases in size, its value, and hence the marginal value of additional books, increases; when the library becomes large, additional books may be difficult to retrieve, lowering their marginal value. The value curve is superimposed on the cost curve to give an optimal level of information.

260. Wilson, John J., Jr., and Barth, Joan W. "Cost Analysis for Community Information Services." In Information for the Community, pp. 171-182. Edited by Manfred Kochen and Joseph C. Donohue. Chicago: American Library Association, 1976.

Before establishing a community information service center, planners must carefully think through several major economic factors. (1) User benefits: community needs must be determined, and services should be provided only if benefits equal or exceed costs to the community. Information activities may already be conducted by several community agencies; a consolidation of these efforts must be considered in the context of interagency benefits. (2) Pricing: fees that would cover all costs may be very high, so a sliding scale should be considered. (3) Costs: important factors are location, record keeping, work allocation, information packaging, and postage. Accounting methods are discussed, and the authors recommend a system appropriate for information services; information system inputs, outputs, and collateral services are defined. (4) Funding sources. (5) Program budgeting: it is stressed that planners must be prepared to present facts and figures for several years in advance.

261. Wilson, John H., Jr. "Costs, Budgeting, and Economics of Information Processing." In Annual Review of Information Science and Technology, 1972, pp. 39-67. Washington, DC: American Society for Information Science, 1972.

Costing techniques as required for planning in libraries, information centers, and storage and retrieval systems are reviewed in this extensive literature survey; 180 books, articles, and papers are referenced. In a section on cost analysis and reporting it is pointed out that there is sufficient cost and system analysis information available for library managers. For proper cost-effectiveness analysis, objectives must be clearly stated; a simple model uses the equation "total costs = fixed costs + input costs + output costs." Cost-effectiveness analysis for storage and retrieval systems, libraries, and computer systems is reviewed.

Utilizing Planning, Programming, and Budgeting Systems (PPBS), managers plan by objectives rather than by operations; PPBS makes it easier to compare alternative ways of accomplishing a given objective.

It is difficult to judge the market value of information; Wilson discusses several articles concerning the use of fees for information services. Cost-benefit analysis is a tool of interest to information managers who are trying to quantify the benefits received from information. An interesting conclusion is that an information system has to be doubled in size for every 5 percent increase in user benefits.

262. Wolfe, J.N.; Aitchison, Thomas M.; Brydon, Donald H.; Scott, Alexander; and Young, Ralph. The Economics of Technical Information Systems. Praeger Special Studies in International Economics and Development. New York: Praeger, 1974.

The methodology and results of a study conducted in Great Britain to develop cost-effectiveness techniques for the evaluation of the provision of nonprimary information are reported. Technical information services (within a firm) and secondary information services (independent agencies outside a firm) were studied; emphasis was placed on the degree to which user wants were satisfied. Not much data is available in this area, so one of the objectives of the study was to develop methods for generating relevant data; in contrast to most economic studies, consumers were surveyed by questionnaire to provide data on benefits. User groups consisted of R&D personnel in chemical, aircraft, electrical engineering, and textile firms, and in agriculture.

Some measures of effectiveness utilized were: (1) value of time saved by R&D workers in using secondary information services; (2) value of time required by the workers to achieve their former level of output if they were deprived of secondary information; (3) increase in salary required if the workers were deprived of information services. Cost measures were the total identifiable costs of each information system.

Among the major conclusions are: (1) relative effectiveness of various systems depends on the number of R&D workers served; (2) cost-effectiveness techniques depend on surveying the workers; information officers provided substantially different evaluations; (3) pure abstracting services provide the greatest benefits among various secondary information systems. Extensive detail for both methods and results is provided in the text and supplemented with tables, figures, and appendixes.

H. PRODUCTION FUNCTIONS/PRODUCTIVITY/ECONOMIES
OF SCALE

263. Brand, Horst. "Productivity in Telephone Communications." Monthly Labor Review 96:11 (November 1973)
3-9.

Output per man-hour in the U.S. telephone industry more
than tripled from 1951 to 1972, growing at 6.5 percent per
year. Gains were somewhat higher in the 1950s than in the
1960s. Productivity has slackened in recent years due to
fewer opportunities to improve already high productivity and
to the business slowdown of the early 1970s.
There are several major factors in productivity gains.
Output almost quintupled over the two decades, reflecting
intensification of user demand due to the rising incomes,
growth in the number of households, growing dispersion of
the population, and increased geographic mobility. New
technologies tend to yield higher productivity levels; improvements in transmission technology have significantly increased
productivity in toll service. Occupational structure of the
industry has changed due to new technologies that involve
higher levels of skill and training; the number of operators
has declined, while plant and professional personnel have
increased.
Future growth in output is likely to result primarily from
increases in the number of households and changes in the
variety of services offered.

264. Bransford, Louis A., and Potter, James G. "Aggregation
of a Public Service Satellite Market." Satellite Communications 2:8 (August 1978) 39-42.

The Public Service Satellite Consortium (PSSC) consists of
over 90 public service agencies; it was created in 1975 to
inform public service users of the capabilities of satellite
technology and to serve as a mechanism for aggregating user
requirements. Most U.S. public service organizations can't
afford access to sophisticated information systems on an individual basis. Cost-effective networks can be created if a
user market is aggregated and if suppliers can be induced to
respond to the market. PSSC is facilitating the process by:
(1) aggregating user requirements to maximize use of facilities
and software; (2) aggregating resources to spread costs over
a broad base; (3) making bulk arrangements for facilities to
minimize first costs; (4) encouraging cooperative decision
making.

A key decision will be what mix of public services to offer. The authors discuss requirements, problems, and possibilities in health and education as examples; the present structure of public education appears to be inimical to wide use of a telecommunications network. The federal government, because of its major role in funding public services, must coordinate the development of a public service communications satellite network.

265. "Break It Up, Lads." The Economist, 7 July 1979, pp. 84-85.

Recently the British Post Office admitted it is unable to handle all the mail clogging its sorting offices. This editorial states that the basic problem is low and declining productivity and agrees with the industry secretary that the government should review the Post Office's monopoly. The separation of posts and telecommunications is also recommended; such a split has been opposed by the Union of Post Office Workers (UPW), which fears that on its own the telecommunications business will develop alternatives to conventional mail.

Early in 1979, the UPW membership rejected proposals to increase postal efficiency. New productivity measures have been suggested, including mail traffic measurement and diversion of mail from overloaded sorting offices. Negotiations will be protracted, and in any case the British experience is that raising low productivity is very difficult. Postal workers have also blocked moves to gain new, profitable services in the postal industry. The editorial recommends competition as a stimulus for the service; firms of letter-carrying motorbike messengers might be licensed in the larger cities.

266. Conference on The Economies of Scale in Today's Tele-communication Systems, Washington, DC, 1973. Digest. Edited by Aruthur D. Hall III. New York: Institute of Electrical and Electronics Engineers, 1973.

Seven papers presented at the workshop are included. Hall gives an overview of economies of scale in existing U.S. communications systems; he defines the term and discusses related cost concepts. He points out the need to view economies of scale from both the engineer's and the economist's point of view. Economies of scale must be distinguished from economies of technological innovation; telecommunication is a field with a particularly high rate of technological change.

Other contributions include the following: (1) Leroy Mantell estimates production functions from actual telephone statistical data and shows that what appear to have been economies of scale in the Bell system were actually due to technological improvement; (2) Bernard Yoged relates scale economies to a communications network model; (3) in a non-technical paper, Christopher Skipp discusses "The Impact of Organization Size on Employee Motivation"; (4) Thomas Leming points out that the Bell System is structured to serve the public telephone market and is not oriented to providing special services; (5) Max Beere discusses the economies of "value added networks"; and (6) William Melody shows how the theory of natural monopoly is built on the notion of economies of scale; traditional regulatory policy has been structured on the assumption of economies of scale. Melody discusses such public policy issues as the role of competition, cream-skimming, and discriminatory rate reductions; a most significant issue for the future will be data markets. Economies of scale in voice communication may be diseconomies for data.

267. Eldor, D.; Sudit, E.F.; and Vinod, H.D. "Telecommunications, CES Production Function: A Reply." Applied Economics 11:2 (June 1979) 133-138.

These comments are a reply to an earlier article by Gideon Fishelson ("Telecommunications, CES Production Function," entry 268). The authors claim that the multiplicative (Vinod's model) and the additive (Sudit's model) nonhomogeneous production functions, which use variable elasticity of substitution, provide a more reliable test for the telecommunications industry than Fishelson's Constant Elasticity of Substitution hypothesis. (See Vinod, entry 278, and Sudit, entry 277.) Fishelson had criticized the present authors for not specifying technology as an input. In this article they reestimate the same functions with a technology variable that produces improved result. The expenditures on research and development of Bell Telephone Laboratories are used as a proxy variable for technological change. This variable is found to yield maximum impact after six years. The results indicate increasing returns to scale for the aggregate Bell system, confirming the authors' earlier findings. They therefore question Fishelson's assumption of constant return to scale and constant elasticity of substitution.

268. Fishelson, Gideon. "Telecommunications, CES Production Function." Applied Economics 9:1 (March 1977) 9-18.

Fishelson takes a critical look at some previous production function studies and their application to Bell Canada and Bell U.S.A. data (see Eldor, entry 267, for reply). Dobell et al.

("Telephone Communications in Canada: Demand, Production, and Investment Decisions," entry 40) were mistaken in their assumption of constant elasticity of substitution (CES) between labor and capital. Vinod ("Nonhomogeneous Production Functions and Applications to Telecommunications," entry 278) and Sudit ("Additive Nonhomogeneous Production Functions in Telecommunications," entry 277) are criticized for derived results concerning negative marginal product of labor and negative elasticities of substitution. Fishelson argues that the application of nonhomogeneous functions is not justified for the telecommunication system, although experimenting with such functions was popular in the fifties.

The author incorporates profit maximization in estimating capital costs and identifies rates of factor-augmented technological progress. In observing the U.S. Bell system, a CES function is generalized to permit changing elasticities of substitution over different time periods. Using CES specifications for the telecommunications sector, a close similarity emerges in this analysis between U.S. and Canada Bell data. The production functions are also similar.

An interesting potential area of research is whether the regulated firm responds to changes in factor prices with the same elasticity as an unregulated firm. Fishelson's findings show that the regulated firm does respond, but research on the optimal timing of introducing an innovation is needed.

269. Gandy, Oscar H., Jr. "Audience Production Functions: A New Look at the Economics of Broadcasting." Paper prepared for the International Association for Mass Communications Research, Warsaw Congress, September 1978.

U.S. TV audiences are products that are sold to advertisers for varying prices depending on the demand for certain demographic characteristics. Inputs to this product consist of such program attributes as violence, suspense, humor, and sex; programs are scheduled with various attribute mixes to attract an audience. Media managers are concerned that this production technology will be increasingly subject to interference by regulatory and other devices to restrict program content, particularly in the area of violence.

Using program descriptions generated by the Cultural Indicators Project at the University of Pennsylvania, Gandy analyzes the effects of several violence attributes (seriousness of the violence, significance to plot, number of violent acts) on audience sizes. Regression analysis was performed at the industry level and at the network level; with each network treated as a separate firm, the effects of the attributes of simultaneous offerings can be seen. CBS programs seem to

have had the best formula for violence; the less significant
and serious the violence was, the more it contributed to audience size. This method can be used to improve program
planning, since the marginal product of individual attributes
can be estimated.

270. Goddard, Haynes C. "Analysis of Social Production
     Functions: The Public Library." Public Finance Quar-
     terly 1:2 (April 1973) 191-204.

The two objectives of this research were to (1) specify
through econometric analysis a previously unstudied public
production function, that of the public library, and (2) estimate marginal costs of book circulation as a guide for investment studies. Circulation, which is the principal service of
U.S. public libraries, was used as the measure of output;
this measure is comparable to any marketed output, and it is
not to be considered a measure of benefits or utility. The
statistical production function shows circulation as a function
of bookstock, labor, materials, and capital. A marginal cost
function is derived from the production function.
Data from a sample of 133 Indiana public libraries were
used for the empirical analysis. The results of four stepwise
regressions are presented; high coefficients of determination
show a good fit to the data; bookstock and capital variables
are significant at the 0.5 level. The evidence shows a tendency toward increasing returns to scale, which indicates
potential gains in economic efficiency as systems increase in
size. A subsample of nine libraries was used to estimate
long-run marginal, average, and total costs; the estimated
marginal cost of book circulation is about $.25.

271. Kilgour, Frederick G. "Economics of Computerized Library
     Networks." In The Organization and Retrieval of Eco-
     nomic Knowledge, pp. 181-189. Edited by Mark
     Perlman. Boulder, CO: Westview Press, 1977.

Libraries are a very labor-intensive industry, and there
have been virtually no gains in staff productivity over the
past century. Library pre-unit costs have been rising much
faster than costs in the economy as a whole. Computerized
library networks, which consist of a computer and telecommunications hook-up, have the potential to increase library
productivity dramatically. Kilgour describes the development
of labor-intensive library procedures and compares them to
the "American System" with its interchangeability of parts,
specialized machinery, and assembly line, all of which make
possible economies of scale and reduced costs.

The computer will introduce the American System to libraries; productivity will be greatly increased in cataloging operations, because only one entry will be needed for multiple libraries. The more times each cataloging record is used, the greater are the economies of scale. In 1975 the largest operating network was the Ohio College Library Center; its principal objective is to reduce the rate of rise of per-unit costs. Kilgour estimates that cataloging productivity in the OCLC system is as much as seven times greater than manual productivity.

272. Lewis, J. Patrick. "Postwar Economic Growth and Productivity in the Soviet Communications Industry." Bell Journal of Economics 6:2 (Autumn 1975) 430-450.

Little research has been done on the Soviet communications industry because it has not been a major contributor to industrialization and also because industry data are usually aggregated with transportation data. The Soviet communications economy is divided into seven branches, referred to as the "network of general use": (1) postal service; (2) telegraph; (3) long-distance telephone; (4) city telephone; (5) rural telephone; (6) radiofication (wired broadcasts to home loudspeakers); and (7) radio/TV broadcasting. Departmental use and military networks are not included in this study.

U.S. and Soviet industry structure and outputs are compared for selected years 1950 to 1970. Three major differences are: (1) U.S. communications accounted for 3 percent of GNP in 1970, while Soviet communications accounted for one-half of 1 percent; (2) in the U.S.S.R., the postal service is the single largest branch of the industry; (3) telephones have been much slower to replace the telegraph in the U.S.S.R.. The Soviet industry has had impressive growth rates since World War II, but it is still quite backward in comparison with the United States.

Production function analysis of the communications industry shows that output per unit of input (factor productivity) accounts for less than one-fifth of the annual growth in output; growth rates are primarily attributed to additions of capital and labor. The Soviet communications industry continues to be highly labor-intensive.

273. Mandanis, George P. "An Empirical Analysis of Economies of Scale and Specialization in Communications." In New Dimensions in Public Utility Pricing, pp. 324-388. Edited by Harry M. Trebing. MSU Public Utilities Studies. East Lansing: Michigan State University, 1976.

The results of a study performed by Systems Applications, Inc., for the U.S. Office of Telecommunications Policy are summarized. The chief objective of study was to determine the presence, sources, and magnitudes of economies of scale in domestic telecommunications networks. Mandanis points out that increases in scale in telecommunications usually involve the installation of technologically advanced facilities, so it was impossible to assess economies of scale separately from economies of technological innovation. The study focused on urban areas and on the more conventional services that will be sufficient for most customers until 1982. Both a static and a dynamic analysis were performed.

In the static analysis, a scale economy coefficient (SEC) was devleoped to measure operational efficiency. The SEC expresses the relationship between unit costs and scale. The approach taken in the dynamic analysis was to study a functionally complete network interconnecting 14 East Coast cities; this analysis utilized a computerized model called the Network Analyzer.

Through both the static and dynamic analyses, substantial economies of scale were found for long-haul transmission and toll switching; scale economies were much more modest for local distribution. Detailed results are presented with extensive tables and graphs.

274. Mantell, Edmund H. "Factors Affecting Labor Productivity in Post Offices." Journal of the American Statistical Association 69:346 (June 1974) 303-309.

It is often alleged that the U.S. Postal Service operates inefficiently, but there is little concrete knowledge of post office labor productivity. Mantell applies canonical correlation analysis to the joint production function that is characteristic of intra-post office activities to determine factors affecting labor productivity. These activities consist primarily of sorting letter mail; the inputs are unsorted mail, the outputs are sorted mail. Data used in the analysis come from a cross-section sample of post offices scattered throughout the United States; data were collected and reported through the Postal Source Data System, an electronic monitoring system.

Variables with high explanatory power in analyzing the "productivity vector" include: (1) labor input factors distributed over time of day; (2) utilization of letter-sorting machines (LSMs); (3) flow of mail distributed by time of day; (4) percentage distribution of classes of mail.

Significant conclusions from the analysis are: (1) productivity is dominated by variations in productivity of the outgoing letter-sorting operations; (2) there is a systematic relationship between productivity and the temporal flow of mail; (3) variations in the class of mail account for some productivity differences; (4) productivity increases with the use of LSMs; (5) from this analysis, conclusions cannot be drawn as to scale effects.

275. Merewitz, Leonard. "Costs and Returns to Scale in U.S. Post Offices." Journal of the American Statistical Association 66 (September 1971) 504-509.

The objective of this econometric study is to specify a production correspondence for "intra post office activity" in U.S. post offices; such activity accounts for 41 percent of postal expenditures. In addition, derived demand and cost functions are estimated for over 156 post offices in 1966. Results indicate decreasing returns to scale over the 156 offices; yet when the sample is broken into groups of small, medium, and large offices, increasing returns to scale are apparent in the small and medium offices; and decreasing returns only in the largest. Merewitz's calculations indicate an optimally efficient size to be 1,400 employees; most U.S. post offices should therefore be combined for economic efficiency. However, there are noneconomic benefits and services provided by small-town post offices.

Using costlines as a measure of technical efficiency, significant differences were found among various regions of the United States; the Northeast and Far West seem to be less productive.

Marginal costs were calculated for handling the various classes of mail and window service; particularly striking was the low marginal cost of third-class mail.

276. Rosse, James N. "Daily Newspapers, Monopolistic Competition, and Economies of Scale." American Economic Review 57:2 (May 1967) 522-533.

In this econometric study of the economies of scale available to smaller daily newspapers, it is found that such economies extend to all scales of newspaper production. Rosse has used Chamberlin's monopolistic competition model, because the newspaper in the United States serves as a prime example of Chamberlin's variable product.

The author highlights the modification of the economic theory of monopolistic competition by differentiating between newspaper firms that practice economies of scale and those that cannot (i.e., the small firms). Such a difference is reflected in the demand for each firm's product. In this case demand cross-elasticities are not close to 0. Rosse defines scale economies as declining average cost and applies the concept to circulation and advertising space.

Two empirical tests of the scale economy hypotheses were conducted. The first test covered 59 isolated, nonmetropolitan, middle western newspaper firms publishing a single weekday edition. This test proved the existence of short-run scale economies in advertising, news space, and circulation. The second test used small-size firms and a short time-span. Elasticities of demand for column inches of space were assumed constant for advertising. The evidence indicated that scale economies in subscriber-inch advertising output have been constant since 1939. Results of both studies substantiate the importance of scale economies as a determinant of the "isolated structure" of the daily newspaper industry. (See also Grotta, entry 54.)

277. Sudit, Ephraim F. "Additive Nonhomogeneous Production Functions in Telecommunications." Bell Journal of Economics and Management Science 4:2 (Autumn 1973) 499-514.

Sudit offers an alternative to H.D. Vinod's nonhomogeneous production function ("Nonhomogeneous Production Functions and Applications to Telecommunications," entry 278). He uses the additive method in preference to Vinod's multiplicative function, claiming that an additive function has economic properties more in keeping with neoclassical production theory; it is also more applicable to telecommunications production. The data used are the same as in Vinod's study.

Major differences are discovered in implied economic behavior. The main difference in the additive system stems from the impact of technological changes that should have been specified as inputs in the model. Similarities in both models relate to economies of scale and the behavior of marginal elasticities of labor and capital.

Sudit concludes by cautioning that economic findings based on different production functions may be radically diverse and yet plausible, particularly in their application to telecommunications. (See also Eldor, entry 267, and Fishelson, entry 268.)

278. Vinod, H.D. "Nonhomegeneous Production Functions and
     Applications to Telecommunications." Bell Journal of
     Economics and Management Science 3:2 (Autumn 1972)
     531-543.

    Vinod begins his analysis by using an extension of the
conventional Cobb-Douglas production function which is linear
in its parameters and can be estimated by least squares. The
analysis is then carried forward to a nonhomogeneous production function in which marginal productivity, marginal
elasticities, and marginal rate of substitution are not assumed
away. After discussing the elasticity of substitution, Vinod
puts forward a production function that has variable returns
to scale and variable elasticity of substitution.
    Substitution behavior between inputs cannot be observed
by simply varying the inputs and assuming the output to be
fixed. Variable elasticity of substitution when applied to
inputs shows less bias in the nonhomogeneous function than in
the Cobb-Douglas one.
    An appropriate production function is a useful tool for
improved description of the real economy and for policy recommendations. The use of appropriate time series makes it
possible to derive empirical estimates of marginal productivity
in a precise manner.
    Two studies are presented to support the theoretical
analysis: (1) A microeconomic study of Western Electric
Company's manufacture of an electronic device called a
sealed contact. Vinod points out the relationship that exists
between certain cost and scale elasticities. From these data
he concludes that nonhomogeneous production functions are
particularly suitable in the application of neoclassical production theory. (2) An aggregative production function for
the Bell System. Econometric estimation of neutral technical
change is used as a surrogate for technology. This study
supports the use of the nonhomogeneous function in macroeconomic policy-making. (See also Eldor, entry 267; Fishelson,
entry 268; and Sudit, entry 277.)

              I. FUTURE OF COMMUNICATIONS

279. Anderson, James A. "Public Television in 1976: A Pro-
     jection of Station Operation and Costs." Journal of
     Broadcasting 18:2 (Spring 1974) 223-245.

    Programming has been the major focus of most public
television studies. However, the foundation for programming
consists of such factors as costs, personnel, and facilities. In
this study, data were collected by questionnaire from 62 U.S.

public television stations on the following six items: (1) time schedules, with type of service provided on various days and at various times of day; (2) local program needs in seven areas of programming; (3) local program costs, fixed and variable; (4) local broadcast costs; (5) optimal funding mix from federal, state, and private funds; and (6) personnel, operations, and capital equipment costs. The stations were asked to give data for 1971 and 1972 and to make projections for 1976; it is the 1976 projection that is presented in this article.

It was found that programming costs are extremely low compared with those for commercial television. Another important finding is the existence of a high critical funding point, which means that quite massive funding is needed to obtain a large increase in output. Finally, stations in larger markets have location-specific costs which means that large-market stations are less productive per dollar of funding.

280. Australian Telecommunications Commission. National Telecommunications Planning Branch. Telecom 2000: An Exploration of Long-Term Development of Telecommunications in Australia. The Commission, 1976.

The National Telecommunications Planning (NTP) unit was established in 1973 to explore future needs and demands for telecommunications, to recommend policies and plans, and to clarify the role of the Australian telecommunications authority. Long-term planning is particularly required for telecommunications because of the intrinsically long life of its capital equipment; therefore the year 2000 was set as a goal for the NTP. This report is a summary of the NTP's work to date. It includes scenarios of social, economic, and technical futures in Australia; growth rates of GDP are projected, and funds available for investment in telecommunications are projected as a proportion of GDP. Demand forecasts indicate that, by the year 2000, investment needs will be $1,500 million to $2,000 million. Feasible upper and lower bounds of future demand for such services as mobile telephones and cable TV are given. It is anticipated that by 2000 nearly all houses will have a telephone, and some 10 percent of homes will subscribe to some additional service.

Tariffs should reflect the costs of providing services, but for some basic services, a purley economic approach may be impracticable; telecommunications services are important in promoting social equity.

As Australia is transformed to a postindustrial society, telecommunications will assume a central role in the economic infrastructure. The Telecommunications Commission will play a major role in setting public policy; one crucial area will be the promotion of harmonious development of the telecommunications and computer sectors.

281. Bennett, B.C. "Economic Forecasting for a Television Company." Long Range Planning 11:5 (October 1978) 63-71.

There are many objections to forecasting, such as the emergence of totally new and unexpected factors, statistical imperfections, and the tendency of forecasts to be self-fulfilling. Nevertheless, forecasting must be done because decisions about the future cannot be avoided. This article discusses the forecasting methods used by Southern Television, a small British company that accounts for about 8 percent of national television revenue. Their forecasts are concentrated on advertising revenue, the major source of income. Forecasters analyze individual product markets and also general trends, which during the 1970s indicated a world-wide move away from advertising. Forecasts are for no more than one year in advance and are done by analyzing recent time series, watching cyclical patterns, and making estimates for the months ahead. Political, sociodemographic, and technological factors are also taken into account.

282. "CATV Equipment Market To Double Over Next Decade." Information Hotline 10:10 (November 1978) 1, 9-11.

From the beginning, U.S. CATV systems achieved steady growth in rural areas. In 1972 the FCC began to encourage CATV entry into larger cities; however, because of the larger variety of signals available in the cities people were not so eager to pay for television. The future of CATV looks more promising now because of the growth of pay TV and satellite program transmission. It is predicted that pay TV revenues will multiply eight-fold by 1986. Over-the-air Subscription Television Stations (STV) may provide competition for CATV pay services, but the costs for STV are very high, indicating that they will be profitable in only the largest cities. Development of a low-cost, pay-per-view security device would also benefit CATV.

Earth station costs have been high, but in 1977 the FCC allowed the use of lower-cost, smaller antennas. The addition of distant programming, made possible by satellite transmission, could bring new subscribers and make CATV economically viable. Other developments that will benefit CATV are the declining costs of fiber optics and the use of CATV for business services.

A forecast of annual equipment revenues from 1977 to 1986, broken down into the major components of CATV systems, shows that by 1986 $309 million will be spent, as compared to $148 million in 1977.

283. Chidambaram, T.S. "A Forecasting Model for Evaluating the Potential of a New Communications Service." Tele-communication Journal 45:10 (October 1978) 541-546.

New communications services, such as electronic mail, videophones, broadcast satellites, and teleconferencing, are in various stages of testing and development throughout the world. Most forecasting models are based on the use of historical demand data; Chidambaram presents a procedure for evaluating the potential of a new, as yet nonexistent, service. It is a computer-based interactive model utilizing the fore-caster's subjective judgments. The model is particularly useful for services offered to large numbers of users and subject to the usual market forces.

Three objectives in forecasting new services are: (1) es-timating when the services will be introduced; (2) determining economic viability of the services; (3) estimating demand. The model is diagrammed in detail, including input factors, input variables, model blocks, computational steps, and output. Three model blocks, or stages, corresponding to the three objectives, are discussed: (1) a network analysis procedure for estimating a time likelihood profile; (2) computations for deriving profit margin factors at various price levels; (3) demand forecasts based on information on rate of imple-mentation, pricing policy, and the habit formation factor. The model also evaluates the reliability of the forecasts.

284. Crandall, Robert W., and Fray, Lionel L. "A Reexamin-ation of the Prophecy of Doom for Cable Television." Bell Journal of Economics and Management Science 5:1 (Spring 1974) 264-289.

Recent studies of U.S. cable television indicate that it will do very poorly in the nation's larger markets; the return on capital will be very low. Yet, as Crandall and Fray point out, investors are hurrying into this new market. The authors demonstrate that pessimistic conclusions are due to pessimistic forecasts of certain critical parameters. They first review other researchers' assumptions about these parameters: (1) demand predictions were kept too low because the only services considered were the retransmissions of broadcast signals; however, it is very likely that many additional services will be offered via CATV; (2) revenues per sub-scriber were set at low levels in various models, because such auxiliary sources of income as motion-picture channels were not included; (3) common sense rejects certain estimates of operating costs for smaller systems, as a wave of bankruptcies would have resulted; (4) based on data from operating systems, capital costs are shown to have been set too high.

The authors then present their own estimates of profitability based on revised assumption; the major revisions are higher subscriber penetration levels and higher annual revenue per subscriber. Projected rates of return indicate a healthy future for the CATV industry. The rates may even be on the conservative side since possible cost reductions and prospective technological improvements were not included in the model.

285. Dunn, Donald A. "Limitations on the Growth of Computer-Communication Services." Telecommunications Policy 2:2 (June 1978) 106-116.

The cost of computer-communication services has been dropping steadily; within the next decade it should be within the budget range of the average U.S. household at about $10 per hour. The current market consists of about 500,000 terminals; it could increase to 50 million terminals. However, certain cost and regulatory limitations may constrain this growth.

User learning costs are a continuing constraint. These are fixed costs that must be included with other costs when estimating a market for a computer service. Information service providers may compete more effectively in the future by making new services easier to use.

Regulations governing the telecommunications industry can inhibit the growth of information services. Regulations designed to keep telephone rates low, such as low rates of return on capital and the assignment of long lives to capital equipment in determining depreciation allowances, make it difficult for telephone companies to finance the equipment needed for a computer-communication network. A complete computer-communication service involves four levels of service: (1) communication links; (2) switching; (3) computers and user terminals; (4) provision of a complete specific service. For each level, potential regulatory constraints are described. The most serious difficulty might be at level 4, where competition is crucial to the growth of the industry.

286. Gappert, Gary. "Some Potential Benefits and Costs of Cable Television." The American Journal of Economics and Sociology 33:1 (January 1974) 59-63.

Gappert reviews some general propositions that bring him to the conclusion that the possible costs and benefits of cable television are not easily predicted because they depend on such complex economic circumstances. While high revenues are virtually guaranteed, start-up costs are also very high, and investment is risky. Cable operators will receive income from several sources; consumers will pay for improved reception and specialized programming, and there will be better access to advertising for small businesses. However, precise supply and demand schedules cannot be specified for owners of cable systems, operators, equipment manufacturers, program producers, advertisers, broadcasters, producers of local public services, and subscribers. A major policy issue is the advisability of government ownership of a CATV system; there will be "monopoly profits" generated by the development of a cable franchise. If it is possible to capture some of the "surplus" generated by a cable system, how should this surplus be invested?

An analogy with one's trying to predict the costs and benefits of CATV is as if one tried, in 1902, to predict the costs and benefits of the automobile culture. CATV policies should be approached in a spirit of experimentation; great public wealth will be created by CATV.

287. Goodfriend, Herbert E., and Pratt, Frank T. "Community Antenna Television." Financial Analysts Journal 26:2 (March/April 1970) 48-57.

In an analysis based on CATV performance in the 1960s, the authors conclude that CATV is an attractive area of speculation for investors. It is predicted that by the end of the 1970s, 50 to 60 percent of U.S. households will be wired for cable; once subscribers are obtained, a steady stream of revenue (about $5/subscriber each month) is assured. The history of CATV is briefly described, and a system description showing the basic equipment is provided. The three significant areas of growth for CATV are: (1) locally originated programming: over-the-air broadcasters have to rely on advertising revenues and have avoided programs without mass appeal; (2) segmented local advertising, in which subscribers in different areas viewing the same program could see different commercials; and (3) two-way communication, useful for data retrieval and home shopping and banking.

A financial model for a hypothetical system shows costs, revenues, and depreciation; by its third year this system is earning a profit and could be sold for $300/subscriber. The legal and regulatory framework of CATV is presented in some detail. One important issue has been the "100 largest markets" rule, under which CATV has not been permitted to import distant signals into the largest markets; economies of scale are important for CATV as more subscribers per dollar of capital expenditure are obtained. FCC policy seems to be based on the concern that CATV poses a threat to local TV stations, especially UHF, and many of its decisions have been to protect over-the-air broadcasters to the detriment of CATV.

The most promising method for increasing the number of available channels is CATV; the authors urge that the public interest be served.

288. Grotta, Gerald L. "Prosperous Newspaper Industry May Be Heading for Decline." Journalism Quarterly 51:3 (Autumn 1974) 498-502.

In recent years, the U.S. newspaper industry has been propsering due to great progress in production technology and the trend toward "one-ownership-cities." However, considering the rapid rate at which the knowledge industry is expanding, Grotta questions whether the newspaper industry will continue to capture its proper share of the knowledge market. Newspapers are doing poorly as measured by two indicators: (1) the growth rate of the GNP has greatly exceeded that of newspaper advertising revenues; (2) population growth rate has exceeded daily newspaper circulation.
Newspapers must pay more attention to marketing and consider their product as seen by the consumer. Grotta cites newspapers' varied responses to a newsprint shortage as evidence that newspapers really don't know what their customers want. Evidence indicates a low elasticity of demand for newspapers, yet publishers are reluctant to raise prices. Newspapers must also consider cross-elasticities with competing products; to survive, newspapers must find what they can do best.

289. LaBlanc, Robert E., and Himsworth, W.E. "Outlook for the Telephone Industry in a Whiplash Economy." Public Utilities Fortnightly 96:3 (31 July 1975) 26-33.

Potential investors wonder how the U.S. telephone industry will fare in an economy of high unemployment and inflation. Positive factors include the industry's essential nature, excellent growth record, and technological innovations; negative factors include the fear that the industry is reaching saturation, the effect of antitrust suits, and the need to attract ever-increasing amounts of capital. Inflation affects the industry in many ways: (1) as consumers suffer from a loss of real income, pressures against utility rate increases will mount, although local phone service rates have increased only 29 percent during the period 1960-1974, when the consumer price index increased 67 percent; (2) during the 1930s Depression, three million phones were removed from service; (3) for the investor, dividend growth has barely kept pace with inflation; (4) during the period 1957-1965, the industry benefited from great gains in productivity, but, since then, wage increases have erased the gains.

The telephone industry is highly capital-intensive; the average industrial company requires $0.55 of capital investment for each $1 of revenue generated, while communications companies require $2.60 per dollar. The industry has had to resort to debt financings in recent years, during a period of high interest rates.

Nonetheless, because of its essential nature, the authors predict the industry will continue to grow and attract investors.

290. Lindquist, Mats D.   "Growth Dynamics of Information Search Services."   Journal of the American Society for Information Science 29:2 (March 1978) 67-76.

An on-line information search service (ISS) typically exhibits a pattern of initially rapid growth in number of users and then a dramatic levelling off well before complete market penetration is achieved. To help management decision making, Lindquist analyzes the causes of this growth behavior using a systems approach. An ISS system is described through a series of diagrams illustrating feedback loops that affect the number of users, the number of queries, and the size of the staff. For example, a positive loop, or effect, encouraging growth behavior of an ISS is simulated over a period of 240 weeks; numerical values chosen for such factors as initial staff size, number of queries, delivery delay, and potential market are typical of an ISS in an academic setting. The behavior of the simulation model is realistic in terms of actual experience; there is rapid growth in the number of users for the first 60 weeks, then the typical decline in growth occurs. It is concluded that the observed growth and stagnation pattern is a natural consequence of market responses to an ISS service.

Three possible managerial actions and their effects are discussed: (1) marketing; (2) increasing the size of the user population beyond the "organizational host"; (3) user education.

291. McCombs, Maxwell E.   "Mass Media in the Marketplace." Journalism Monographs 24 (August 1972) 1-104.

The "constancy hypothesis" of mass media consumption is tested against data from the past 40 years and found to be quite accurate. The hypothesis states that the amount of money spent on mass communication is relatively constant and is closely related to trends in the general economy, rather than to competitive and technological changes within the industry. Mass communication has become a staple, like food or shelter, and consumer spending for mass communication remains a constant proportion of total consumer spending.

Gains by one medium tend to offset losses by another, thus keeping a constant total; when television stormed the market, movies declined dramatically; specialized magazines have offset the loss of mass circulation magazines. The years of television's surge into the market, 1948-1959, are investigated in detail, and it is demonstrated that TV's share of the consumer dollar was drawn from other media rather than from nonmedia expenditures.

The existence of any mass medium depends on: (1) its operating cost; and (2) the constraint posed by the constancy hypothesis, which will determine whether there is enough money available to meet the operating cost. The ultimate constraint on the growth of mass media may be scarcity of consumer time.

292. Maisel, Richard. "The Decline of Mass Media." Public Opinion Quarterly 37:2 (Summer 1973) 159-170.

The two-stage theory of social change and media growth is compared to a newer three-stage theory. The first stage is preindustrial, characterized by face-to-face communication; the second stage is industrial, with mass communication; the third stage is postindustrial/service-oriented, characterized by specialized communication. The author tests the three-stage theory by measuring and comparing the growth rates of various U.S. media during the period 1950-1970.

The specialized media tested are the education system and the personal message system (telephone, telegraph, mail). The data show that these specialized media are growing much more rapidly than the mass media. Further more, within the education system, higher education, the more specialized area, is growing more rapidly than primary education. Within the mass media, the more specialized media such as books and specialized magazines have grown more rapidly. The author concludes with data showing that the mass media are shrinking in size compared with the total U.S. economy.

293. Okundi, Philip O. "Pan-African Telecommunication Network: A Case for Telecommunications in the Development of Africa." IEEE Transactions on Communications COM-24:7 (July 1976) 749-755.

African leaders have realized that a viable telecommunications infrastructure will encourage the economic integration of the continent, which in turn will accelerate economic growth. Before describing the development of PANAFTEL, the Pan-African Telecommunications Network, Okundi discusses the difficulties confronting telecommunications growth in Africa.

In 1971 Africa had the lowest telephone density in the world; a
very low percentage of resources was devoted to telecommunications. Severe geographical, political, and language barriers
have thwarted development. The European colonial background
has resulted in much traffic being inefficiently routed through
Europe at high rates. Facilities are not sufficient for governments to exercise even basic administrative functions. Between countries there are large differences in tariffs with no
apparent relationship to distance.

In 1962 ITU organized a conference at Dakar, Senegal, at
which the first plan for an African network was outlined. In
1968 ITU and UNDP began preinvestment surveys of the requirements for a network. It was concluded that the most
appropriate system would be a combination of coaxial cables
and radio relay systems. At an implementation meeting in 1972
it was decided that $100 million U.S. would be required to
finance the network. Okundi outlined such aspects of the
project as traffic studies, financing agreements, and technical
training seminars. He estimates that by 1980 the originally
proposed network will be operating. However, it will be a
minimal network; there will be congestion, some countries are
not included, and some links are too long.

The next stage will be the development of complementary
systems. An African domestic satellite communication system
was called for at a Kinshasa meeting in 1975, and a feasibility
study was authorized. Longer links could be more efficiently
routed via satellite.

294. Park, Rolla Edward. "The Growth of Cable TV and its
     Probable Impact on Over-the-Air Broadcasting." Ameri-
     can Economic Review 61:2 (May 1971) 69-73.

Cable television carries distant signals, and the resulting
diversity in programming may reduce the size of local audiences for local stations, thus reducing local station revenues.
Local stations may even be forced out of business, reducing
service available to cable nonsubscribers. U.S. FCC policy
has been to promote diversity of programming, and, consequently, the FCC has restricted the growth of cable in the top
100 markets, since such markets already have "adequate" and
diverse programming from several local stations.

The author has constructed a model to show the impact of
unrestricted cable growth. Such factors as cable penetration,
audience shares, and revenues are included. Results of this
mathematical model show that (1) overall loss of revenue due to
cable is small enough that it could be wiped out by one year's
typical revenue growth; (2) stations in larger markets would
be relatively unhurt by cable growth, while stations in smaller
markets would suffer severe revenue reduction; and (3) UHF

stations will gain from cable growth, because cable technology gives UHF reception comparable to that of competing VHF stations.

295. Polishuk, Paul. "Opportunities in Communications." Telecommunications 10:9 (September 1976) 22-27.

Addresses delivered at a seminar sponsored by the Communications and Industrial Electronics Division of the Electronics Industries Association are summarized. Spokesmen from a wide range of U.S. telecommunications industries describe their current market situation and predicted growth rates. CATV has annual revenues of one billion dollars and is growing 15 percent per year, yet only 12 percent of homes are on cable, signifying high growth potential. Paging systems have grown more than 30 percent annually in the United States, increasing from 240,000 units in service in 1972 to more than 500,000 in 1975; paging service rates are quite low in comparison to competitive services. The slow but steady growth of CB radio is due to a great deal of consumer education, and a very large market potential is predicted for this industry. Other industries described include satellite systems, electronic aviation equipment, microwave radio transmission, and mobile radio.

Third World nations are increasing their telephone systems at the rate of 25 percent a year. The emerging nations are viewed by both U.S. and foreign manufacturers as primary markets in which to maintain their traditional growth. Because of the shortage of trained personnel in the Third World, marketing of switching equipment must include a broad program of training and other assistance.

296. Staelin, David H. "Expanding Broadband Switched Communications Networks." Satellite Communications 3:1 (January 1979) 26-30.

Based on the current rapid expansion of broadband high data rate services, Staelin predicts the eventual integration of these links into a U.S. national broadband switched communications network. Short-term economic requirements are spurring present growth, but in the long run the two primary motives for creation of a national network would be its impact on national productivity and quality of life.

The size of a network can be estimated by determining an upper limit and a lower "threshhold of utility." Staelin's analysis is based on market studies that showed the potential for substitution of business travel by teleconferencing. Assuming maximum substitution, an upper limit for the number of required video channels is computed. Factors that might raise this upper limit include the possibility that increased efficiency might lead to a demand for more meetings; a factor that might lower the limit is regulatory restrictions. The lower threshhold of utility is determined by the minimum number of participants required to maintain the interest of an individual user.

For acceptance of the network, prices must be kept low; Staelin estimates costs for various system configurations. He suggests that national leadership from an agency such as NASA and favorable regulatory policies will be required to develop this important national resource.

297. Stine, G. Harry. "The Economics of Future Space Communications Systems." Satellite Communications 2:9 (September 1978) 20-23, 25.

The results of a study of space industrialization conducted by Science Applications, Inc., show that by the year 2000 revenues from space communications/information services could be $100 billion. Communications/information services was one of four areas investigated using a typical industrial marketing methodology. Fifteen potential services were identified through a screening process that eliminated activities with very difficult technology requirements and/or cheaper and easier terrestrial alternatives. For each activity, technical requirements, timing, and potential users were studied; market forecasts were generated for best and worst cases.

Specific results for three potential activities are outlined in this article: (1) personal portable communications (the "wrist radio" concept); (2) large-scale data transfer; (3) locater systems. In each case, starting dates; initial and later prices, revenues, market penetration, and investment requirements are predicted. The fact that such services are highly capital-intensive bothers many people; it must not be forgotten that present terrestrial systems are capital-intensive but are also highly profitable.

298. "Video on Your Screen." The Economist, 26 May 1979, pp. 122-123.

It is predicted that, by 1990, most European and American homes will have home video equipment with a ready supply of prerecorded programs. The business consequences of this new communication development are analyzed, emphasizing the marketing possibilities and problems for firms engaged in producing the equipment. It has been predicted that videotape recorders (VTRs) would provide a shot in the arm for flagging consumer electronics industries; while VTRs have been a major growth area for Philips (of Europe) and certain Japanese companies, the VTR market has not grown nearly as fast as corporate planners had assumed. VTR prices are too high; they are more expensive in real terms than was color TV in the mid-1960s. Consumers believe that VTR prices will fall, as did color TV prices. Other major VTR problems include: (1) lack of a standard recorder; (2) high cost of cassettes; (3) shortage of ready-made films. A newer product, the videodisc player, poses a significant competitive threat to the VTR; its price is lower, and discs of recent and popular films are very cheap. Philips launched this product, but Japanese and American production and marketing skills may push Philips out of the market.

Section 4

Impact of Communications on Economic Systems

299. Blackstone, Erwin A., and Ware, Harold. "Quantification of Some Benefits of Mobile Communications." In Communications for a Mobile Society: An Assessment of New Technology, pp. 259-274. Edited by Raymond Bowers, Alfred M. Lee, and Cary Hershey. Beverly Hills, CA: Sage, 1978.

It is difficult to quantify the benefits of mobile communications because of a lack of reliable data and also because communication is an input to production; its economic benefits are the result of its influence and leverage on other processes, and the amount of this influence cannot yet be accurately estimated. The authors first review the suitability of the following systems for specific purposes and functions: (1) one-way paging services; (2) conventional and trunked systems; (3) cellular systems. They then show methods to quantify benefits for each of the systems. The benefits of paging systems are much lower than for two-way systems and vary with the user's proximity to a telephone.

Conventional and trunked systems are primarily used for dynamic routing (redirecting vehicles after they have left their base); such use can increase the productivity of vehicle fleets by 20 percent. An equation for estimating yearly savings realized through use of dispatch service is explained, and examples are given. If doctors used such systems, and saved one hour per week, the annual gross savings would be $850 million. If better communications improved the productivity of service workers by 5 percent, gross annual savings would be $30 billion.

Cellular systems have the most versatility; the authors assess their additional benefits. The impact of Automatic Vehicle Monitoring systems on bus service is described; the

178

number of buses required for a given level of service could be
reduced by 5 percent, leading to savings in energy consumption.

The potential benefits of mobile communications are both
private and social and may not stimulate sufficient demand
because of their "public good" nature. The government may
need to subsidize new systems.

300. Cherry, Colin. World Communication: Threat or Promise?
     A Socio-Technical Approach. Revised ed. Chichester,
     Eng.: John Wiley, 1978.

Two chapters are especially pertinent to the economics of
communication. In "The Communication Explosion" it is shown
that rapid communication growth since World War II has had
three aspects: (1) geographical; (2) number of messages
carried; and (3) technical complexity. A key distinction is
made between domestic and business uses of media; for example, although the United States has 40 percent of all the
world's telephones, it has only slightly more proportionally in
the business sector than the United Kingdom. Less than 10
percent of international telephone traffic is in the domestic (or
private) sphere. Modern communication systems require large
capital outlays; careful planning requires accurate forecasting
of demand, which is difficult because new technology not only
satisfies existing demand but it also creates new demand.
This regenerative growth is typical of service industries.
Effective communications may facilitate coordination and re-
gionalization among smaller, poorer nations, enabling them to
close the widening gap between rich and poor nations.

In "Communication and Wealth" Cherry points out that
communications media are not commodities but rather "poten-
tials," or "powers." Informational media, such as newspapers,
TV, and movies, are differentiated from organizational media,
such as telephones and telegraph. In developed countries
the informational media are more similar to private consumer
products, while in LDCs they are often the responsibility of
the government to utilize for economic growth purposes.
Correlations between communications media and wealth indicators are shown; telephones appear to be more closely
correlated with wealth than do newspapers.

Communication costs are falling for several reasons:
(1) technological advance: (2) once a system is installed, new
and varied uses are made of it; and (3) trunking costs are
lowered as more traffic is sent over a single route. Richer
countries benefit more from falling costs, as they have much
greater demand for communications.

301. Cholmondeley,   Hugh.   "CANA: How   the   Caribbeans
     Solved   Their   Newspooling   Problem."   Media Asia   3:3
     (1976) 163-164.

    The 13 English-speaking countries/territories of the West
Indies, with their common background and economic vulner-
ability, have sought regional integration.   In 1967, at the
annual Heads of Government meeting, a resolution asked advice
from Unesco on establishing a regional news agency; it was
thus recognized that communications could foster integration.
Cholmondeley summarizes the difficult and lengthy negotiations
that resulted in the Caribbean News Agency (CANA) in
January 1976; it is an independent news service owned by 17
media institutions.
    CANA   will   have   great   impact   on   regional   economic
development through making available reports on price fluctuations, market conditions, availability of commodities from
outside the region, and shipping schedules.   Furthermore,
there is a growing group of subscribers outside the region,
including the United States, U.S.S.R., China, and Cuba;
their awareness of Caribbean conditions will be of mutual
economic benefit.

302. Clippinger, John H.   "Can Communications Development
     Benefit the Third World?"   Telecommunications Policy 1:4
     (September 1977) 298-304.

    Less developed countries are planning to exploit com-
munication technologies for various development objectives.
Advocates believe that sophisticated communications systems
can help reduce costs and speed up the accomplishment of
many objectives.   Critics argue that modern communication
technologies are very expensive, difficult to maintain, often
fall short of performance expectations, and fail to help the
poorer part of the population.   In many LDCs, for example,
telephony promotes development only in urban areas, thus
widening the gap between urban and rural groups.   The
information exchanged through international data networks is
often inappropriate to local needs and may even divert research resources from important local needs.
    The major problem is that in most LDCs there is insuf-
ficient income for users to be able to express preferences in
the marketplace.   Governments must therefore set priorities;
they must be careful to involve information users in the
decision-making process and to develop appropriate technologies.   The chief criterion should be that communication
technologies meet human needs.

303. Colpitts, Andre B. "Use of Input-Output Tables for
     Analysis of Communication Needs of Developing Coun-
     tries." M.S. Thesis, Massachusetts Institute of Tech-
     nology, 1974.

A complex economy requires coordination through a
developed system of communications. The cost and value of
communication are therefore part of economic exchange. Colpitts measures the expected increase in communication demand
that accompanies economic development, using input-output
tables for 13 countries with a wide range of economic and
communications development. The communications systems that
are considered are mail, telegrams, and telephones. An
important finding is that in developed countries with adequate
communications the total value of communication output will
equal about 1.0 percent of total production. It was also found
that in all countries service industries use about two-and-a-
half times as much of the communication/dollar of production
than do manufacturing industries. Results showed that for
the most underdeveloped countries in the study, communication
capacity will have to grow nearly two-and-a-half times to
provide industry with an adequate level of communications.

304. Cruise O'Brien, Rita. "Is There a Link Between Tele-
     communication and Development?" Intermedia 7:4 (July
     1979) 26-29.

There has been economic growth in developing countries
in recent years, but such problems as inequitable distribution
of income, insufficient employment, and a widening gap with
developed nations persist. Telecommunications and the mass
media have also grown, and it is possible that they reflect
and even reinforce these negative trends. However, if
communication is planned together with other sectors certain
inequalities might be mitigated. The study described in this
article was commissioned by Unesco to relate communication/
economic indicators to communication planning; indicators can
be used to monitor the outcomes of planned policies.
     Despite problems with the poor quality of much available
data, the study team developed a composite communication
indicator called commindex; the index indicates for each country the quantitative relationship between four communication
indicators and other development indicators. Graphs of the
results for India and Spain are shown as examples of irregular
and regular growth, respectively. It is considered premature
to draw conclusions regarding causality between communications
and development; the problem is whether to consider communications an investment item or a consumption item.

305. Dertouzos, Michael L., and Moses, Joel, eds. The Computer Age: A Twenty-Year View. MIT Bicentennial Studies, no. 6. Cambridge, MA: MIT Press, 1979.

In this collection of essays on the future of computers and information processing, the editors have stressed topics that they expect to be of importance in the next twenty years. All of the contributors are noted writers in the areas of computer science and information processing; two of them, Herbert Simon and Kenneth Arrow, have won Nobel prizes in economics. All of the contributions were written for this book. They are organized into the following four sections: prospects for the individual, trends in traditional computer uses, socioeconomic effects and expectations, and trends in the underlying technologies.

Sections three and four are of particular importance to the economics of communication. Section three includes articles by Daniel Bell on the role of informational activities in our society, by Herbert Simon on computers and the centralization/decentralization of organizations, and by Martin Shubik on computer modeling of social and economic systems. In section four the cost reduction trend in computer and communications hardware and the problem of software costs are discussed. B. O. Evans' essay on computers and communications provides an overview of this topic; Evans predicts that communications cost performance and price will be major factors in the growth of electronic computers.

There are short critical evaluations by John McCarthy at the end of each essay, plus a long critical essay by Joseph Weizenbaum at the end of the volume.

306. Dordick, Herbert, and others. "The Network Society." Intermedia 7:4 (July 1979) 23.

"Network Information Services" (NIS) is a new industry based on the combined technologies of computers and telecommunications. The information consumer interacts with a terminal to obtain information from remote files in a rapid, economic, and convenient form. The systems can handle many remote users. Unfortunately there is no cohesive structure in the industry, and there is consequently much inefficiency and overlap of operations. Dordick hopes the pattern of television development won't be repeated in the NIS industry: commercial, short-term, economic interests are favored over public, long-term, social criteria.

NIS can provide a much more efficient economic marketplace: products/services can be offered, buyers and sellers can be located, and transactions can be concluded via this information network. Dordick describes NIS as "a completely

new medium of communication," operating "at a much higher
density than human conversation, much greater speed than the
postal system, and much greater selectivity than the mass
media."

Although the technology has been available for some time,
development of these new services has been slow for the
following reasons: (1) restrictive regulations on the cable
industry; (2) no government investment; (3) human behavioral
change is very slow.

307. Eckstein, Otto. "National Economic Information Systems
     for Developed Economies." In The Organization and
     Retrieval of Economic Knowledge, pp. 67-79. Edited by
     Mark Perlman. Boulder, CO: Westview Press, 1977.

Economic analysis has three traditional functions:
(1) analyzing the historical record for systematic regularities;
(2) forecasting; and (3) assessing public policy alternatives.
It is carried on in five institutional settings: (1) universities;
(2) research institutes; (3) government agencies; (4) private
industry and financial institutions; and (5) households. The
National Economic Information System (NEIS) is primarily suited
to the needs of government agencies and private industry,
where forecasting and policy analysis are the major functions
of economic analysis. The NEIS has five components; Eckstein
gives details on each component in relation to his own system,
Data Resources Inc. (DRI): (1) computer systems; (2) communications network; (3) software; (4) data banks; and
(5) econometric models.

The goal of an effective NEIS is to produce an optimal
organization of economic information and analysis for use in a
market economy.

In the discussion section following the paper, the question is raised as to whether DRI would survive competition
with other firms or whether such services should become
public goods.

308. Fisher, Franklin M.; Ferrall, Victor E., Jr.; Belsley,
     David; and Mitchell, Bridger M. "Community Antenna
     Television Systems and Local Television Station Au-
     dience." Quarterly Journal of Economics 80:2 (May
     1966) 227-251.

The effects of CATV competition on the audience and
revenues of U.S. local off-the-air stations are estimated;
specifically, the economic impact of not being carried or dup-
licated by CATV is measured. CATV affects audiences of local
stations in three ways: (1) CATV subscribers are excluded

from watching local stations on other channels; (3) CATV brings in different programming from different stations. The growth rate of CATV continues to increase; therefore its economic impact is important for policy decisions.

CATV affects the revenues of local stations through advertisers; if an audience changes, so does the station's attractiveness for advertisers. An audience-revenue relationship is formulated, in which revenue is a function of average prime-time audience. Audience size is then related to potential size and viewing habits; a key variable is the number of program alternatives.

Findings include: (1) CATV has substantial economic impact on local station revenues; (2) significant number of local stations will have to reduce costs to withstand CATV penetration; (3) potential station entrants, particularly UHF, will be discouraged from entry by CATV. CATV will probably lead to a reduction of local TV service and an expansion of national service. Congressional and FCC policy have long favored as much local service as possible.

309. Frey, Frederick W. "Communication and Development." In Handbook of Communication, pp. 337-461. Edited by Ithiel de Sola Pool and Wilbur Schramm. Chicago: Rand McNally, 1973.

In this lengthy review article, emphasis is placed on the role of communications in the development process. Frey discusses the difficulty of defining and conceptualizing "development." He then summarizes in maps and tables world patterns of development and measures of communication development. Several development and communication indicators are considered: GNP per capita, energy consumption per capita, literacy rates, and newspaper circulation and pieces of mail per 1,000 population. Rates of growth in newspaper circulation and radio and TV receivers are included. These data concern media availability; Frey then presents data on media exposure. Exposure to media is found to vary greatly within developing countries, depending on such factors as sex and literacy.

Frey reviews various theories of development, grouped as economic, psychological, political, and communications; in the first three areas he emphasizes the role of communications. It is pointed out that economists have paid little attention to communications, treating it as an adjunct to transportation. Yet the price system, which is central to economics and tends not to function well in LDCs, is essentially a communications system. Other communications systems, including legal, postal, and administrative systems and scientific and technical knowledge, have a key role to play in development.

Development and mass media growth go together, but the direction of the causal relationship cannot now be determined. It is not known whether the mass media generate development.

310. Garbade, Kenneth D., and Silber, William L. "Technology, Communication and the Performance of Financial Markets: 1840-1975." Journal of Finance: Papers and Proceedings 33:3 (June 1978) 819-832.

The impact of three communication innovations on the behavior of securities prices in geographically dispersed markets is treated. The authors hypothesize that speedier communications would reduce intermarket price differentials and increase market integration. The three innovations are: (1) introduction of the U.S. domestic telegraph system in the 1840s; (2) the opening of the trans-Atlantic cable in 1866; (3) introduction of the consolidated stock market ticker tape in 1975. Statistical data show that the first two innovations led to a significant narrowing of price differentials, while the third made no apparent difference. The reason for the differing results may be that the first two innovations both speeded up the delivery of information and provided a quicker mechanism for orders to execute a trade, while the consolidated tape only accelerated the flow of information. The authors also speculate that the differing results may stem from the fact that the telegraph and the cable were private sector initiatives, while the consolidated tape stemmed from the regulatory authority of the Securities and Exchange Commission.

311. Gold, Martin E. "India's Motion Picture Industry." Indian Journal of Economics 52 (October 1971) 143-157.

India is the world's second largest producer of feature-length films and is a major film exporter. Among medium-scale Indian industries, film ranked second in capital investment and fifth in number of people employed in 1960. Gold explains that India's position is not due to comparative advantage; he compares costs across several countries and shows that India's are not particularly low. Rather, it is Indian demand for films that has produced rapid growth in the industry. Films are consumed because such forms of entertainment popular in other countries as social gatherings, clubs, alcohol, and sports are viewed negatively by Indians. Also, there is a huge population in India. There is natural protection for Indian films provided by Indian culture; foreigners haven't produced films and Indians demand native songs and dances in their films. Strict censorship and certification requirements have also protected Indian films from foreign competition.

Gold next describes benefits to the Indian economy provided by films. In the past, India has had to import all its raw film; however, by the late 1960s, film export earnings were greater than the costs of importing film, a positive influence on foreign exchange earnings. In 1967 India began producing its own raw film. Industries connected with film and the number of people employed in them are listed, including cinemas, refreshments, distribution, chemicals, and various professional groups. An appendix provides extensive data on film production, imports, and exports.

312. Golding, Peter. "Media Role in National Development: Critique of a Theoretical Orthodoxy." Journal of Communication 24:3 (Summer 1974) 39-53.

In many theories of development, Western Europe and North America are viewed as the goals to be attained by LDCs. Indices of underdevelopment are based on these "modern" societies. This view has had great impact on communication studies of development; Golding outlines and critiques three approaches to development that underlie much work in the mass media area: (1) the index approach in which tables of progress are compiled; (2) the differentiation approach, in which underdeveloped societies are assumed to have simple structures and unspecialized roles; (3) theories of exogenously induced change.

Three theories of mass media's role in development are grounded in the above approaches: (1) the correlation approach, based on the index approach, with both simple association and causal models; (2) the psychological approach, which implies that change and differentiation require new attitudes and values that can be conveyed by the mass media; (3) the diffusion approach, which is a theory of exogenously induced change; the variable in this approach is mass media exposure, which takes no consideration of program content and use.

Golding criticizes these approaches for stressing Western values of deferred gratification and individual entrepreneurship and also for their incorrect interpretations of the history of many LDCs, which under Western colonialism actually regressed from a complex level of development.

313. Grant, Stephen. "Educational TV Comes to the Ivory Coast." Africa Report 16:2 (February 1971) 31-33.

The first national educational TV experiment in Africa took place in the Ivory Coast. The program was designed to contribute directly to economic growth and national development

needs. It was felt that the traditional educational system was
failing to contribute to economic development in that as many
as 40 percent of students were repeaters in or drop-outs from
primary school; money and teachers were thus wasted on
overcrowded classes, and school drop-outs became a drain on
the national economy. It was hoped that ETV would enable
children to progress at the same rate through the primary
grades.

Grant describes the projected costs and benefits of the
program. A cost of $500 million was anticipated for the first
12 years, 90 percent to come out of the Ivory Coast's education budget. Costs are divided into production, transmission,
and reception categories. It is predicted that there will be
large increased annual returns to education in terms of lower
drop-out rates.

314. Grindlay, Andrew. "The Information Industry: A Huge
      Opportunity for Canada?" Business Quarterly 44:1
      (Spring 1979) 88-90.

By creating a name for itself in the fast-growing information industry, Canada could relieve current economic problems
through increased job opportunities and export earnings.
There are seven sections of the information industry: main-
frames, components, peripherals, software, telecommunications
facilities, computer-related supplies, and education of computer
people and users. The first two should be left to the United
States and Japan; the investment required and the risks of
entry are too great. Canada has certain advantages that will
help in the other five areas: (1) a high literacy rate, which
makes job training easier; (2) a strong base of computer
companies linked to parents in other countries, thus providing
access to the latest technology; (3) a leadership role in telecommunications technology.

Grindlay recommends the following strategies: (1) no
protective tariffs or quotas should be imposed; (2) the cost of
data transmission in Canada should be reduced; (3) tax incentives should be provided; (4) government should be kept
out of the industry.

The demand for home computers is growing rapidly and
will fuel demand for "canned" programs.   There will be a
software industry similar to the record industry.

The information industry will create some displacements in
the job market. Manual workers and some office workers may
not be trainable for the new industry. Grindlay expects to
see a certain polarization in society, with information workers
at one end and the rest at the other.

315. Gunaratne, Shelton A. "A Critical Look at the 'New Paradigm' of Communication and Development." Southeast Asian Journal of Social Science 4:2 (1976) 9-20.

According to communication scholar Everett Rogers ("The Rise and Fall of the Dominant Paradigm," entry 347), the dominant paradigm of development (which emphasizes economic growth, capital-intensive technology, centralized planning, and internal causes of underdevelopment) is no longer the accepted model in the Third World. Rogers criticizes this model for many reasons, including that it ignores equality of distribution of development benefits, it doesn't take into account quality of life, and it ignores the possibilities of autonomous development. Gunaratne presents Rogers's redefinition of development as "a widely participatory process," and then criticizes this new paradigm because of the self-contradictory nature of many of its elements; for example, self-reliance may lead to further inequality of distribution because of disparities in human skills among different localities.

Rogers sees two main roles for mass communication with his new paradigm of self-development: (1) providing technical information in response to local requests; and (2) circulating information about the self-development accomplishments of local groups. Gunaratne again stresses the contradictory nature of these elements; some kind of centralized planning will be required to see that less active localities do not lag behind the more active ones.

316. Hai, S. "Telecommunications Development in Israel: The Growth of Public Services and Lessons from Developing Countries." Telecommunications Policy 3:2 (June 1979) 134-146.

The development of a modern economy depends on its public services sector. Public services can be considered as social or economic in nature; for historical reasons, such as the need to absorb immigrants, Israel has experienced greater growth of social services. In 1977, economic infrastructure services contributed about 13 percent to Israel's GNP, while in the West the contribution was over 20 percent. Telecommunications has been quite inadequate in Israel, with a growing demand surplus and a decline in quality of service. While telecommunications is considered important for its contribution to economic growth, it will be crucial in the future as an essential part of information transfer technology.

Although Israel has a relatively well-developed economy, its telecommunications system shares many features with less developed nations. Causes of imbalanced telecommunications development include: (1) use of telecommunications surpluses to cover deficits in postal services, leading to a lack of investment capital; (2) scarcities of skilled workers, who are attracted to the private market; (3) too much concentration on developing advanced systems for national prestige, and consequent lack of attention and money for traditional services; (4) poor administrative methods; (5) inflexible pricing policies. The article is concluded with policy recommendations to correct these problems.

317. Havrilesky, Thomas. "The Information Explosion, Technological Innovativeness and the Competitive Ethic." Land Economics 48:4 (November 1972) 347-356.

Havrilesky uses the antipollution movement as an example of how the information explosion has been a driving force behind recent cultural change. The antipollution minority has utilized the grants mechanism to buy media time and space to proselytize; consumer tastes and more importantly lawmakers' opinions have been changed. New regulations affect prices, which leads to shifts in market demand away from polluting products. Subsidies to communications media via antipollution groups increase the supply of communications, thus lowering the price and increasing the quantity of information available to the consumer. A new consensus on such collective goods problems as the environment has been molded. The increased supply of communications is making people wary of such traditional norms as the "oligopoly-dominated market exchange system" and the "welfare-warfare state," and there is a growing repudiation of the competitive ethic.

With the reallocation of resources away from pollution activities, technologists will find employment on the supply side of the pollution control market. They also can have great impact as advocates; legislation is needed to encourage the flow of information from the technological community. Public policy that fosters information flow helps facilitate people's adaptation to new technologies.

318. Hilewick, Carol Lee; Deak, Edward J.; Kohl, Kay K.; and Heinze, Edward. Socio-economic Impact of Investment in Transportation and Communication: A Methodology Utilizing a Multi-Industry Multi-Regional Forecasting Model Modified to Incorporate Investment in Communication. Washington, DC: U.S. Department of Transportation, 1976.

The two objectives of this study were to explore the influence of transportation and communication (T/C) on rural economic development and to identify rural industry sectors most likely to be affected by investment in T/C. It was hypothesized that improved accessibility through upgraded T/C would enhance rural development. Chapter 1 is an extensive literature search covering location theory, T/C and development, the diffusion of innovations, and economic impact models.

Two rural counties in Pennsylvania and North Carolina were selected; economic, transportation, and communication profiles are given for each. An econometric forecasting model was used to simulate the impact of investments in T/C in the two counties. The model was modified to include communication through the development of an Industrial Communication Index (ICI). The bulk of the study is devoted to transportation; transportation improvements are measurable in terms of direct cost savings. The simulation predicted significant savings for both road and rail improvements in both counties.

The ICI is used as one of the parameters in the location equations; it is a measure of aggregated economic activity in six sectors: (1) printing and publishing; (2) office and computing machines; (3) communication equipment; (4) communications (telephone and telegraph service); (5) radio/TV broadcasting; and (6) business services. A policy of "normalization" was simulated; forecasts for each county were made on the basis of investment in communications sufficient to bring the county up to "normal" national output levels. Because of the aggregated nature of the communications data, such specific measures as direct cost savings cannot be made.

319. Hudson, Heather E.; Goldschmidt, Douglas; Parker, Edwin B.; and Hardy, Andrew. The Role of Telecommunications in Socio-Economic Development: A Review of the Literature with Guidelines for Further Investigations. N.p. Keewatin Communications, 1979.

For the purposes of this literature review, telecommunications is defined as including basic telephone service plus other services that use a telephone channel. Materials were included only if they were applicable to a developing country environment. An overview chapter provides a discussion of the environment of developing regions, focusing on rural development. The developmental benefits of communications are reviewed, including the following: social services delivery, economic development, stemming urban migration, participation in national development, and quality of life. Some representative statistical studies are reviewed and critiqued; the problem of demonstrating the relationship between telecommunications and development is discussed, and some approaches are suggested. Many studies do show that the benefits of telecommunications accrue to society in general;

telecommuniations has public good properties. For example, it has been demonstrated that telecommunications improves the cost-effectiveness of rural social services delivery.

In a separate chapter, the potential of satellite communications for remote and rugged areas is discussed; because they are cost-insensitive to distance, satellites are more economic for such areas than terrestrial facilities. The Alaskan satellite system and its specifications are described in some detail. It is concluded that telecommunications system planning must be integrated with national and regional development plans, and funding agencies must not consider telecommunications in isolation.

320. Hudson, Heather E., and Parker, Edwin B. "Telecommunication Planning for Rural Development." IEEE Transactions on Communications Com-23:10 (October 1975) 1177-1185.

The installation of a telecommunications infrastructure should be a high priority item in development planning, particularly because of its potential in rural development. Technological innovations have reduced the cost of extending services to remote areas; satellite systems have made possible two-way communications services with cost independent of distance. Planners must carefully consider the communications technology they will use; North American telecommunications are designed to maximize economic returns through use in urban locations with heavy traffic. Different technologies will be required to suit different development objectives.

In Alaska and Northern Canada, two-way telecommunication links in radio and satellite have made effective health care available in remote villages. Such links can also contribute to (1) both formal and nonformal education; (2) economic development, through the dissemination of marketing information and the formation of cooperative buying and selling units; (3) community development, through coordination and reduction of duplication in services.

Planners must translate development needs into system design requirements. Important factors for rural development include intraregional communication capability, conference call capability, and accessibility to all residents.

Communication capability must be viewed as an essential element of infrastructure rather than as a consumption item to be supplied in response to demonstrated demand.

321. International Telecommunication Union. Telecommunica-
    tions Economic Studies: Economic Studies at the National
    Level in the Field of Telecommunications (1973-1976).
    Geneva: ITU, 1976.

    National telecommunications adminstrations can use this
loose-leaf volume as a handbook to provide advice and methods
for planning telecommunications development. The first three
chapters treat the impact of telecommunications on the national
economy. Telecommunications is an essential tool in the production of goods and services and for the sale and distribution
of industrial products. Business expenditures on communications are taken as an indicator of their impact. Telecommunications is also a necessary item of private and social
consumption; social needs in both urban and remote rural
areas are considered. A socioeconomic cost-benefit calculation
is provided. In the chapter on planning, examples are given
from Australia, Sweden, the United States, and Poland.
    Chapters four and five deal with budgeting and account-
ing for a telecommunications administration. Detailed examples
include an analysis of operating costs. The final chapter
concerns personnel policy and covers planning, training, and a
method for measuring productivity. Many charts and tables
are included, and each chapter has a bibliography.

322. Jones, David W., Jr. Must We Travel? The Potential of
    Communication as a Substitute for Urban Travel. Stan-
    ford, CA: Institute for Communication Research, 1973.

    New electronic communications technology will enable users
to approximate closely the communication capacity of face-to-
face meetings. There are three likely stages in the diffusion
of two-way information utilities: (1) links between corporate
headquarters and branches; (2) the "wiring" of the transaction
sector of the economy (banking, brokerage, and consulting
services); (3) home and neighborhood information utilities.
Jones estimates the amount of home-to-work, rush-hour travel
that is susceptible to substitution by communications; sus-
ceptibility is defined as the capability of a worker to maintain
via communications the necessary relationships to data/per-
sons/things.
    Occupations falling into susceptible categories, which
stress ideas, communications, and decision-making activities,
are identified; travel data are drawn from a 1965 study performed in the San Francisco Bay Area. Twenty-two percent
of morning rush-hour travel was found to be prone to substitution; for trips terminating in the Central Business District,
potential for substitution was 47 percent. Communication
substitution could lead to dispersal of transactional economic

functions to locations with lower land costs; the composition of companies could also change, with routine communication and clerical tasks being performed by specialist, out-of-house agencies; urban congestion would be relieved. There would be a large impact on the automobile industry and public transit.

323. Jones, Rebecca.   "Satellite Communications: Indonesia's Bitter Fruit."   Pacific Research and World Empire Telegram 7:4 (May-June 1976) 1-6.

     Indonesia, with a per capita income of $120 per year, is the first Asian country and only the fourth country in the world with a domestic satellite communications system.   Jones explains that implementation of the system has little to do with any national goals for improving the living standards of Indonesia's people.   Rather, foreign investors desired improved communications between their Jakarta offices and their extractive enterprises on other islands.   Executives of multinational corporations that manufacture communications equipment have bribed Indonesian officials to purchase a new system.   The Indonesian military wanted the system to increase their ability to monitor dissent and control information activities.
     The system is too expensive for Indonesia; Jones specifies suitable alternatives and other satellite systems that would have cost much less.   The chosen system will increase Indonesian dependency on foreign technology.   U.S. firms manufacture the equipment in the United States; very few jobs will be created in Indonesia.   The system will increase centralized control over the society for "national security" purposes.

324. Jones, William K.   "The Future of the Telecommunications Industry: Propsects and Problems."   Public Utilities Fortnightly 90:8 (12 October 1972) 27-36.

     Telecommunications will have an important impact on four current social problems.   Telecommunications helps control environmental pollution by providing an alternative to transportation; greater use of telecommunications could improve land use and traffic patterns and reverse the rural-to-urban migration.   Poverty could be ameliorated through use of telecommunications to provide job information, training, and skills to be impoverished.   Telecommunications can contribute to inflation control by improving productivity; rates for telecommunications services must be kept as low as possible.   In an increasingly urbanized society, access to telecommunications can help relieve individual isolation and provide a sense of community.

The telephone industry will continue to play a very important role within the broader telecommunications industry. In analyzing possible industry configurations, Jones looks at traffic patterns, interconnection, growth of various telecommunications entities, and ways to allocate functions within the industry. On the latter two points, he concludes that entities other than the telephone industry will grow the fastest and that competition is preferable to regulation as a method for allocating contested functions.

325. Jordan, Paul L. Communications Satellites, Technology Transfer, and Economic Development. Santa Monica, CA: Rand Corp., 1970.

Expansion of the educational system is essential for developing countries, which typically suffer from a shortage of skilled workers and entrepreneurs and low productivity rates; television can be an effective tool in improving education. Jordan reviews the general conditions of primary, secondary, and higher education in developing countries; primary education is characterized by low enrollments and high drop-out rates. Secondary education is needed for the training of technicians, and higher education is needed for the production of managers, administrators, and professional persons.

Economic models are presented in which output is a function of capital, labor, and the level of applied technical knowledge, and change in the latter is a function of level of education, theoretical level of technology, and actual level of applied technical knowledge. Economic growth can therefore be generated by changes in the level of education. There is currently much discussion of the use of satellite-based ETV to improve education; Jordan warns that dissemination of the signal is only one part of the overall ETV system. A country must be able to effectively utilize the signal.

326. Jussawalla, Meheroo. "The Economics of International Communication." Third World Quarterly 1:3 (July 1979) 87-94.

Communications technology has had a large impact on international economic relationships. Examples of the effect of instant communications on trade, currency fluctuation, capital flows, and multinational corporations are given; the media are capable of restoring or destroying confidence in a currency.

Third World countries require telecommunications systems for development, particularly for export-oriented development strategies; they must have knowledge of developed country markets for their products. Developed countries need to export their communication goods/services since their own information sectors are saturated. There is thus a two-way process linking trade flows with communication flows.

The genesis of the New Economic and Information Orders is briefly described; within both orders a more balanced flow, whether of commodities or information, is stressed. LDCs will no longer be the passive recipients of first world information. Improved communications will promote the development of social service systems within LDCs, as well as help them to organize regional trade blocs and promote trade. The two orders converge at the level of technology transfer and the investment required for it.

327. Jussawalla, Meheroo. "The Economics of Telecommunications for Development." In Pacific Telecommunications Conference Papers and Proceedings, pp. 1D-1 - 1D-11. Edited by Dan J. Wedemeyer and David L. Jones. Honolulu: 1979.

The author provides an overview of the broad impact of telecommunications on development. It is hard to state whether telecommunications causes change or facilitates it; it is evident, however, that economic scarcity is linked with communication scarcity. There is currently a large demand in third world countries for telephones, and such countries are giving priority to telecommunications projects; projects in Mexico, Iran, Egypt, Indonesia, Kenya, and other areas are briefly described. Telecommunications systems must be restructured to meet overall development needs; the World Bank, for example, lends money for telecommunications on a commercial basis which favors urban development.

Problems in implementing telecommunications projects for development include: (1) rate of return - it must be at least high enough to pay the interest on money borrowed for projects; (2) bureaucratic delays; (3) elitism and neglect of rural areas. Benefits of telecommunications include: (1) improved human services delivery; (2) less immigration to urban areas and consequent decentralization of employment; (3) reduced transactions costs for government, industry, and agriculture; (4) more equitable distribution of development gains.

India's experience with telecommunications is described in some detail. It is stressed that telecommunications must be treated as a public good and that in international lending the indirect benefits of telecommunications must be emphasized.

328. Jussawalla, Meheroo F. "The Future of Communications in Development Planning in India (the 80s)." Paper presented at the AIES Conference, Manhattan College, New York, 10-12 August 1979.

Communications must be included as a determining variable in development planning. A definitive connection between communications and economic growth cannot now be drawn, but links are plainly visible. The multiplier effects of investment in communication technology can be investigated. Communications will create structural changes in the socioeconomic system that will increase the productivity of the working population; communications delivery systems that improve the quality of life in terms of health, education, and nutrition are vital to the development effort. The World Bank considers telecommunications the "nervous system" of a society and its economy, and this view is reflected in Bank lending policies.

Jussawalla describes the major Indian communications industries: radio, TV, newspapers, telecommunications, and satellite communications. Actual and potential contributions to Indian development by each industry are reviewed, along with facts and figures on investment and costs. A national communications policy is called for; priorities in communications investment must be assigned, especially in light of the shift in emphasis from urban to rural development.

329. Kimbel, Dieter. "Policy Research for Information Activities: The OECD Programme on Information, Computers and Communications Policy." Telecommunications Policy 1:5 (December 1977) 367-373.

In 1977 OECD created the Working Party on Information, Computers and Communications Policy (ICCP), with a mandate to investigate the socioeconomic and industrial implications of advancing information technologies. Eleven topics ICCP will investigate are listed, and two are discussed in detail. The first is the problem of transborder data flows and the issue of protection of privacy versus the right of access to information. The second is the macroeconomic analysis of information activities and the role of advanced electronics and telecommunications technologies. The new technologies will become the basis for future economic and social development. As ancillary products, they are transforming the watch industry, automobile industry, and instrument industry, among others. They also serve as production factors, by making available correct information to manage complex systems. New policies will be needed to give direction to the impact of advancing technologies on employment, economic growth, industry, structure, and international trade.

330. Lunz, William E. "Rural Telecommunications Develop-
     ment." In Pacific Telecommunications Conference Papers
     and Proceedings, pp. 1D-29 - 1D-33. Edited by Dan J.
     Wedemeyer and David L. Jones. Honolulu: Pacific
     Telecommunications Conference, 1979.

     Investment in telecommunications is considered to be
essential to economic growth. In many LDCs, few resources
are available for such investment, but careful planning can
serve to maximize the benefits of what is available. Telecommunications investment has typically been oriented to urban
areas for the following reasons: (1) urbanization is seen as
being synonymous with development; (2) because of population
density in urban areas it is thought more people will benefit;
(3) urban development is seen as necessary to attract multinational corporations; (4) it is prestigious to have a developed
urban sector.
     However, telecommunications investment should be di-
rected to rural areas because the economies of most LDCs are
dependent on extractive or agricultural activities located in the
rural sector; telecommunications will facilitate such activities.
Also, the actual proportion of the population living in rural
areas is higher, and more people will be benefited.
     Lunz considers some financial, maintenance, and logistical
problems of installing rural telecommunications and proposes
satellites as a cost-effective solution. A microwave network is
more expensive in terms of both installation costs and time.

331. Lyle, Jack; Jussawalla, Meheroo; and Rahim, Syed. "T3:
     Transportation Telecommunication Trade-Offs." Paper
     presented at the East-West Energy Interdependencies
     Seminar, East-West Center, Honolulu, Hawaii, 3-8 De-
     cember 1978.

     Shortages of petrochemical fuels and increasing urban
congestion are leading people to ask whether at least some
transportation could be replaced by telecommunications. In
the past, transportation has been an essential component of
industrialization, and communication has depended on transportation, because the people carrying the ideas had to be
transported. However, as new methods of telecommunications
are implemented, such as video-conferencing, less transporting
of people will be required.
     Half of commercial air travel and automobile commuting is
for the generation/exchange of information; using a wage rate
of $4.50/hour, the cost of commuting time for office workers in
1975 was $34 billion. The cost/benefit implications of T3
include the following considerations: (1) transportation costs
more in terms of pollution, land requirements, natural re-

sources, and energy; (2) T3 would mean dislocation in construction and other industries; (3) T3 would mean decentralization of work and social/cultural activities from city centers,
with loss of tax revenues for cities; (4) less commuting time
would mean greater leisure time.

The impact of communications on GNP is increasing;
communication inputs to GNP have been growing twice as fast
as transportation inputs. LDCs may not be ready for T3 yet,
but the fact that many of them don't have heavy investment in
traditional transportation/communication infrastructure will give
them a competitive advantage in implementing advanced telecommunications systems.

332. Marsh, Donald J. "Telecommunications as a Factor in
      the Economic Development of a Country." IEEE
      Transactions on Communications COM-24:7 (July 1976)
      716-722.

Marsh reviews techniques for formulating correlations
between national telecommunications systems and economic
development in the context of investment requirements in
several Latin American countries. A cause and effect relationship between telecommunications and development is difficult to
establish because of the complex interdependencies among
such variables related to telephone demand as population,
income, price, and economic infrastructure. In Latin America,
population growth is primarily an urban phenomenon, so
telecommunications development should be concentrated in
urban areas. Governments have frequently maintained telecommunications prices at levels too low to generate sufficient
profits; government policy is thus the major factor in the
development of this industry. Marsh concludes that telephone
density in Latin America is far too low and requires extensive
investment to assure future economic development.

333. Martin, James. The Wired Society. Englewood Cliffs,
      NJ: Prentice-Hall, 1978.

Earth's ecology is strained to the breaking point; we must
develop those technologies that are in harmony with nature.
This book is concerned with one such technology, electronic
communications. There are no visible limits to its growth, and
it could restructure society in terms of work patterns, leisure,
education, health care, and industry. Martin describes in
nontechnical terms the capabilities of the new technology in a
vast number of areas: medical facilities, new uses for TV,
news, electronic funds transfer, instant mail, information storage and retrieval services, radio gadgets, satellites, trade-offs

with transportation, education, shorter work weeks, and work at home.

The most important impact of telecommunications will be on industry; countries with the best facilities will achieve the highest growth rates. The information-handling process consumes 5 to 30 percent of an organization's expenses; a letter is much more expensive than a telephone call. New communications channels will do much to lower costs.

Martin details economic and social forces that block the development and use of new technologies, such as large investments in obsolete equipment, unions, and regulatory devices. The impact of electronic communications on less developed societies is considered. The final large question is who will pay for this new technology; Martin presents arguments in favor of government subsidization.

334. Morgan, Kevin. "National Satellite System: A Note on Possible Economic Impacts." Media Information Australia, no. 9 (August 1978), pp. 46-48.

Cost estimates vary so widely that it is difficult to assess the potential impact of a domestic satellite system; in this paper, Morgan intends only to suggest possible impacts on the structure and costs of telecommunications services in Australia. Since there already exists a vast public investment in a terrestrial system, the potential disutilities of a satellite system must be looked at.

Three methods for funding a satellite system are described; in each case there would be a large increase in the level of indebtedness in the telecommunications industry. The key question is whether sufficient new revenue will be generated to offset costs. The answer seems to be no, for although the new system will double telecommunications capacity, traffic cannot grow proportionately; adding 5,000 remote subscribers will not provide the revenues needed to sustain the huge investment. The massive oversupply of service would destroy the pricing policy of Telecom, the Australian telecommunications authority. The impact on Telecom under each of the three funding methods is described. It is concluded that while the project would create 100 new jobs, it would destroy thousands of others throughout the industry.

335. Nooter, Robert, and Weiss, Charles. "External Financing
     for Communication and Information Development." In
     Aspen Institute Program on Communications and Society,
     Conference Report, pp. 20-24. Aspen, CO: August
     1978.

     The characteristics of loans made by World Bank and
AID for communications projects in developing countries are
described. World Bank concentrates on strengthening the institutional capability of national telecommunications authorities.
AID stresses projects using communication hardware and
software for specific development purposes, such as education
and family planning, rather than communications infrastructure
in its own right.
     After the authors' presentation, several issues were
brought out in a discussion session. First, there was a
strong consensus in favor of communication aid programs; it
was suggested that it would be more fruitful for the United
States to focus attention on aid programs and shift attention
away from more political issues such as the WARC. The need
in developing economies for reliable two-way, real-time communications systems was stressed. The lack of evidence as to
the worth of investment in rural telecommunications projects
was mentioned. Other speakers pointed out the need for
reliable communications to coordinate dispersed productive
units in the economy.

336. Oshima, Harry T. "Development and Mass Communica-
     tion - A Re-examination." In Communication and
     Change: The Last Ten Years - And the Next, pp.
     17-30. Edited by Wilbur Schramm and Daniel Lerner.
     Honolulu: University of Hawaii, 1976.

     The old strategy of economic development is urban-based
and capital-intensive, stressing the growth of large-scale
industry. This strategy has failed because effective aggregate
demand cannot grow fast enough to keep up with supply,
resulting in excess capacity and unemployment. Oshima
demonstrates that in underdeveloped nations there aren't
enough families with sufficient income to purchase goods from
capital-intensive industries. These problems are exacerbated
by the population explosion. The new strategy of economic
development is rural-based and labor-intensive, reflecting the
need to create more jobs and produce more food.
     Mass communication functions as a catalytic agent, an
input in the production process, in the new strategy. Four
development tasks for mass communication are: (1) to help
revolutionize agriculture through increased productivity; (2) to
promote small industries through improved entrepreneurship

and skills; (3) to provide a two-way flow of communication from the center to rural areas for participatory planning and decision making; and (4) to help overcome the opposition who are against a labor-intensive strategy.

The role of mass communication is greater in the new strategy because more people in more remote regions must be reached. It is more complex for several reasons: labor must be reeducated, intermediate technology must be discovered, diffused savings in small bits must be collected, and new institutions and values must be established.

337. Parker, Edwin B. "Communication Satellites for Rural Development." Telecommunications Policy 2:4 (December 1978) 309-315.

Effective consumer demand in urban areas can make telecommunications economically self-supporting, but it can also obscure the fact the telecommunications are part of a country's essential infrastructure. Rural areas have less apparent demand, because they are poorer, but actual demand should be treated as unknown until it is tested; actual demand was greatly underestimated in Alaska, for example. Telecommunications links people in ways that make their work more effective; in rural areas, better management, coordination, and education can be provided to relatively untrained personnel supplying such services as health care. Telecommunications is an investment in human capital.

For rugged and remote areas satellite communications may be more economical than terrestrial systems. Satellite systems are cost-insensitive to distance, more reliable and easier to maintain than terrestrial systems, and have more flexible capacity. Since most satellites have been designed for heavy traffic routes, some specifications will need to be changed for rural use. Parker suggests demonstration projects to test different specifications. Hybrid systems utilizing both satellite and terrestrial technology are likely to be least costly.

338. Parker, Edwin B. "An Information-Based Hypothesis." Journal of Communication 28:1 (Winter 1978) 81-83.

The gap is widening between the rich and poor nations and also between urban and rural areas in the poor nations. Parker hypothesizes that increased effectiveness in the transfer of knowledge can foster development and yield a more equitable distribution of wealth; the amount of physical resources may be limited, but the application of knowledge to these resources can lead to unlimited growth.

Parker argues for a development strategy utilizing labor-intensive information services to mobilize the labor and brain power of an entire society, especially the rural areas. This strategy depends on the use of new telecommunications technologies, including both two-way interactive and one-way broadcast transmission of messages. Such low-cost technologies as communications satellites make it possible to install telecommunications in remote rural areas even before electrification and roads. By utilizing telecommunications links to provide information and support, development can begin in rural areas with a lower initial level of training, education, and social organization.

339. Parker, Edwin B., and Dunn, Donald A. "Information Technology: Its Social Potential." Science, 30 June 1972, pp. 1392-1399.

Cable TV, computer systems, and communication satellites technologies could be utilized to create an "information utility" network that would provide equal access to information for all Americans. Retrieval systems would contain information, entertainment, news, library records, and education, available to anyone at anytime. Because more education could be provided without extra building and labor costs, there would be increased economies of scale leading to a large reduction in unit costs. Education would be more widely available to people of all ages; a more highly educated population would lead to greater economic productivity and consequent economic growth.
Present and future cable systems are described technically, and costs are estimated for several configurations; systems built in the future will have improved performance at lower costs. The total capital investment required for a national utility would be similar to that required for the nation's telephone plant. The hardware and software segments of the industry will grow and create many employment opportunities. There would be less need for energy-consuming transportation.
The authors suggest that federal planning and coordination of such a network is required; the first step should be experimental pilot projects.

340. Parker, Edwin B. "Social Implications of Computer/Telecoms Systems." Telecommunications Policy 1:1 (December 1976) 3-20.

Government and business institutions can be changed to make better use of technology for development purposes; telecommunications policy can help solve problems in economic policy.   Before giving specific examples, Parker provides a background description of current thinking about the information/communication sector of the economy.   The United States is becoming an information society because: (1) the cost of information. technology is declining; (2) productivity gains have resulted from increased expenditures on information activities; (3) increased use of information can correct market inefficiencies.

Particular problem areas in national economic policy where information/communication will make a difference include: (1) productivity - since the information sector is now the largest, we should look for policies to stimulate productivity in the information sector itself rather than in the industrial sector; (2) natural resource constraints - consumer preferences must be shifted away from resource-intensive goods, such as by substituting telecommunications for travel; (3) inflation - consumers may pay more for goods/services because of inadequate information; (4) international interdependence - the more developed countries must sell information goods/services to the LDCs in exchange for natural resources.

A key social/political aspect is access to communications networks; ownership of facilities is not important if access is open.   Other policy areas include privacy, property rights in information, and changing patterns of work and leisure.

341. Pierce, William B. and Jéquier, Nicolas.   "The Contribution of Telecommunications to Economic Development." Telecommunication Journal 44:11 (1977) 532-534.

In many developing countries there is insufficient investment in telecommunications systems because benefits are not seen.   Many experts feel that expanded telecommunications will benefit only the more affluent classes, not touching the lives of the masses, especially in rural areas.   The purpose of a new joint ITU/OECD project is to analyze the benefits of national investment in telecommunications and to show how it contributes to development; project planners hope to demonstrate the multiplier effects of such investment.

The authors give several examples that illustrate the benefits of investment in telecommunications.   In LDCs, industrial firms have been unable to expand production because of low-quality telephones and telex; many employment opportunities are lost.   Automobile traffic congestion is aggravated when business people and civil servants cannot telephone one another.   Current knowledge of prices and market conditions will enhance farm production.   Inexpensive public heath services and agricultural extension can be provided via telecommunications.

Investment in telecommunications is costly and must be balanced against other needs; however, the costs of communication technology are declining.

342. Polishuk, Paul, and O'Bryant, Michael A. Telecommunications & Economic Development: Papers Presented at the First International Telecommunication Exposition, Atlanta, Georgia, October 9-15, 1977. 2 vols. Dedham, MA: Horizon House International, 1977.

A wide variety of topics were presented at the Exposition, focusing on telecommunications technology and its applications. Over 200 short papers are included in the Proceedings, grouped in the following 15 sections: telecommunication needs of developing countries, market opportunities in telecommunication, satellite communications, switching, transmission, data communications, broadband and narrowband services to the home and business, fiber optics communications, local telephone network, economics of telecommunication, social impact of telecommunication, test equipment, mobile communications, applications, and teleconferencing. Authors represent public and private communications entities, research groups, universities, international organizations, and governments from North and South America, Europe, Africa, and Asia.

343. Pool, Ithiel de Sola, and Corte, Arthur B. The Implications for American Foreign Policy of Low-Cost Non-Voice Communications: A Report to the Department of State. Cambridge: Massachusetts Institute of Technology, 1975.

New low-cost, high-speed communication technologies, such as data communication via computer networks, packet switching, and satellites, will affect international interactions in government, business, science, and culture. Impact of the new technologies on U.S. State Department interests are summarized in Chapter 1. Telecommunications can complement travel by helping in maintaining contact after initial meetings; it can substitute for some travel, the costs of which are escalating. The telecommunications industry is growing rapidly and will affect the U.S. balance of payments by earning dollars abroad; improvement of telecommunications will facilitate trade by locating shipment, lessening delays, and providing fast documentary evidence by facsimile. Data base operations are characterized by high fixed costs and low variable costs; the resultant economies of scale will help the United States to continue in its predominant position in the communications industry, which will promote U.S. political and social influence abroad.

In Chapter 2 the new technologies are described in a nontechnical manner. International telecommunications is growing at a rate of 18 percent per year, while long-haul costs are decreasing. Benefits are outlined in the following areas: (1) business activities can be located in an economically viable fashion; some decentralization will be possible; (2) technology transfer to LDCs will be facilitated; (3) the delivery of such services as education, health, and banking will be facilitated.

In Chapter 3, issues to be negotiated at ITU, the UN, and Intelsat are discussed: rates and standards, satellites, spectrum allocation, copyright, and a system of payment for services via international networks.

The report is concluded with recommendations for U.S. policy. Five appendixes supplement the text.

344. Pool, Ithiel de Sola. "International Aspects of Computer Communications." Telecommunications Policy 1:1 (December 1976) 33-51.

Computer communications is defined as any communication in which the message is stored in computer memory and then processed or transmitted under computer control. There are six distinct services, from the user's point of view: (1) time-shared remote computing; (2) computer-aided instruction; (3) distributed management information services; (4) funds transfers; (5) information retrieval from remote data bases; and (6) message delivery.

The cost of computer communications will become increasingly insensitive to distance; satellites are making distance even less important. Opportunities flowing from increased computer communication due to falling costs and improving technology include: (1) economically optimal location of activities and less duplication of information facilities; (2) acceleration of technical progress; (3) more access to information for LDCs; (4) economic efficiency in world trade; and (5) increased diversity of cultural expression.

Problems blocking realization of these opportunities include: (1) lack of international standards in such areas as software, symbols, and spectrum allocation; (2) the complexity of international payment for communications systems; (3) demands for information security; (4) protection of sunk investments; and (5) nationalistic fears of foreign data flows.

345. Reid, Alex. "The Social and Economic Effects of Technological Change in Communications." Paper presented at the IBI General Meeting, Mexico City, 1-5 September 1974.

Actual and potential technological changes in telecommunications services are described. Restraints on new services include: (1) the large investment in existing plant, which slows the rate of change and reduces the potential of cost savings from new plant; (2) the fact that only a few services among the many possible can be developed, because an initial mass of users must be assembled for start-up and to achieve economies of scale; (3) regulations. The decision to provide a new service should be based on market demand; "need" is too fuzzy a concept.

There are several factors involved in substituting a newer medium for an older, established one: (1) the older media are versatile and durable and will not be entirely eliminated; one study shows that only about 30 percent of mail can be substituted for by electronic communications; (2) the price structure is complex, because each medium has different cost elements, there are wide variations between costs and prices for historical/political reasons, and the extent to which a medium lends itself to advertising varies; (3) institutions that have grown up around a certain medium are hard to change; (4) a new medium can stimulate demand for more of the old.

346. Research Institute of Telecommunications and Economics (Japan). Research Report Summaries. Tokyo: The Institute, 1970-1976.

A wide variety of topics in the general area of telecommunications and economics are under study at the Research Institute. In these annual publications, from eight to 15 research studies are summarized. Many are concerned with the impact of telecommunications on economic systems. Some topics in the 1976 report are: "A Study of Regional Quality of Life and Its Implications for Telecommunications," "The Roles of Telecommunications in the Developing Countries," "Prospects of the Demand for Data Communication," and "An Analysis of Information Flow and Its Impact on Regional Development." Further information about reports of interest can be obtained by writing to the Research Institute.

347. Rogers, Everett M. "The Rise and Fall of the Dominant
     Paradigm." Journal of Communication 28:1 (Winter 1978)
     64-69.

     The dominant paradigm of development stresses economic
growth through industrialization, capital-intensive technology,
centralized planning, and the use of per capita income as the
main index of development. The credibility of the paradigm
has been weakened by such events as the sudden wealth of
previously poor OPEC nations and the realization by the West
that alternative pathways to development are being followed by
China, Cuba, and Tanzania. Rogers gives his own definition
of development: "a widely participatory process of social
change in a society, intended to bring about both social and
material advancement (including greater equality, freedom, and
other valued qualities) for the majority of the people through
their gaining greater control over their environment."
     A key element in the new development approach is local
participation, with the responsibility for planning being at the
local level. The dominant paradigm implies a one-way flow of
communication from the government to the people; self-development implies that government development agencies will
communicate mainly in answer to locally initiated requests.
Another aspect of the use of communication in development has
been the return to such lower-cost communication channels as
radio, after the 1960s enthusiasm for such "big media" as
television. (See also Gunaratne, entry 315.)

348. Shapiro, Peter D. "Telecommunications and Industrial
     Development." IEEE Transactions on Communications
     COM-24:3 (March 1976) 305-311.

     A correlation has been demonstrated between industrial
development and telecommunications system development.
Causality applies in both directions; telecommunications provides the infrastructure for exchange of business information,
and industrial development provides capital, expertise, and the
demand needed for telecommunications growth.
     In planning a telecommunications system to help achieve
development goals, three sets of issues must be considered:
(1) The technical capabilities of the system affect the availability of service. A "critical mass" of telephone density
must be achieved before telecommunications can attain full
value. In countries where universal service can be only a
long-range goal, screening devices can be used to provide
adequate service first to those industries with the most to
contribute to economic growth. (2) Equipment supply must be
arranged. Local manufacture can be an important component
of industrial development. (3) The tariff structure allocates

telecommunications to various segments of the economy; a common discrimination is between business and residential customers. An attempt to recover all costs through revenues may lead to tariffs that are too high; because of the potential benefits of telecommunications, governments may choose to subsidize their development.

349. Starling, Jack M. "Cable Television: Prospects for Marketing Applications." Akron Business and Economic Review 7:3 (Fall 1976) 28-35.

Now that cable television (CATV) is authorized to operate in the top 100 U.S. TV markets, new programs and services must be developed to ensure commercial success. In this study CATV's potential to provide such marketing services as remote shopping, marketing research, and advertising is evaluated. Data were collected by interview and mail survey from CATV operators, department stores, and advertising and marketing research agencies. CATV services presently offered or planned include: advertising, opinion polling (including market surveys), remote shopping, meter readings, and gas leak detection.

Marketing firm evaluations are given for both one-way and two-way interactive service (the latter is now in the experimental stage). Seventy-nine percent of department store respondents see a profitable use for shopping channels with telephone order placement; 68 percent see profitable opportunities with subscriber home terminal order placement. Seventy percent of marketing research agency respondents and 85 percent of advertising agency respondents believe CATV will provide them an effective medium. The primary benefit of the medium is that it provides a fast, low-cost means of conducting research, especially when two-way systems are available; a major limitation is the lack of randomness in sample selection. In the near future, advertising will be CATV's most lucrative source of marketing service revenue.

350. Valerdi, Jorge. "A Communications Plan for Mexico: Opportunity for Recovery." Telecommunications Policy 1:4 (September 1977) 271-288.

The communications sector in Mexico is in an unsatisfactory condition for development purposes; only 30 percent of the population has access to a telephone, and only 47 percent can receive TV. Policies and strategies for communications development are proposed; the primary objective of communications is to support the development of the population with a balanced, efficient communications infrastructure. There must be diminished technical dependence on other countries. Increased rural communications, increased productivity of services, and major support given to the industrial and services sectors.

The organizational, regulatory, and legal structure of communications services is described. The present role of communications in three areas of the economy is discussed: (1) contribution to GNP; (2) government investment in communications; (3) national production and imports/exports of communications equipment. Demand for telephone, telex, and TV services is estimated for the year 2000 based on population and GNP projections. There will be a very significant growth in the telephone service, estimated at 7 to 11 times the number of lines available in 1975. The country must develop a national industry to supply the equipment.

351. Voge, Jean. "Information and Information Technologies in Growth and the Economic Crisis." Technological Forecasting & Social Change 14:1 (June 1979) 1-14.

Voge briefly summarizes studies that define and measure the information economy. The information ratio (which can be defined as the percentage of information workers within the work force) is approaching 50 percent in the United States; however, growth in the information sector is leveling off, and there is a trend to saturation. Bureaucracy will soon account for one quarter of total economic activity. Economic growth in the material sector has slowed down because productivity increases cannot compensate for the loss of manpower to bureaucracy. Voge suggests that when production is equally divided between material and information an economy has reached its maximum maturity. We may have to accept maturity and its consequences, including a blockage in per capita buying power and level of investment.

There are many similarities between economic growth and growth patterns of physical and biological systems. As in biology, the solution to the current economic crisis could be evolution, defined as "far-reaching and discontinuous changes in structure." The major communications media and data processing systems have been based on a hierarchical model, and centered on urban areas; Voge sees in communications and other systems a possibly evolutionary trend towards a decentralized, cellular model. Distributed data processing systems and the success of minicomputers are pointing the way. In several industrialized countries there are ongoing experiments in such community media as teletext and Citizen's Band radio.

352. Wellenius, Bjôrn. "On the Role of Telecommunications in the Development of Nations." IEEE Transactions on Communications COM-20:1 (February 1972) 3-7.

Telecommunications systems require initial investments higher than for any other public utility; priorities must be set and choices must be made, especially in the less developed countries where needs greatly exceed resources. The economy must be analyzed to find where investment in telecommunications will contribute most to the national or regional product; telecommunications must also be allocated for the maximization of social integration. Telecommunication planners are unable at present to give objective criteria for the amount of resources to be allocated to their sector.
    Wellenius reviews the literature to learn what knowledge is available on the relationship between the economy and telecommunications. Many studies have demonstrated a correlation between telephone indicators and various economic figures, but no cause/effect relationship is established; therefore inferences of optimal levels of investment cannot be made. A few studies have shown how telephones affect given economic activities. Wellenius participated in a study in Chile concerning the relative effect of telephone service on the efficiency of production for different types of agricultural production units. Innovative studies are needed on the effects of telecommunications services on the individual, the community, and the environment.

353. Wellenius, Bjôrn. "Telecommunications in Developing Countries." Telecommunications Policy 1:4 (September 1977) 289-297.

The telecommunications sector of a typical developing country is described; telecommunications organizations are usually state-owned independent corporations or parts of government departments. Telecommunications services tend to expand at very rapid rates in LDCs, yet supply can rarely catch up with expanding demand; there is large hidden demand in most LDCs.
    Telecommunications will benefit a country most if it is managed as a business; prices should be kept high enough to recover costs and generate funds for expansion. Annual operating costs and revenues per main telephone and annual rates of return are given for selected developing countries. Figures indicating the large range in productivity in the telecommunications industry are also given.
    Telecommunications contributes to economic development by removing physical constraints on business organizations, permitting increased productivity, and increasing access to

goods and social services. A major issue is the development of telecommunications in rural areas; these areas must be supplied, even if at a loss, because rural development programs depend on telecommunications. Also, demand can't surface until people become familiar with a service. The employment of locals, and local production of equipment, must be encouraged by government policies.

354. Wells, Alan. "Mass Media Systems, Economic Development, and the Public-Private Continuum." Southeast Asian Journal of Social Science 4:2 (1976) 21-30.

The media are an important input to development, but there is much debate over the extent to which they actually fulfill development needs. Their uneven performance in the development context stems from programming content and feedback mechanisms. Since the type of media system influences programming, Wells analyzes media systems to find the types best suited to development.

A private "free" system of media control is often contrasted with a "totalitarian" system of public control. However, the commercial U.S. pattern, with private ownership of broadcasting facilities and financing obtained from advertising, stimulates consumer buying rather than economic development in LDCs. The "totalitarian" model may be better suited to developmental needs, because it can be nationalistic, project local life styles, and be used for educational purposes.

Wells finds the above dichotomy too simplistic and prefers a typology in which control of the electronic media is classified as state-operated, public-corporation, public-interest partnerships, or private-enterprise. He finds the first two types most appropriate to development purposes. Besides media control, Wells also discusses finance, programming, target audiences, and feedback mechanisms, and specifies for each the methods most conducive to development.

355. "Where Rise in Postal Rates Will Hit Hardest." U.S. News & World Report, 22 February 1971, pp. 56-57.

Postal rate increases in the United States add to the cost of such business operations as advertising and bill collections. Magazine publishers are the hardest hit, with second-class postal rates increasing 145 percent from 1971 to 1976. Publishers say the rate increases will drive up prices and advertising rates. Postal rates for magazines and newspapers have been kept low in the past because of a policy that wide dissemination of information was in the public interest. When the U.S. Postal Service was created in 1970, all classes of mail were required to cover their costs of operation. Publications had been paying only 56 percent of the direct costs of their handling; now they will have to cover direct costs plus contribute to postal service overhead.

Publishers feel the rate increases are too high. It is difficult to recover the added costs because of outstanding subscriptions and advertising contracts. Publishers say the price hike may cause a monopolistic situation, reducing the diversity of published opinion, by killing some magazines and preventing new magazines from entering the market.

356. White, C.E. "Telecommunication Needs of Developing Countries." Telecommunications 10:9 (September 1976) 49-53.

Some general problems in the design and installation of telecommunications systems in less developed countries are outlined. Systems must be chosen that can incorporate as much information within limited facilities as possible. Because of a lack of untrained personnel, there is a need to centralize equipment in just a few locations. The large amounts of money required to capitalize a new system may be a considerable portion of the entire budget of a developing country.

Mr. A.R.K. Al Ghunaim of the Ministry of Communications in Kuwait has offered a novel approach to the long-range telecommunication objectives of developing countries. In this idealistic plan, joint discussions by interested parties could lead to standardization of plant and equipment capable of mass production and universal application; factories would then be allotted to each region in the most efficient way possible.

Telecommunications growth to date and short-term plans for Brazil, Peru, the Middle East, Africa, and Asia are briefly summarized. Data for Brazil are presented in some detail; implementation of its plans for the period 1976-1980 requires $15,000 million, of which 82 percent will come from internal resources. Brazil views telecommunications as a major factor in the development of the electronics industry.

357. Wood, Fred B.; Coates, Vary T.; Chartrand, Robert L.; and Ericson, Richard F. "Videoconferencing Via Satellite: Opening Government to the People." The Futurist 12:5 (October 1978) 321-326.

Two-way communication between citizens and their elected representatives is essential to the American political system. In 1977 an experiment was conducted to determine if satellite videoconferencing will be a viable mechanism for this dialogue. Four demonstrations were completed, including a question/

answer session between a representative and high school students in North Carolina and a subcommittee hearing in which public witnesses in Illinois gave testimony on a bill. The demonstrations all proved to be technically feasible. Such conferences are useful because more people are reached more effectively, time and energy are saved, and person-to-person contact is established.

Estimated costs in the 1980-1982 time frame will be about $300/hour for conferences between Washington DC and one field location. Costs include earth terminals, TV studios, and satellite transmission time. Direct savings from videoconferencing that can be measured in dollar terms include air fare, travel time, and per diem. Benefit-cost ratios for four typical applications are 2.5 or 3:1, and the benefits are probably understated since only those factors that can be expressed in dollar terms are included. A critical factor in the establishment of videoconferencing will be the availability of low-cost small earth terminals and mobile terminals.

358. World Bank, Telecommunication: Sector Working Paper. Washington, DC: World Bank, 1971.

This pamphlet is part of a World Bank series dealing with sectors in which the Bank lends for development purposes. There is unsatisfied demand for telecommunications services throughout the developing world, even at relatively high prices; this is to be expected, since a growing economy will have expanding communication needs. Communication contributes to economic growth via increased efficiency of administration in government and business, improved market information, movement of goods, reduction of inventories, and tourism; telecommunications can substitute for mail where literacy is low.

An overview of world telephone distribution, rates of growth, and investment in 1970 is given. Special characteristics of telecommunications are outlined: (1) the value of a single connection increases as the total number of connections increases; (2) technological advances have yielded steadily decreasing unit costs for circuits; (3) the demand for telecommunications is highly inelastic to price; since supply is usually a monopoly condition, prices can be set to cover costs and generate funds for reinvestment.

The World Bank Group is the principal multilateral source of finance for telecommunications development.

International Exchange of Communication Goods/Services

359. Almaney, Adnan. "Governments' Resistance to the Free Flow of International Communication." Journal of Communication 22:1 (March 1972) 77-88.

Economic barriers, such as customs charges and taxes on imported information materials, and political barriers, such as censorship, inhibit the flow of communications between nations. Unesco has made efforts to lower these barriers through several international agreements, but not many countries have signed these agreements because of: (1) ideological differences; (2) desire of governments to promote their own economic interests; (3) countries' attempts to preserve national cultural identities. Ideological differences seem to be the most formidable problem. There are two major economic reasons for governments' resistance to joining Unesco agreements: (1) protection of national industries from foreign competition; (2) desire to retain revenues from taxes on imported materials (certain Unesco agreements do not permit this).

360. Chung, Kun Mo. "Commercial Transfer of Foreign Technology to the Electronics Industry in Korea." Asian Economies, no. 13 (June 1975) 5-27.

Recent national economic policy in Korea has stressed the development of six export-oriented industries; this paper focuses on the electronics industry, which is targeted to account for 25 percent of Korean exports by 1981. Electronics is a high-technology industry, and to date virtually all electronic technology has had to be imported into Korea.
Foreign techniques are brought to Korea through six channels: (1) books and journals; (2) foreign experts;

(3) technical assistance programs; (4) imported goods and equipment; (5) transfer contracts of patents, licenses, and technical know-how; (6) direct foreign investments and operation of offshore plants by foreign firms. Older knowledge comes through the first four channels, but newer knowledge comes through the last two, which are commercial channels. Commercial transfer of foreign technology is regulated by the Korean government; Chung explains the procedures and lists the benefits that the vendor of the technology may receive. These include tax exemptions, reinvestment provisions, and special treatment in labor relations.

As of June 1974 22 percent of commercially imported techniques concerned electronics technology. Chung analyzed these transfers and makes the following observations: (1) the majority were bought from Japanese firms; (2) most are routine and not of major importance; (3) only rarely has imported technology been adapted to local conditions; (4) there have been many duplicate transfers. He recommends reduced dependence on Japanese firms, more development of the local science and technology base, a shift from consumer to industrial electronics, increased dissemination of imported technology to other domestic users, and increased technological cooperation with other "emerging nations."

361. Clippinger, John H. "The Hidden Agenda." Journal of Communication 29:1 (Winter 1979) 197-203.

The value of access to the radio spectrum is increasing with increased demand for international communication. The 1979 WARC will test the ability of international institutions to handle the tricky issue of spectrum allocation. Many communication/information issues will shape the WARC meetings, particularly Third World demands for a New World Information Order. The NWIO advocates that governments should have the right to say what information enters and leaves their borders and that information is a government-controlled public good. In the United States information is a commodity whose value is determined in the marketplace; the government must only guarantee its "free flow." The United States may continue to advocate free flow only as long as it remains an exporter of information/communication technologies; U.S. markets are already open to foreign competition, and it is possible that the United States will restrict the flow of information on computer technologies if the United States loses its comparative advantage in this market.

The United States has promised technical assistance to LDCs in communications development; yet it must be remembered that information transfer is not the same as technology transfer. The Third World needs the capability to utilize the information.

The hidden agenda of WARC is acceptance by the United States of the contention that there should be a redistribution of the world's resources.

362. "Colour Television: Japan's Global Strategy Adapts to New Realities." (Part I and Part II). <u>Multinational Business</u>, no. 3 (1978) 23-30; no. 4 (1978) 18-27.

Japan has dominated world markets in consumer electronics through its highly successful global marketing strategy. Sony is said to have pioneered this strategy, which consists of high quality, high prices, and high reliability, coupled with world-wide marketing to obtain scale of production. In 1976, for example, more than half of the color TV tubes sold worldwide were made in Japan. However, recent international trends are affecting Japan's phenomenal export industry, including appreciation in the value of the yen, stagnation in the domestic market, very few new markets to open up, protectionist pressure in Europe and the United States, and the fact that color TV is passing into the saturation phase.

Voluntary export curbs in Europe, the role of color TV patents, and marketing difficulties in the United States are explained. Japan's satellite plants in Singapore, Taiwan, and Korea, and overseas operations in the United Kingdom and the United States are described. Despite a currently stagnant market, the TV market will grow because TV will be adapted for the reception and presentation of data.

In Part II of this article the development of new products is described, focusing on the VTR. The Japanese plan is to make the VTR a mass market product, but it is possible that it will remain a luxury optional extra. A problem in expanding the VTR market is the continuing cost of tapes.

363. Frame, J. Davidson, and Baum, John J. "Cross-National Information Flows in Basic Research: Examples Taken from Physics." <u>Journal of the American Society for Information Science</u> 29:5 (September 1978) 247-252.

The transfer of technology at the research level, where it consists of information flows, can be measured by how often scientists in one country reference scientists in another. In this study, information flows among several countries in three subfields of physics were tabulated by counting references appearing in relevant articles identified in <u>Physics Abstracts</u>. Ratios were constructed showing references from country A to country B as compared to references from country B to country A. Only the United States has ratios consistently lower than 1; in these fields of physics, U.S. scientists reference

the work of foreign scientists only 66 to 72 percent as frequently as foreign scientists reference U.S. scientists. While
the United States has a negative balance of information flow,
the U.S.S.R. has a strong positive balance.

Ratios were then adjusted for the respective sizes of the
research efforts of the various countries; even accounting for
its size, U.S. research is still the most highly referenced in
the world, while Soviet research is underreferenced.

In conclusion, it is asked whether the United States is
suffering a net loss of scientific information and whether U.S.
taxpayers are supporting foreign research efforts.

364. Guback, Thomas H. "Film as International Business."
     Journal of Communication 24:1 (Winter 1974) 90-101.

The international film business is strictly a commercial
operation; little thought is given to a film's aesthetic and
cultural impact on a country's social development. This
survey of the film business reveals extensive American domin-
ation; the American film industry accounts for half of the
global film trade. Besides exporting films, American multinational corporations have subsidiaries that make, distribute,
and exhibit films. In the United States, the film industry is
the industry most dependent on foreign earnings; by the late
1960s, 53 percent of total film rentals came from abroad. The
U.S. government has encouraged the expansion of film trade
through such devices as the Webb-Pomerene Export Act, which
allows domestic competition to cooperate in trade through an
export association, the Motion Picture Export Association.
(The motion picture is the only U.S. enterprise that negotiates
on its own with foreign governments, many of whom earn more
income through taxes on American films than do the producers
of the films.)

Western Europe is the largest market for U.S. films.
Furthermore, there is such extensive financing of European
films by American firms that many European film makers feel
totally dependent on the American film industry.

365. Guzzardi, Walter, Jr. "The Great World Telephone War."
     Fortune, August 1977, pp. 142-147, 150, 154.

Third World governments are treating telecommunications
as high priority, although there is uncertainty over the cause/
effect relationship between communications and development.
Planned investments in telecommunications are enormous, and
large equipment suppliers are now engaged in mortal combat
over new contracts. Because of rapid technological advances,
a once labor-intensive industry has become a capital-intensive

one, and equipment suppliers now have excess capacity in the form of surplus employees; first world suppliers must export because of the pressure of extra capacity, the high costs of research and development, and saturated home markets.

Difficulties of doing business in the Third World include: (1) difficult terrain; (2) lack of such infrastructure as roads and potable water; (3) language; (4) government ownership of telecommunications. Governments often insist on keeping telephone rates low to maintain popularity with the people, but low rates mean poor service; governments often insist that multinationals build plants in the host country, yet these plants are high-cost and may be expropriated. Recent tortuous contract negotiations in Kuwait, Iran, Saudi Arabia, and Egypt are described.

366. Lebowitz, Abraham I. "Some Factors Relating to the Economic Basis of International Systems for Information Storage and Retrieval." In International Conference on Information Science, Proceedings, pp. 299-304. Edited by Lydia Vilentchuk. Tel Aviv: National Center of Scientific and Technological Information, 1972.

Scientific and technical information is a necessary input to research and development. It can be generated locally or transferred from other countries. In terms of locally produced information, the gap between developed and underdeveloped nations seems to be increasing; Lebowitz provides OECD data on R&D expenditures. Technology transfer (TT), as an alternative to local R&D, is usually a "bilateral transfer of information based on a specific contractual . . . relationship between the parties." Another method of TT is the importation of information in the form of existing primary and secondary publications; this method, as a factor in national development, has been neglected because of its magnitude, complexity, and cost. It would be quite difficult for a developing country to set up a system large enough to handle a high percentage of the world's scientific publications.

Many developing countries have depended on the bibliographic services of the larger countries, but some of these are being phased out in favor of automated systems, due to the increasing costs of the scientific information explosion. Another difficulty for developing nations is the unfavorable ratio of the price of foreign books and journals to local salaries; these prices reflect the high labor costs in industrialized nations.

The long-term solution to the world's information problems must be an international system in which all benefits are available to all countries regardless of their contribution to operating costs; costs might be allocated in proportion to the amount of research performed in a country.

367. Liebich, F. K.   Removing Taxes on Knowledge.   Reports
     and Papers on Mass Communication, no. 58.   Paris:
     Unesco, 1969.

The elimination of international trade barriers to educational, scientific, and cultural materials will facilitate economic
progress. Liebich first gives an overview of measures that
have liberalized international trade and then gives a more
specific history/overview of measures aimed at the trade of
knowledge materials.   The League of Nations and then Unesco
have sponsored agreements to facilitate such trade.   In developed countries, such obstacles to free movement as import
duties and quota restrictions are designed chiefly to protect
local industries, but in LDCs the problem may be a shortage of
foreign currency to purchase foreign materials.   Unesco has
arranged special currency deals to mitigate balance of payments problems; other Unesco initiatives include: (1) temporary loans/exhibitions of foreign materials; (2) rapid delivery
of delicate scientific instruments; (3) lowered postal and air
freight charges for knowledge materials.
     Extensive statistical data showing the dollar value of
knowledge imports/exports for 1963 and 1965 are included.
The bulk of the report details the current situation in and
gives recommendations for various segments of the knowledge
trade: books, newspapers/periodicals, music, maps and manuscripts, works of art, musical instruments, films, sound
recordings, visual and auditory equipment, and scientific
instruments.
     Liebich recommends that the greatest possible elasticity in
applying customs and other regulations should be obtained and
that import duties should be eliminated.

368. Nordenstreng, Kaarle, and Varis, Tapio.   Television
     Traffic - A One-Way Street?   A Survey and Analysis of
     the International Flow of Television Programme Material.
     Reports and Papers on Mass Communication, no. 70.
     Paris: Unesco, 1974.

For 50 countries, the proportions of domestically produced
versus imported television programs are shown; data on international networks for sales and exchanges of program material
are included.   Data were obtained through a questionnaire
survey completed in 1973.   On the questionnaire, program
output was divided into 13 categories based on format.   The
United States, Japan, People's Republic of China, and the
U.S.S.R. import very little program material; in Europe, one-
quarter to one-third of programs are imported, although for
individual countries the statistics are highly dispersed; Latin
American programming is heavily dominated by the United

States. The major program-exporting countries are the United States, United Kingdom, France, and West Germany; distribution patterns for each of these four nations are given. In the 1960s the United States exported more than twice as many programs as all other countries combined. The two major trends are: (1) one-way traffic from the major exporting nations, and (2) the dominance of entertainment material by exported programs.

The results of a 1973 symposium on the International Flow of Television Programs are reported in Part II. The consensus was that economic imperatives (TV hardware, technical know-how, relative cheapness of American TV series, wealth and resources of the industrialized nations) have determined the one-way flow, rather than any political/cultural intent. Ways to redress the imbalance are recommended.

369. Organisation for Economic Co-operation and Development. "Policy for the Transfer of Results." In Economics of Information and Knowledge: Selected Readings, pp. 239-262. Edited by D.M. Lamberton. Middlesex, Eng: Penguin Books, 1971.

As the volume of research grows, the transfer of information and discoveries becomes more complex. Government intervention may be necessary, because individuals on their own cannot satisfy their needs for information; government is better able to bear the costs. The U.S. government has paid great attention to information policy, which includes the collection of information and its transfer to users. Federal expenditures devoted to scientific and technical information are presented; in the mid-1960s, they amounted to 1.5 to 2 percent of federal research and development. The activities of several specialized government information agencies are described, including the Defense Documentation Center of the Defense Department and the Division of Technical Information of the Atomic Energy Commission.

The Committee on Scientific and Technical Information (COSATI) has been created to coordinate the various information agencies; one result of COSATI activities is the standardization of technical reports on microfilm, which has created a large new market with substantial cost savings.

Aspects of information policy are grouped and discussed under six headings: (1) media (journals, reports, conferences); (2) information processing (collection and storage); the pressure of demand for information is very high; (3) personnel; (4) specialized establishments; (5) modern equipment; and (6) international problems (compiling information on scientific activities abroad).

The transfer of information and technology from the immediate purposes of the creating agency to other purposes and other agencies/individuals is a crucial element in economic growth. NASA is given as an example; it is required to transfer to the industrial/scientific community information arising from its space activities.

370. Porat, Marc Uri. "Global Implications of the Information Society." Journal of Communication 28:1 (Winter 1978) 70-80.

Porat first summarizes his research which shows that the United States can be characterized as an information economy. By 1967, 25 percent of GNP came from the production, processing, and distribution of information goods and services; another 21 percent was generated by purely internal uses in both public and private bureaucracies. In 1970, information workers earned 53 percent of all labor income. As a resource, information has unusual properties; it is infinitely renewable, and it doesn't depreciate with use.

New growth for the information economy must come from either domestic or foreign demand. Porat considers foreign demand in this article. Multinational corporations are aggressively marketing information goods and services. In 1975, $2.4 billion worth of computers and telecommunications systems were exported from the United States. This massive export has led to many policy problems that must be resolved: (1) along with U.S. information goods, American accounting and administrative procedures are also exported; (2) information technology may be used for internal surveillance and military systems rather than economic development; (3) U.S. television and radio programs may be considered "cultural imperialism"; (4) problems of protection of privacy have arisen with the export of data bases.

371. Silverstein, David. "Sharing United States Energy Technology With Less-Developed Countries: A Model for International Technology Transfer." Journal of International Law and Economics 12:3 (1978) 363-419.

Although the United States had pledged itself to international energy cooperation, it has paid little attention to the energy needs of the non-oil producing LDCs, where rising energy costs are taking large shares of slim budgets and thus constraining economic growth. The development of energy technology in the United States is concentrated in the private sector; technology transfer (TT) to LDCs will take place at the discretion of multinational corporations, but there is a maze of domestic and foreign legal barriers to such transfer. Silverstein reviews the principal legal barriers; U.S. export control, antitrust, and tax laws are strong constraints on international TT.

Using econometric analysis, Silverstein presents a model of energy TT based on the hypothesis that the rate of indigenous discoveries and innovations and the rate of transfers from other countries are directly proportional to the level of proprietary protection. Through a series of equations it is shown that if U.S. laws produce a smaller U.S. energy technology base, then a smaller LDC energy technology base will result.

The article is concluded with a proposed model bilateral treaty between the United States and an LDC for their mutual benefit in promoting energy TT.

372. Teece, D. J. "Technology Transfer by Multinational Firms: The Resource Cost of Transferring Technological Know-How." The Economic Journal 87-346 (June 1977) 242-261.

Data from 26 recent international technology transfer projects were tested to see if the costs of the actual transfer were a significant part of total project costs and also to find which variables most influenced costs. All the projects involved the transfer of the capability to manufacture a product or process from firms in one country to firms in another; each project was conducted by a multinational firm with headquarters in the United States. Transfer cost was defined as the costs of transmitting and absorbing all the information required to utilize effectively new physical equipment or hardware. It was found that transfer costs averaged 19 percent of total project costs, with a range from 2 percent to 59 percent.

Two groups of variables were tested statistically: characteristics of the technology/transferer, and characteristics of the transferee/host country. Two particularly significant variables were found to be the number of previous applications of an innovation and how well the innovation is understood by the parties involved. The more experienced enterprises had lower transfer costs, which indicates the importance of the accumulation of skills in facilitating the technology transfer process; a major implication of the study is that technology transfer is a decreasing cost activity.

373. Uttal, Bro.   "Japan's Big Push in Computers."   "Exports Won't Come Easy for Japan's Computer Industry." Fortune, 25 September 1978, pp. 64-66, 68, 70, 72; 9 October 1978, pp. 138-140, 142, 146.

American computer industry spokesmen fear that Japan is about to invade world computer markets; the Japanese profess to be not so confident of their ability to export computer equipment successfully.   Uttal feels that, although it is too early for Japan to make large inroads, the Japanese are nonetheless beginning to implement the export strategy that was so successful for them in television sets, cars, and consumer electronics.   In the first of these two articles, Japan's home market is described as background for a discussion in the second article of Japan's future in exporting computers.

The home field is badly overcrowded and is in the midst of a price-cutting war; also, the industry faces severe competition from U.S. imports, the duties on which have been progressively lowered.   The Japanese feel that after a home "shake-out" in the industry, the remaining companies will be able to obtain high enough profits to finance foreign expansion.   Japan's export strategy is to concentrate on simpler equipment in just a few segments of the market; after sufficient volume has been built up, the expertise, knowledge of consumer needs, and economies of scale are transferred to additional products.

Another economic benefit of a large computer industry, in addition to export earnings, is that it will assure Japan of the technology necessary to continue to improve industrial productivity; Japanese workers are highly educated and receptive to computers.

374. Vaitsos, Constantine.   "Patents Revisited: Their Function in Developing Countries."   Journal of Development Studies 9:1 (October 1972) 71-97.

Vaitsos evaluates the economic effects of the patent system as it functions in developing countries.   A patent is actually a monopoly grant; the patent system is based on the assumption that patents provide incentives for creative activity, but on a world-wide basis they may hinder inventiveness, especially in LDCs.   In developing countries patents are owned almost entirely by foreign individuals or companies.   Concentration of patents in large multinational corporations enhances corporate market control; the main function of such patents is to help profit maximization by large corporations.

It is often argued that patents stimulate foreign investment in LDCs.   Vaitsos demonstrates that this is untrue because nearly all patents granted by developing countries are unexploited. Unexploited patents serve to restrict the right to use or imitate key industrial technologies, thus preserving secure import markets for foreign corporations. Patents block the transfer of technology related to the patented products; they also can block domestic research activities in developing countries. Vaitsos gives examples of several types of restrictive business practices exercised through patent licenses: (1) price fixing; (2) discriminatory rates; (3) tie-in arrangements; (4) domestic and export restrictions. Patents create unfavorable terms of trade for LDCs. Vaitsos concludes by questioning the need for patents in developing countries.

375. Varis, Tapio, "Aspects of the Impact of Transnational Corporations on Communication." International Social Science Journal 28:4 (1976) 808-830.

Varis presents a historical overview of the development of transnational communication enterprises (TNCEs) and then analyzes the current world situation. TNCEs are largely involved with international marketing and distribution operations and play a major role in advertising by providing a global network. Many TNCEs are part of larger conglomerates; Varis gives extensive examples and provides income and sales figures for several European and American companies. He gives a detailed analysis of the transnational development of Dutch Philips (hardware producer) from 1919 to date, and of the global expansion of the three American networks, ABC, CBS, and NBC.
     TNCEs affect the media structure in host countries; in Canada, four times as many American magazines as Canadian magazines are sold. They also affect host country employment and culture in general; TV in particular serves the commercial interests of the TNCEs.
     TNCEs are part of the international dependency structure. Varis gives data that show the one-way flow in the international distribution of films, TV programs, printed materials, news and advertising.

376. Varis, Tapio. "Global Traffic in Television." Journalism of Communication 24:1 (Winter 1974) 102-109.

International television broadcasting is an economic, social, and cultural transaction; it is economic in that programs are treated as commercial commodities to be bought and sold. The results of this survey of 50 countries to find the sources of programming show an imbalance in the television market situation. Radio programs for international distribution are often primarily propagandistic, but television programs are intended primarily to earn money; competition has led to concentration in a few major countries. In the 1960s the United States exported more than twice as many programs as all other countries combined; some countries import more than two-thirds of their total programming. Even Western Europe imports about one-third of its programs. The distribution of newsfilm is concentrated in three world-wide British and American agencies.

Section 6

Social/Political Implications of Communication Economics

377. Arrow, Kenneth J. The Limits of Organization. New York: W.W. Norton, 1974.

In this collection of four lectures, Arrow discusses organizations as systems for the allocation of scarce resources. "Organizations are a means of achieving the benefits of collective action in situations in which the price system fails." One important way in which the price system fails is in the presence of uncertainty; the acquisition of information through the collective action made possible by organizations is an effective way of managing the problem of uncertainty. To collect relevant information, an organization must possess information channels; the choice of channels is determined by their benefits and costs. There are few conclusive statements that can be made about the benefits of information; the costs of communication channels are determined by such factors as the individual's limited capacity for acquiring and using information and the irreversible capital investment required. Factors that determine the agenda of organizations are investigated; decisions are a function of information, and there are decisions to act and decisions to collect information. The final issue Arrow treats is the necessity to balance the authority of decision makers with their responsibility to those who carry out the decisions. Decision-making structures should facilitate the flow of information.

378. Blankenburg, William B.   "Nixon Vs. the Networks: Madison Avenue and Wall Street."   Journal of Broadcasting 21:2 (Spring 1977) 163-175.

During the Nixon years, the media were subjected to an unusual amount of hostility and even threats from the White House. Blankenburg has studied the economic performance of the commercial television networks from 1968 to 1974 to determine whether advertising revenues and stock prices were affected by White House enmity. The results show that the networks increased their share of national advertising revenues in every year except 1971; in 1971, the continuation of the 1970 recession and the banning of cigarette advertising provide reasons for the temporary downturn. The hypothesis that network stock prices fell following White House attacks is not supported; none of the correlations between stock movement and White House antimedia activity was significant. Blankenburg concludes that the size and diversity of the networks make them difficult economic targets.

379. Conrath, David W., and Thompson, Gordon B.   "Communication Technology: A Societal Perspective."   Journal of Communication 23:1 (March 1973) 47-63.

Communication is central to an organization or a society. Which communication technologies we choose to pursue now will be crucial to our future. In allocating resources for and evaluating alternate technologies, we emphasize economic measures to the neglect of other societal needs. Three dimensions along which the impact of communication systems on social values might be measured are: (1) ease of access to stored information; (2) scope of shared interaction space; (3) possibility of feedback. At present, we have no clear way to measure any of the three; eventually, as, for example, in the first case, we would like to be able to say that one innovation has twice the value of another along this dimension. It may be possible to adapt such economic measures as indifference curves to these social indicators.

Many communication innovations now being proposed bring little return in societal benefits; the cashless society, for example, results only in logistics efficiency. The authors conclude by presenting their concept of a universal information storage and retrieval system with high values in all three proposed dimensions.

380. Høyer, Svennik; Hadenius, Stig; and Weibul, Lennart.
     The Politics and Economics of the Press: A Developmental
     Perspective. Sage Professional Papers in Contemporary
     Political Sociology, no. 06-009. London: Sage, 1975.

     Historical data concerning the newspaper industry in
several industrialized Western nations, emphasizing the Scan-
dinavian countries, are presented; findings point to a phase
development in the growth and consumption of newspapers.
The initial, introductory phase may be rather lengthy; it is
followed by a short but hectic period of expansion, and then a
period of consolidation.   This is the S-curve typical of the
diffusion of innovations.
     Since World War II there has been a general trend toward
the consolidation of newspaper markets.   This trend toward
local monopolies means that political parties have lost their
ability to participate directly in the industry, while the economic system, through advertising, has gained in importance.
Studies show that monopoly newspapers tend to become politically neutral.   The authors recommend the prohibition of
advertising in newspapers; although this would require
dramatic increases in subscription prices; it would give the
market to readers.   In Scandinavia, governments have taken
responsibility through subsidies to secure a politically com-
mitted press.
     TV broadcasting has reduced the role of the press in the
political system especially as TV becomes more localized and
challenges the local newspaper market.   The press is changing
from being a political instrument controlled by the market to
being part of a communication system controlled within broad
limits by Parliament, paid for by the taxpayer rather than the
consumer.

381. Johnson, Nicholas.   "Harnessing Revolution: The Role of
     Regulation and Competition for the Communications In-
     dustries of Tomorrow." Antitrust Bulletin 13 (Fall 1968)
     881-887.

     A national communications policy is needed in the United
States; there is no alternative to planning, but it must be
decided who is to do it.   The familiar approach is to determine
whether sectors of the industry should be competitive or
subject to regulation; this is an important way to decide the
optimal allocation of resources, but the social values at stake
in the structure of communications systems transcend such
concepts as competition, regulation, and resource allocation.
     Communications is not just a matter of business, it is
competition in the marketplace of ideas.   Currently there is too
much concentration of control in the hands of owners who have

too many economic and political interests. If consumer sovereignty and political democracy are national goals, then communications planning decisions must be responsive to the people. It must be realized that competition and regulation are not ends in themselves; opportunity must be allowed for structural changes brought about by technological advances. Those in control of communications must not be permitted to prevent innovation.

382. Porat, Marc U. "Communication Policy in an Information Society." Bulletin of the Institute for Communication Research (Keio University, Tokyo), no. 11 (1978), pp. 1-13.

The United States has become an information economy. In 1967, information activities engaged 46 percent of the work force, which earned 53 percent of all labor income. The U.S. labor market is glutted with information workers; the economy will not easily absorb more.

Two types of issues must be addressed by major policies. The first type concerns the arrangement of the information infrastructure, dealing with such issues as common carrier policy, competition, and investment in new technologies. Porat calls this communication policy and points out that there are enormous economic stakes here; more than 10 percent of all investment in the United States is attributable to the telephone industry, for example. The second type concerns the application of information technologies across all sectors of the economy, including postal service, publishing, finance, media, education, etc. This is information policy, and the major issue here is that many industries will tend to converge as they utilize the same information technologies, leading to problems of intense competition among traditionally separate industries.

383. Schiller, Herbert I. "Computer Systems: Power for Whom and For What?" Journal of Communication 28:4 (August 1978) 184-193.

Schiller asks how the advent of computer communications will affect the information dependency of peoples and nations. Most of the hardware is produced by a small number of private companies; IBM has at least 50 percent of the computer market in most major, developed countries. The poorer nations will have no opportunity to influence the design and production of new information hardware. In terms of software, in 1975 the United States held 89 percent of all records in organized data banks; 79 percent of these data are scientific-technological in nature. U.S. companies are gaining ever-larger aggregations of data bases.

The utilization of data bases and information systems depends on transmission systems; communication satellites are largely under the control of the same U.S. firms that dominate the computer and telecommunications industries.

Schiller wonders whether the new technology will be utilized to help in the development effort. New technology alone is useless without concomitant changes in the socio-economic structure that facilitates developmental uses of the technology.

384. Seiden, Martin H. Who Controls the Mass Media? Popular Myths and Economic Realities. New York: Basic Books, 1974.

The American system of mass communications is rooted in commerce, not politics. It is supported by the advertising dollar, which has protected the mass media from government control as much as has the First Amendment. A current myth is that the mass media have enormous power to influence and mold the American public through content and advertising. Seiden demonstrates that because of the industry's economic structure this is simply not so; the media tend to mirror society, rather than molding it. The key to influencing people has always been ideas, not technology.

The basic economic structure of each major mass medium is described, and then it is shown that, because of the myth of media power, government regulations have been impinging upon the freedom of the media, particularly in the area of broadcasting. A key chapter focuses on advertising, which accounts for 75 percent of newspaper and nearly 100 percent of commercial broadcasting revenues; these are the means by which the media have secured independence. Other subjects treated include public opinion, antitrust and the media, journalists, the underground press, TV programming choices, the use of mass media in education, and American media abroad.

385. Shubik, M. "Information, Rationality and Free Choice in a Future Democratic Society." In Economics of Information and Knowledge: Selected Readings, pp. 357-365. Edited by D.M. Lamberton. Middlesex, Eng.: Penguin Books, 1971.

The traditional economic concept of people as rational, optimizing individuals who possess perfect information and exercise freedom of choice is questioned in terms of current social/economic/political developments. As technology and markets expand and population grows, the proportionate share of information an individual can "know" decreases; as the

speed and volume of transmissions increase, limitations become
even more marked.

We must rethink our model of the political/economic person
to consider "the uncertain decision-maker acting under severely restricted conditions of information embedded within a
communications system upon which he is becoming increasingly
more dependent." Individuals will become increasingly interdependent as the pace of communications quickens.

The size and growth of our society will erode our traditional economic/political values; computers and communications,
if carefully planned, can be utilized to preserve and extend
freedom and individual choice by providing the means to treat
individuals as individuals rather than aggregates.

386. Silbermann, Alphons. "Communication Systems and
     Future Behavior Patterns." International Social Science
     Journal 29:2 (1977) 337-341.

Silbermann reviews the 1976 report of the Commission
for the Development of the Technical Communication System
(Federal Republic of Germany). The report emphasized the
technical aspects of communication technology at the expense
of the human user. Members of the Commission seem to see
no difference between economic and social effects, for example,
and view them together; the words "need" and "demand" for
service are used interchangeably, although their meanings
and connotations are quite different. Silbermann sees in
modern society a trend toward individualism and also toward
a service-oriented economy; current media are mass-oriented,
but to fit social trends we will need individual or "on-demand"
communication. This type of communication must not be rejected on the basis of purely technical and commercial factors,
as it is in the Commission's report.

Author Index

Subject Index

About the Author

KAREN P. MIDDLETON is a graduate of Stanford University (A.B., Economics) and the University of Hawaii (M.L.S., Library Studies). She was a Peace Corps teacher in Seoul, Korea, and then worked as an economist in Washington, D.C. and Cambridge, Massachusetts. She has worked as a librarian and a lecturer in library studies at the Law School and the Graduate School of Library Studies of the University of Hawaii. From 1978 to 1980 she held a research position at the East-West Center, where she specialized in the economics of communication. She is currently living and working in Jakarta, Indonesia.

MEHEROO JUSSAWALLA is a graduate of Madras University (M.A., Economics) and Osmania University (Ph.D., Economics). She was Professor of Economics and Dean of the Faculty of Social Sciences at Osmania University, Hyderabad, India before migrating to the U.S. in 1975. She had served on the Research Programs Committee of the Planning Commission, Government of India from 1968 to 1970, and from 1971 to 1975 was a member of the Board of Directors of the State Bank of India. In 1957-58 she was awarded a grant under the Wheat Loan Program for studies at the University of Pennsylvania. In 1969-79 the American Council on Education awarded her a Visiting Professorship at Hood College, Frederick, Maryland. During that period she guest lectured at Vassar, Elmira, and Cedar Crest Colleges. From 1975 to 1977 she served as Professor of Economics at St. Mary's College, Maryland, and joined the Communication Institute of the East-West Center in Honolulu as a Research Associate/Economist in 1978. She has published books and articles in professional journals on development economics, money and banking, and recently on communication economics. Her special interest is in the field of communication policy and planning.